NIGHTMARE ON LIME STREET

Nightmare on Lime Street

Whatever happened to Lloyd's of London?

Cathy Gunn

SMITH GRYPHON
PUBLISHERS

First published in paperback
in Great Britain in 1993 by
SMITH GRYPHON LIMITED
Swallow House, 11-21 Northdown Street
London N1 9BN

First published in hardback in 1992
by Smith Gryphon Limited

A CIP catalogue for this book
is available from the British Library

The right of Cathy Gunn to be identified as author of this work has been asserted by her in
accordance with the Copyright, Designs and Patent Act 1988

ISBN 1 85685 042 0

Typeset by Computerset, Harmondsworth, Middlesex
Printed and bound in Great Britain by Butler and Tanner Ltd, Frome

CONTENTS

ACKNOWLEDGEMENTS

Many thanks to all those people who kindly agreed to see and talk to me in the course of my researches, or allowed me to spend time in Lloyd's with them. Thank you too, to my editor, publisher and agent; to Edward and sundry friends; and to Dave's Disc Doctor service which saved me from the new nightmare of every 1990's author – the vanishing book.

Part of Chapter 5 first appeared in the *Digest of Lloyd's News*, October 1991.

For my parents

1
A Dark and Stormy Night

*Money, th' only power
That all mankind falls down before*

(SAMUEL BUTLER, *HUDIBRAS*, PART III, CANTO II, L. 1327)

O
n the night of 15 October 1987 winds racing at speeds of up to 100 m.p.h. tore diagonally across southern Britain, ripping up trees, tearing off roofs and snapping telephone lines from Cornwall to Norfolk. They hit central London around 2 a.m. on the 16th and swept north eastwards through the financial district, the City, to wreak further havoc on the English countryside. One Londoner getting up at 5 a.m. to prepare for a business flight to Europe awoke to no electricity and the unaccustomed darkness of a city with no street lights. Turning on the radio he caught the tail-end of a news reporter's description of the chaos outside: '. . . nuclear winter out there.' My God, he thought, it's happened. They've dropped The Bomb.

He soon realized his mistake. But for the people who were still picking up the bill five years later, he might just as well have been right. The British hurricane of 1987 was just one of an unprecedented catalogue of natural and man-made catastrophes – the Piper Alpha oil rig explosion in the North Sea, the Lockerbie air disaster in Scotland, Hurricane Hugo in the Caribbean and southern USA, the San Francisco earthquake, and storms and floods across Europe, and more – that struck the world's insurance markets at the end of the 1980s just as a slow-burning but no less devastating fuse sparked off another series of massive claims: this time against the cost of repairing decades-old pollution.

Many of these bills landed on insurance syndicates belonging to the 300-year-old insurance club that is Lloyd's of London, just when their resources had already been depleted by huge payments of claims for personal injury against American firms involved in the asbestos industry. All this happened against a grim background of overcapacity, tough competition, and falling premiums in the world's insurance markets, and struck just as the United Kingdom and America slid into economic recession. An ill wind indeed.

Lloyd's of London is not only the globe's oldest insurance market but traditionally also the one that underwrites some of the highest risk and biggest catastrophe insurance cover in the world. For it, the impact of this combination of mishaps was unmitigated financial disaster.

Insurance is supposed to be about catering for the unexpected, but this time there was not enough money held in reserve in the club's kitty to meet the sort of claims, and forewarnings of claims, that came from policies written during 1988 – £509 million too little, it turned out, and the shortfall was even worse on policies issued in 1989. Fears grew that the final tally, when 1988, 1989 and 1990's losses were all added up, would be £3 billion, to be paid for out of club members' dwindling personal wealth. By 1992 Lloyd's was fighting for its life.

The whole point of insurance is to even out the impact of the unforeseen accident or natural catastrophe. At Lloyd's the insured person or firm pays a fee or 'premium' up front in return for the recipients agreeing to club together in a syndicate and put up enough capital to cover the cost of any future accident(s). There may be conditions and certain exclusions, but the basic principle is to spread the cost between many people so that the assured does not go bust if the worst happens, or, in the words of the early insurance Act from the days of Elizabeth I, to ensure that 'the loss lighteth rather easilie upon many rather than heavilie upon fewe.'

Naturally the groups or syndicates of people receiving the fee for 'underwriting' the risk hope there will be no accident and that they can enjoy the income without shelling out for the disaster. If lots of risks are underwritten the premiums that flow in should generate enough income to cover the cost of the occasional claim and still leave money over for the syndicate members to share out amongst themselves.

The principle has worked – with the odd hiccup – for over 300 years. It took root in a seventeenth-century coffee house run by Edward Lloyd near the Tower of London around the 1680s, and later in nearby Lombard Street. Lloyd's staple then was shipping insurance, with the coffee house acting as an informal club for shipowners in search of news, and for prosperous men prepared to back their ventures by adding their 'name' to the list of people who would underwrite vessels and cargoes as Britain's overseas trade burgeoned. From these early days onwards, Lloyd's remained a club, not a company. Three hundred years later, its members were still well-to-do individuals prepared to underwrite insurance risks in their own name with their own money. These 'Names' put up their personal wealth as the capital on which to underwrite 'lines' of insurance risks placed through this market. Premium income was shared pro rata to the percentage of each insurance risk for which each Name had signed up.

The system meant that each member of Lloyd's was effectively a sole trader. As such, he or she did not have the protection of the limited liability – behind which to shelter – that was enjoyed by the incorporated insurance companies which had sprung up from 1717 after scandal and corruption among Lloyd's underwriters led to dissatisfaction and an early breakaway movement. For members of Lloyd's everything was ultimately at risk if a valuable ship failed to come in. But in the main, the rewards of taking this risk had been considerable over the centuries – so much so in our century that for the bulk of the 1970s and 1980s people and practitioners at Lloyd's became complacent and too inward-looking. Officials became sloppy, and dazzled by the money pouring in, costs were allowed to ratchet up, while nearly everyone overlooked some of the subtler changes that were under way in the wider, world insurance markets, and the impact of inflation on the value of future claims – with disastrous consequences. Belonging to Lloyd's seemed to be a way of making money from old rope. In 1991, the rope snapped.

The unprecedented number and sheer size of claims that struck an ill-prepared market, starting from late 1987 and lasting beyond the end of the decade, meant personal ruin threatened thousands of people, as Lloyd's syndicates called upon their Names to stump up enough extra money to meet the unprecedented flood of actual and notified claims. Lloyd's future has always depended on maintaining its long reputation of meeting valid claims promptly – for example the Kuwaiti government's insurance claims running in to $300 million for its state-owned airline's planes, seized by the Iraqi forces in August 1990, had already been paid by the time the Allied forces retaliated the following January – and therefore Names had to plug any gaps at once in readiness for the huge claims known to be coming in.

Normally, because Names have to deposit some wealth at Lloyd's and each syndicate also keeps some of their earnings in reserve to meet claims, there is enough cash in the kitty to cope. But in the late 1980s the system went badly on the blink. On some syndicates not only were all the Names' deposits and reserves soaked up to meet claims, but many of the 26,500 Names themselves had to be tapped for more cash. To make matters worse, 70 per cent of the £509 million shortfall on 1988's business fell on just 30 per cent of the members – about 7,000 people, from minor Royalty to showbiz stars, members of Parliament, lords of the realm, and even Essex housewives. A year before Lloyd's syndicates had made that amount of money between them. How had the market managed to do a £1 billion turnaround into the red in one short year? While acid questions were asked and tempers flared, fears mounted that the shortfall in the accounts for 1989, due to be finalized in 1992, would top the £1 billion mark. The truth was to prove even worse than that – and there were further losses still gathering on the horizon.

By mid-1991 one businessman, who had been persuaded by an acquaintance over dinner some fifteen years before in 1976 to become a member of Lloyd's already faced net calls for fresh injections of money totalling £400,000. 'If I have to pay it, I'm finished,' he said, pacing round and round his plush West London home, now itself at risk. 'I have nothing left.' Lloyd's is supposed to be in the risk business – so win some, lose some, you might say. But the scale of the losses was too great for members to take quietly, especially those who now believed themselves the victims of poor advice and negligence on the part of those supposed to be looking after them, and shoddy underwriting by their syndicates.

When the tidal wave of disasters met the gathering clouds of new pollution and old asbestosis claims blowing in from the USA, they sparked another sort of highly charged storm over Lloyd's of London: a massive row about how the finances had been allowed to get so bad. Bitter recriminations, accusations of incompetence or worse, and lawsuits flew like the leaves, branches and roof tiles ripped off in the 1987 hurricane. Not only were the people running some of the worst-hit of the Lloyd's syndicates sued, but also the Corporation of Lloyd's itself, which provides the umbrella organization under which all the syndicates of members operate. It also came under heavy legal fire from angry and highly litigious American Names dissatisfied with its stewardship of the market who now challenged the legality of its syndicates canvassing in the US for members in the first place.

Lloyd's problems were compounded by its being the market that traditionally underwrites the riskiest of insurance business – catastrophe cover, product and employers' liability cover, shipping, and other large and expensive items like aeroplanes and oil rigs. In the past, the insurance companies with their limited capital had tended to fight shy of taking such big risks on board, whereas Lloyd's, with its scope to increase its underwriting capacity by attracting more and unlimited sole traders as members each year, could underwrite them.

Most people and most companies insure their property and activities with local insurers, who then spread their own risk by reinsuring all or part of these combined risks and individual larger contracts in the international insurance markets. The reinsurers may be bigger, more international insurance companies or a syndicate of individuals at Lloyd's of London – or a mixture of both these. A large reinsurance risk may be spread between several Lloyd's syndicates and half a dozen big insurance companies.

During the 1980s the mix of business underwritten at Lloyd's had quietly shifted even more towards the riskier end of this spectrum as insurance companies grew larger and more international, in direct competition with Lloyd's syndicates, becoming able to take on more of the better quality large risks than they could before. So many insurance companies were keen to write new business, however, that the world moved into a serious oversupply of underwriting capacity. This forced premiums down on the better business and even led to a scramble for the less attractive risks at what proved even more inadequate prices. Meanwhile, fuelled by inflation in the 1980s, the cost of replacing planes and ships, and the value placed by people, firms and the courts on damaged property, impaired health, and lost lives were all rising steeply and pushed up sharply the size of individual claims and settlements. Many of these were awarded against still valid insurance policies written and priced for long before such large claims were envisaged.

In the midst of all this, the insurance groups operating internationally kept a tighter grip on administrative costs than did Lloyd's syndicates in the 1980s, enabling them to undercut Lloyd's premiums and win business. By 1991 the big British and international insurers' London offices were doing nearly half the non-life insurance business placed in the City of London.

After a bad bout of losses in 1965 when Hurricane Betsy had ravaged America and generated massive claims, Lloyd's had feared it would have insufficient underwriting capacity to compete with its growing rivals, and embarked on a drive to attract new members. It also made it a bit easier to get into the club. What had actually followed was one of the most profitable decades in the club's existence and the 1980s looked set to follow suit. Basking in this sunny prospect, syndicates had let their costs drift upwards.

Practitioners paid themselves well, and enjoyed the perk of cheap membership of Lloyd's for themselves and sometimes for their families too. They failed to notice that the steady encroachment of the rest of the world's insurers into its patch was also lifting the veil on the famous Lloyd's expertise in gauging and pricing insurance risks. The light this slowly shed began to fade its mystique. Knowledge about pricing risks had been handed down at Lloyd's for three hundred years from underwriter to underwriter, each with varying degrees of skill. Now, even where its underwriters were still better able to gauge risk than their newer rivals, the big insurance groups eager for business were able, thanks to their lower cost-bases, to undercut practically any Lloyd's premium. To retain business Lloyd's hungrier and hastier underwriters had cut their prices back a bit too: but not their costs.

To become a Name at Lloyd's, you have to demonstrate a minimum degree of wealth, put some of it on deposit with the market, and sign on the dotted line by the summer of one year to become a member for the following year. However, since you were becoming a sole trader and accepting an unlimited liability to meet insurance claims against your syndicates' underwriting, you effectively put all your wealth at its disposal – and beyond indicating what sort of insurance (Lloyd's divides its broadly into marine, non-marine, aviation and motor) you wanted to 'write', you had no real say over what risks you were agreeing to cover *ad infinitum*.

Your choice of syndicates was suggested by your members' agent, and their business was conducted by a team of skilled (you hoped) professional underwriters who chose what to take on and what premium to charge; what to turn down, how much of the premiums to hold in reserve to meet claims, and how much to distribute to Names as profits. Underwriters paid themselves commissions on the money they distributed to the Names, and until 1990 a slice of that went to the Names' members' agents as remuneration too. So it was in an agent's interest to put his Names on to the most profitable syndicates. But if the syndicate concerned were 'under-reserving' and paying out more of the income stream as profit than was prudent – or 'overwriting' by taking in more premiums on more risks than the Names had resources to back if things went wrong – then trouble lay ahead. So did charges of conflicts of interest against some of the agents who seemed to have channelled their Names on to some of these high-paying syndicates.

However, until disaster struck at the end of the 1980s, belonging to Lloyd's had generated a handy extra income for Names (and their agents) distributed from the insurance premiums, and the investment income earned on them, even after meeting what claims did come in. In the eighties you 'only' had to prove you were worth £100,000 to became a Name at Lloyd's, while people working in or connected with the market did not have to pass a means test (but did have to make a deposit). You had only to deposit with the market, or get your bank to confirm that you could lay your hands on, one-third of that demonstrated wealth – and by 1988 it wasn't hard to be worth £100,000. Anyone with a big gain in the value of their home, land, or holiday cottage thanks to booming house prices, past inflation, and a fat South Eastern salary, could do it. New money flocked to Lloyd's, eager for a share of the profits that had been distributed regularly each year for the past two decades. Rich and newly rich foreign investors also liked to be Lloyd's Names. It was a great way to make your assets work twice over; and it had terrific social cachet. Few paid much heed to the formal warning given to all Names that this was a risk business, and not every members' agent fell over himself to stress it either.

Members of Lloyd's in the 1980s included Prince and Princess Michael of Kent, and members of the Royal Household such as Britain's premier aristocrat, the Duke of Norfolk, businessmen like Lord Vestey, author Jeffrey Archer, sporting and show-business stars including actress Susan Hampshire, golfer Tony Jacklin and tennis players Virginia Wade and Buster Mottram, and pillars of the establishment such as British Gulf War commander Sir Peter de la Billière. Glad to be part of this élite band at the time were Members of Parliament including Winston Churchill, grandson of Britain's wartime Prime Minister, Secretary of State for Energy John Wakeham, the junior defence minister Kenneth Carlisle, former Cabinet Minister Sir Norman Fowler and John Maples, the Economic Secretary to the Treasury. So were many other leading businessmen – including the late and now disgraced Robert Maxwell – retired people, land-rich but cash-poor farmers, widows whose husbands had made them 'Names' at Lloyd's years before, people who worked within the insurance market, and even secretary Betty Atkins given mini Lloyd's membership as a retirement present by grateful City bosses.

Throughout the eighties boom, they flocked to become members of Lloyd's. By 1988 it boasted a record 32,433 individual members who made combined private assets of £11 billion available for Lloyd's underwriting – the market's 'capacity'. Between them they belonged to more than 400 underwriting syndicates insuring against mishap anything from satellites to ships, buildings, oil rigs, aeroplanes, works of art, dancers' legs, racehorses and stud animals, ritzy advertising campaigns (against their stars doing something disgraceful causing the ads to be pulled), company executives fearful of kidnap, factory workers (against industrial injury or disease) right across the globe, and even against prize money having to be paid if someone captured the Loch Ness monster.

The upsurge in capacity flowed into an already oversupplied world market for insurance, but Lloyd's underwriters cast around to invent new forms of insurance to absorb the flood. Lloyd's was, after all, famous for being the world's most innovative insurance market. New ideas and new syndicates sprang up to meet the challenge. Much of the new capacity went into writing fashionable high-risk reinsurance business and raking in the higher premiums that could be charged for this cover. Initially the trend-setters tried reinsuring old US general liability risks. Older syndicates were delighted to be able to pass on some of the risks they faced on these policies, especially from likely asbestosis claims, and paid the reinsurance premiums. The new syndicates, and some older ones that chose to specialize in this field, wanted the business. Everyone was happy – or almost everyone – and no one was going to rock the boat. If the newer syndicates had miscalculated, that was their problem and their risk. When disenchantment came with that fad, the rising tide of new money was channelled into a new fashion: reinsuring catastrophe cover for one another, passed in first widening and then contracting circles from one syndicate to another, round and round the London market earning a slice of premium income at each place.

By 1988 the insurance club in its shiny new glass and steel building – said by City wags to resemble a coffee pot, with its steaming rooftop vents, reminiscent of the old market's coffee-house origins, and which was opened formally by no less a person than the Queen herself – was on the crest of the wave and riding high . . . towards a crashing fall.

Several things combined to upset the coffee pot, bringing this mighty market low in 1991. Shortly before Britain woke up in 1987 to the after-effects of its first hurricane in 200 years, corporate and judicial America had woken up to the green movement – with a vengeance. Tough new US pollution laws in the 1980s meant firms had to clean up their act, and their old dumps and sites. The cost was massive. So they looked to their insurers to pick up large chunks of the bill, on those policies written forty years before – and US judges grew lavish in their interpretation of the old documents.

Since most of the US companies suddenly caught up in America's green backlash had been reinsured at Lloyd's of London, the people due to pick up the bulk of the unexpected and crippling tab were its members. Claims are paid against policies written at the time that the event – such as breathing in damaging asbestosis fibres – which caused the accident or damage is deemed to have happened; large settlements years later may show the premiums paid at the time to have been hugely inadequate for the eventual degree of risk. This is known as 'long-tail' business: still valid insurance policies that may be activated decades later, and it is where the gravest (though not all) of Lloyd's problems in the late 1980s and early 1990s originated.

Asbestos claims brought severe problems in the mid-1980s but these were nothing compared to what followed them. The first year of really grim reckoning on all fronts was 1988 but, since for reasons of prudence Lloyd's syndicates wait three years for the bulk of any claims to arrive against each single year's underwriting before doing the official tally and sharing out the profits or losses, it was 1991 before the full horror was known.

On 1988's underwriting Lloyd's members faced an expensive and deadly cocktail. The basic ingredients were provisions for the massive pollution clean-up known to be in the pipeline, the bill for the October 1987 hurricane – eventual cost to UK insurers, £2 billion – plus the first claims from the Piper Alpha oil rig and the Lockerbie Pan-Am disasters in 1988.

But there was an extra, vicious twist to the mix supplied by the recent fashion for reinsuring catastrophe cover. Not only had the original cover been spread amongst Lloyd's syndicates, but they had subsequently also divided and subdivided parts of their share of the risk within the Lloyd's market. The reinsurance 'spiral' that resulted narrowed down to a handful of unlucky syndicates left holding most of the parcel, but they were at the end of a hideously complicated web of claims, which led to considerable double-counting of the anticipated bills as each syndicate tried to work out which claims it might have to meet if its own reinsurers in the chain let it down. Meanwhile the brokers who placed and re-placed the cover had earned a fortune in commission.

In subsequent years the double-counting will be unravelled and some syndicate members could heave a huge sigh of relief one day as the cash set aside now means more can then be paid out in profits again later to those still aboard the better syndicates, who live to tell the tale, and to lucky new members – maybe. This assumes there are no more nasty surprises to soak up cash in the meantime. But the immediate effect of the reinsurance spiral was like vigorously shaking a bottle of champagne before popping the cork, or banging a glass down on the table to create a tequila slammer. Its impact on the already explosive combination of the catalogue of disasters and anticipated pollution and known asbestosis claims, which were still flowing in despite hopes that they had passed their peak, was to send the estimated total claim facing Lloyd's syndicates into the stratosphere. Many of its members doubted if they would ever get over the monstrous financial hangover that followed.

Lloyd's syndicates lost a net total of £509 million on their 1988 under-writing as the double-counted likely claims outweighed and swallowed up profits made on other insurance underwritten during that year. When the sum was finally calculated and announced to a stunned financial world in 1991, Lloyd's members erupted in shock and disbelief. Matters were made even worse by the warning that the results for 1989, to be tallied and released in the course of 1992, were expected to be even worse – for there was no respite from disasters as the 1980s gave way to 1990; even 1991 looked 'iffy' in some observers' now jaundiced eyes.

Hurricane Hugo (estimated cost, £1 billion) swept through America in 1989, which was also rocked by the San Francisco earthquake, while pollution claims remained a looming harbinger of financial doom. In 1990, more storms and floods caused massive damage in Europe while early 1991 brought snow, ice and flood damage to Britain. And that is just a sample. To each catastrophe, the reinsurance spiral added extra kick.

For members of Lloyd's on the worst-hit syndicates, the catalogue read like the script of a horror movie. Each big new claim meant another bill for their already reeling syndicate. Instead of raking in a useful extra income as planned, they were plunged into losses that soaked up first their 30 per cent deposits at Lloyd's, then their syndicate's reserves and any extra personal or special reserves they had built up on deposit there as well as any profits they had earned for that year from other more fortunate syndicates, and finally triggered calls on them to make large payments to top up their troubled syndicates' depleted reserves to face the anticipated claims. Lloyd's may be British but it serves an international market and many of its members also hail from all over the world. Its North American Names were to prove just as vociferous and litigious as its UK ones when rows broke out.

For many people in Britain cleaning up the mess of fallen trees, smashed cars, damaged roofs, missing garden sheds and devastated gardens on the morning of 16 October 1987 and preparing their insurance claims, these events were to mean higher insurance premiums on their homes and cars as insurance companies reassessed their charges in the light of the sums they were now having to pay out and the damage done to their own profit and loss accounts. For investors owning shares in the big insurance companies, the huge new claims, coming on top of snow damage in January 1987 and claims for subsidence caused by a series of long hot summers, meant lower dividends and wobbly share prices for quite a time. Meanwhile, the insurance companies took care to offset even more of their own risk in future by reinsuring a large part of their exposure to bad weather claims at Lloyd's and elsewhere than before.

For individuals clearing up after the hurricane who had also risked their money directly in reinsuring those policies and underwriting others through Lloyd's of London, the damage was a far greater blow. Some of them found themselves paying not just for their own storm damage (and claiming for it under their own household policies where they could), but picking up large chunks of other people's claims as well as these fed through the reinsurance spiral to their own Lloyd's syndicates.

For the people whose first year of underwriting at Lloyd's was 1988, and for elderly Names who faced little chance of rebuilding their assets, this year of disasters triggered the worst kind of financial nightmare which even the taxbreaks available to newcomers could not entirely alleviate for many. One serious loser set up a rickshaw hire business in the heart of London to make a living pounding the streets. Whatever their status, few of the members caught in the flood of claims against 1988's underwriting could easily meet the bills that came in, and many faced real financial hardship. Their resources had been eroded by falling share and house prices as the 1980s boom turned into the 1990–3 recession, making it much harder to raise the money to meet the cash calls now coming through. By 1992 some had also lost their jobs.

As the insurance claims poured in on all fronts between 1988 and the end of 1991, some Names faced calls to meet them running into hundreds of thousands of pounds each and the prospect of even greater losses to come. Others looking at calls of even a few tens of thousands were in no better position to meet them. Once-soaring UK house prices had started to tumble after mid-1988, as the bottom fell out of the boom and by 1991 people once considered to be worth £250,000 or £500,000 saw their property assets dwindle in value just as they most needed to be able to borrow against them or cash them in to meet their Lloyd's obligations.

Financial ruin now stared many in the face. But they did not all pay up quietly. Instead some started questioning the competence of those who had acted for them in the market, criticized the way the market itself was governed, formed action committees – and reached for their lawyers in droves, on both sides of the Atlantic. Gradually the dissidents' voices grew stronger and their numbers, too, grew in volume until Lloyd's faced full-scale rebellion that threatened the very fabric of its existence.

In America, Lloyd's method of canvassing for Names came under attack as lawyers there accused it of operating illegally. As well as suing on behalf of angry and litigious US Names, they argued that Lloyd's should have been vetted and approved by the powerful Securities and Exchange Commission (SEC) there before being allowed to sign up US members. Lloyd's said it had been exempt under an agreement confirmed with the SEC as recently as ill-starred 1988; but the SEC decided to re-examine the arrangement, in the light of the monster losses now being declared.

The incumbent chairman of Lloyd's, David Coleridge, a successful and tough-talking, portly fellow who, despite his reputedly formidable brain-power is inclined to sound off first and think afterwards, publicly accused rebellious Names of being wimps and whingers who had enjoyed the fat years but now sought to wriggle out of their obligations in the lean ones. He conveniently disregarded the fact that many now suffering losses had only joined since 1987 and had never had a fat year. He had, however, already appointed a task force under David Rowland, boss of the large insurance broker Sedgwick, to look into the implications for Lloyd's future of all these events.

Lloyd's also created a Hardship Committee to help struggling Names find ways of paying up, headed by Council member and Names' representative, Dr Mary Archer. By early 1992, 300 people had applied. There was no question of anyone being let off the hook, however.

The high drama and bitter recriminations on all fronts reached a crescendo by early 1992. Lloyd's survival hung in the balance as nearly 4,000 Names resigned from the club in 1991 and thousands more either ceased or scaled down their underwriting in line with their own depleted fortunes. Many also refused to pay the cash calls to keep up their syndicates' reserves. This raised a grim spectre indeed: if everyone refused to pay, was there enough money in the Central Fund, the Lloyd's rainy day kitty for such emergencies, to meet claims? If not, Lloyd's was in danger of meltdown. Its governing Council ended 1991 grimly aware that the venerable insurance club could fail to make it into the twenty-first century; and awaited the deliberations of the task force with a mixture of impatience and trepidation. At one stage it considered having the task-force findings printed on (appropriately) blood-red paper to prevent photocopies being made and leaked before the Council had digested them.

To the men and women working in the market, David Coleridge (a descendant of poet Samuel Taylor Coleridge) was a somewhat Rambo-esque figure whose energy and drive could save Lloyd's. Some of the more jaundiced and outspoken badly hit Names regarded him as more resembling the captain of an unruly and even piratical band of adventurers, who had lost and perhaps plundered their fortunes while the commander snoozed. Tempers were running as high as the losses were deep.

But Lloyd's still had its admirers as well as its detractors. And among those who would prefer it to survive these rough seas, smarten up its crew and sail into a new dawn, were some of its greatest (and some of its oldest) competitors: Britain's big insurance companies. They wanted access to a market like Lloyd's, capable of underwriting large or unusual reinsurance risks, in order to spread their own risk and complement their own services to clients.

Lloyd's has long been a magnet attracting insurance business to the United Kingdom that would otherwise have been placed in other countries. Despite its troubles and shifts in the world market for insurance, it was still attracting millions of pounds worth of business to the UK, business that the big insurance companies have piggybacked in the past. Though overseas competition was getting stiffer and the British insurance industry suffered from the effects of overcapacity in the world insurance market, with its income shrinking as a result through the late 1980s, between them Lloyd's and the insurance companies still pulled in just over £3 billion worth of 'invisible' earnings to the United Kingdom in 1990 – money earned from providing services rather than making physical goods, of which Lloyd's contributed £1.69 billion. In 1986, however, the combined sum had been nearer £5 billion. Times were hard in other insurance markets too. In the United States, insurance companies were going down like flies trapped against a hot window pane. Above the general buzz of trouble, however, Lloyd's difficulties were loudest.

The big international insurance groups all have offices in the City of London, established from the eighteenth century onwards to be near the venerable insurance club and the brokers that have clustered around it bringing in underwriting business. In the early 1990s they too were cutting back, merging or pulling out of the London market altogether. Many of them had just clubbed together themselves to rent and kit out an expensive new building to house a London Underwriting Centre, where they could share certain costs and space under one roof even closer to the modern Lloyd's building and, in particular, to the colony of insurance brokers scuttling between them all. While happy to give Lloyd's some serious competition and take a greater slice of its original business, these big insurance companies had not previously conceived of replacing it entirely. Despite the damage to London's reputation by Lloyd's difficulties, there was still more to be lost than gained if Lloyd's were allowed to sink under the waves of disaster after 300 years of plying its remarkable trade. Or was there? By early 1992, some of the international insurers with London offices were beginning to think they could, indeed, replace Lloyd's quite happily if it slowly foundered and slipped beneath the waves of history. All they needed was a little time to move into the gap.

Lloyd's was slow to respond to the dangers on every side. When the terrible news broke in June 1992 that this once great institution had lost over £2 billion on its 1989 underwriting year, the shock waves split the market. As the remedial action was speeded up, the question on everybody's lips was: is it too late to save Lloyd's of London?

2
What's in a Name?

| *A merchant of great*
traffic through the world

(SHAKESPEARE, *THE TAMING OF THE SHREW*,
ACT I, SCENE 1, L. 12)

Lloyd's seems to attract the descendants of nineteenth-century poets who had a taste for opium-eating. The families of both Samuel Taylor Coleridge and Robert Southey have spawned current-day Lloyd's men working respectively in London and South Africa (and of older provenance, on a par with Lloyd's own, in Paris there is La Rochefoucauld in the fold).

Over the years Lloyd's itself has been no stranger to outbreaks of controversy and the occasional scandal, but the events of 1991 and 1992 were cataclysmic even by their standards. In the past it had always managed to stave off the threat of having outside regulation forced upon it, preferring to wash its dirty linen inside the club. The Names' rebellion of 1992 threatened to open the floodgates to external inquisitors with little sympathy for the Lloyd's old guard.

The 300-year-old market, though housed today in one of London's most avant-garde buildings, is still steeped in seventeenth- and eighteenth-century tradition, personal connections, and privilege. It is a bustling, gossipy, buzzing commercial tower of Babel where the language may be English but the business comes from every imaginable corner of the world. By early 1992, it was riven in two: with the old guard trying to update and preserve what they could, and the young turks beginning to look for a much more radical restructuring of the market to ensure its healthy survival into the next century.

Inside the Lloyd's building is the underwriting 'Room' (now four floors round a central atrium) where insurance brokers come to find takers for the risks their clients want insured. In the hurly-burly of talk and paper and brokers rushing to and fro trying to agree terms with this underwriter or that one, it had grown easy for the working élite to look upon the people whose money underpins the whole edifice as mere punters, unskilled and uninformed in the ways of insurance, who could therefore be disdained to a degree if they started to get uppity and ask awkward questions. Hence the attitude expressed by some would-be wits and wags within the upper echelons of the Lloyd's hierarchy at the first signs of rebellion among previously acquiescent Names, that if God didn't intend some people to be fleeced, he would not have made them sheep.

This attitude put outside members of Lloyd's – the vast majority of Names – at a double disadvantage to those Names who work in the market itself. It also stirred up real fury when Names began to suspect they had indeed been fleeced by the Lloyd's practitioners who had been supposedly tending their interests. David Coleridge's accusations, that external Names had reaped the benefits of membership and now sought to escape the whirlwind, overlooked that even the greediest of investors is entitled to expect his agent to do his job; which is to look after the client's interests completely.

Though as a result of past scandals, Lloyd's had moved during the mid-1980s to protect all Names from unscrupulous and even fraudulent insiders, allegations were once again rife in the summer of 1991 that the 'non-working', external Names tended to get the second-class business while the cream was lapped up by the syndicates populated by the working Names, their families and friends, on to which it was virtually impossible for a newcomer to get. Names also suspected that certain reinsurance syndicates had been cynically taken advantage of, to offload asbestosis risks, by other underwriters who realized how bad the claims might be. A Lloyd's catchphrase is *uberrimae fidei* (*with utmost good faith*) and the brokers it somewhat regally allows to place business with Lloyd's syndicates are not supposed to withhold information about their clients' risk from the underwriters taking on the business. So this was a serious allegation.

What was the Council going to do about it? Names demanded to know. Lloyd's said it found no evidence of breach of faith on these insurance contracts, but many of the lawsuits that followed sprang out of this suspicion, and a string of accusations of negligence.

Each outbreak of scandal in Lloyd's past has been followed by a strenuous bout of cleaning up its act, leading to rejuvenation, fat pickings, subsequent complacency, and eventually to a new scandal and a repeat of the whole cycle. Much the same is true of the history of the nearly 400-year-old London Stock Exchange; while the large UK insurance companies dating from 1717 onwards owe their long incorporated lives to the general clean-up of stock and insurance broking and underwriting that followed the great financial scandal of 1720, the South Sea bubble.

Lloyd's, like the London Stock Exchange, began in a seventeenth-century London coffee house – in Lloyd's case, the one run in Tower Street by a certain Edward Lloyd – where Britain's shipowners, merchants and wealthy individuals would regularly congregate to enjoy the fashionable new drink, one of the few pleasures of Puritan England at the time and which had the advantage of keeping them sober, unlike the wine bars beloved of City folk today. While there they would hear the latest news and gossip, and reports of whose ship had come in, whose sunk, whose cargo was sold profitably or lost at sea – and strike the deals designed to spread the risk of their ship and its cargoes going down amongst the many instead of a few.

Whilst shipping gossip became Lloyd's staple diet, and its proprietor even ran a newspaper of shipping news for a time, the first record of Lloyd's coffee house concerns some stolen watches. In 1688, another Edward, Edward Bransby of Derby, was mugged by a pockmarked, black-haired man in an old brown riding coat and a black beaver hat who stole five watches from him. Determined, if he could, to get them back, Mr Bransby advertized in the *London Gazette* describing his assailant and the rather ornate watches, and offering a one-guinea reward to whoever could tell him where they were, either by leaving word at 'Mr Edward Lloyd's coffee house in Tower Street' or direct to Mr Bransby himself in Derby. History does not relate whether he ever saw the watches again; but Lloyd thrived. He moved his premises to Lombard Street, and the shippers followed.

Nowadays considerably more than ships are insured at the modern Lloyd's but in essence remarkably little has changed. The idea was both ingenious and simple. The shipowner spread the risk to himself amongst a wide range of people by insuring against loss at sea, and paid them a fee, the 'premium', for being prepared to underwrite his ship and cargo against such loss. Since not all ships sank this generated a handy income for the 'underwriters', out of which the occasional claim would have to be met.

Individuals underwrote the risk by putting their name down on a 'slip' of paper indicating what percentage of the cost of a ship foundering they were prepared to carry, in exchange for a pro rata share of the premium paid by the ship or cargo owner for the comfort of that insurance cover. Hence the expressions of becoming a 'Name' at Lloyd's and writing a 'line' of insurance on a 'slip'. To show that they were good for their share of the bills if a ship did go down, Names would provide evidence of their personal wealth, and had to be prepared to sell their own assets to meet these obligations if necessary. Since each risk was spread amongst dozens of individual Names, they found themselves forming *de facto* syndicates.

After the scandal of the collapse of the speculative South Sea Company in 1720 triggered new legislation to try and police the conduct of rapidly expanding British trade a bit more, only two companies – the Royal Exchange Assurance and London Assurance – were allowed to provide marine insurance. The Bill passed in parliament forbade other companies to dabble in these waters, but it did not exclude individuals. So it was business as usual for the 'merchant insurers' who from then on were more drawn than ever to their unofficial office at Edward Lloyd's coffee house. But not only shipping insurance was carried out there. All sorts of business was conducted, from auctioning ships by candle (when the candle burned down to a line or even to an inserted nail, the auction was over and the highest bidder at that point had bought the vessel), to betting against the life expectancy of well-known people. Even the length of time a felon survived on the gallows was meat to these gamblers.

The market in shipping insurance eventually moved from there in 1769, mainly to get away from some of the more disreputable business that was going on. The shipping fraternity moved off in high dudgeon to a new coffee house, but kept the Lloyd's name for their society. Over the centuries the coffee-house element faded and the business element dominated – and these kind of premises proved too small. By 1774 the market was on the move again, this time to rooms in the Royal Exchange building, but the club atmosphere, syndicates, and the concept of Names' unlimited liability to meet any bills survived. The red-coated 'caller' who broadcasts messages to people in the modern underwriting 'Room' is also still called a waiter, his top-hatted colleagues man the front entrance, while liveried waiters continue to dance attendance in white-powdered gloves on the Council's weekly silver-service luncheon.

Gradually Lloyd's leading lights also invented other kinds of insurance cover, against fire, burglary and more, until now you can insure practically anything against the unforeseen at Lloyd's – from a composer's ears or a distiller's nose to a space station – if you are prepared to pay the price asked. Public events, art exhibitions, diamonds and gold nuggets in transit, model Suzanne Mizzi, sports and rock stars have all been covered against mishap in mid-event, shoot, play or concert. Skylab was insured by Lloyd's against bits falling to earth and damaging property or killing those below (and it was *Cutty Sark* whisky that wanted cover in case the light-hearted prize it offered for finding the Loch Ness monster were ever collected). Most of the business done, however, is for commercial and industrial groups from all over the world whose brokers come to Lloyd's of London seeking cover for their assets, operations and employees.

A plethora of rules and regulations has grown up around this system but when rebellion broke out in the early 1990s the basic formula had not really changed in 300 years. The rules are made by the Council of Lloyd's; the practical details are seen to by the Committee of Lloyd's and a host of working parties looking into this and that when thought necessary. The chairman of Lloyd's is elected annually and often invited by his peers to stand for a second or even third term.

Even in the eighteenth century, trotting off to Edward Lloyd's coffee house in the City regularly to keep track of the business one had underwritten, or get cover for ships, became a tiresome and impractical business. So Names had appointed agents to handle their underwriting affairs, and shipowners and other businessmen picked insurance brokers to arrange their insurance cover. Agents handling several different Names today put them into a variety of different underwriting syndicates for a good spread of business. A rich Name may be on tens of syndicates, a less adventurous one of more modest means would be on ten to twenty. The new Lloyd's building remains the market-place where the underwriting representatives of all these syndicates come together and are badgered by the insurance brokers who want to get various risks insured for their clients.

For more than two centuries, Lloyd's had regarded itself as a society, with an elected committee which regulated its members. In 1871 it was officially incorporated by Act of Parliament as a society of private underwriters, and continued to run along the old lines. But one hundred years later the insurance companies were giving it serious competition while the Society's in-house regulatory and disciplinary systems were now very stretched after the expansion in membership over the previous century to 18,000 Names. The inevitable scandals followed culminating, in 1978 – a year that was almost as cataclysmic for Lloyd's as 1988 was to prove – in the Sasse affair in which syndicate 762 and its lead underwriter Tim Sasse were taken for an expensive ride in dodgy US and Canadian property assurance, losses on computer leasing, and a mixture of other poor quality risks written in the mid-1970s.

Inquiries were held and the Lloyd's hierarchy tried to sort out the mess from within. But Names facing huge losses suspected that members of the club were instinctively less likely to view co-members' peccadilloes with the cold hard stare that outsiders would focus on them – and refused to pay for what it saw as Lloyd's failure to enforce its own rules. (Sounds familiar, doesn't it?) Writs began to fly. After much argument, a deal was finally struck in 1980 whereby the Sasse syndicate's Names put up £6.25 million towards its 1976 losses and Lloyd's put up rather more at £9 million, and all of Sasse 762's near £7 million loss on 1977's underwriting. In exchange for this aid, the Names dropped their legal actions.

In the midst of this drama, the Committee of Lloyd's decided the time had indeed come for a long hard look at reforming the market, from within – before the government did it for them from outside the club. A working party led by Sir Henry Fisher was set up with a very wide brief. His report eventually came up with proposals for major constitutional reforms that were enshrined in the 1982 Lloyd's Act of Parliament and established the Lloyd's Council with tougher and more efficient regulatory powers than the old committee exercised.

It also meant the separation of underwriting agencies from the insurance brokers, which until now had been able to own both operations. This division was meant to put an end to any potential conflicts of interest between the broker acting for the would-be insured and the syndicates providing the cover. Not all Lloyd's practitioners were happy with this separation of the expertise; but because of past abuses the government of the day insisted on it.

The 1982 Act also gave the Governor of the Bank of England powers to appoint four Council members from outside Lloyd's and created the post of a chief executive, though the first incumbent was soon to find himself often at loggerheads in a decreasingly subtle battle for power with the old-guard chairman of the new Council. The face of Lloyd's and some of its practices were radically changed. So were its premises: the old Committee had decided in the late 1970s that it needed more space and set in motion the search for a design that would eventually yield the stunning new Lloyd's building that dominates Lime Street across the road from its previous home.

Sasse was not to be the last Lloyd's scandal. Gone but not forgotten is the insider's habit of popping oneself and a few colleagues on to a 'baby' syndicate of perhaps as few as half a dozen people which took a slice of the best risks and left the rest to other Names on the main syndicates looked after by the same underwriter. Even David Coleridge had been on one of these in the past – and in 1991 and 1992 the feeling had returned that insiders might have been protecting their own to the detriment of outside Names, this time using the reinsurance spiral to offload high-risk exposures.

Brewing through the 1970s and spilling into the 1980s were a cat's-cradle of interlocking scandals that culminated in the PCW affair, when a Lloyd's syndicate was found to have been defrauded to the tune of £38.7 million by senior men of its underwriting agency, in a complicated reinsurance swindle. Poor underwriting contributed to more huge losses on top of that for the unhappy PCW Names, taking the total calls they faced to meet future liabilities up to £235 million. Once more there was mutiny amongst Lloyd's Names and, again after much huffing and puffing by the Lloyd's establishment, an agreement was finally struck in 1987 that saw the Names carry the £34 million cost attributed just to the poor underwriting; potential defendants of any legal action that the PCW Names might otherwise take putting up £55 million; and Lloyd's own Central Fund provided the balance to create a £134 million pool that could be invested to generate enough gain to meet the £235 million anticipated liabilities.

Once again litigation by angry Names had been headed off. Some of the miscreants involved in other limbs of the complicated affair were disciplined and expelled by Lloyd's but the chief culprits had fled the United Kingdom. Arrest warrants were issued, but by early 1993 the two main accused, underwriters Peter Dixon and Peter Cameron-Webb, still had not been brought to book and were unlikely to be, as Britain's leisurely extradition moves had become time-barred in the USA. In 1990, though, steps were taken finally by the British Secretary of State for Trade and Industry Peter Lilley to disqualify them for fifteen years from being a director of a British company; steps that eventually came to their slow fruition in early 1992.

Lloyd's was not alone in facing embarrassing revelations of wrongdoing in the early 1980s. Its venerable cousin the Stock Exchange and big business had their share, too, in an outbreak of fiddles that were soon dubbed 'velvet-collar crime' in the City. But in its efforts to modernize the securities dealing industry, the Stock Exchange moved in the opposite direction to Lloyd's: bringing its brokers and market-makers (its rough equivalent of underwriters, in this case) together into huge combines ahead of the new rules that took effect in the Financial Services Act of 1986, while Lloyd's brokers had been forced in the 1982 Lloyd's Act to divest their interests in underwriting agencies.

The year 1986 saw the British government ask Sir Patrick Neill QC to lead a new committee to study Lloyd's regulatory framework in the light of what was now planned for the rest of the financial services industry. He came up with a list of seventy-one recommendations which the Council of Lloyd's rapidly agreed – more or less – to implement off its own bat, to avoid legislation. This included increasing the number of Council members appointed from outside the club by the Governor of the Bank of England to eight, doubling the requirement for the four introduced by the 1982 Lloyd's Act. After the first rush, progress implementing the remaining recommendations was steady rather than speedy.

When in 1991, latest Lloyd's chairman David Coleridge (head of Lloyd's underwriting agency Sturge) appointed David Rowland, boss of the Sedgwick insurance broking house, to look into the implications for Lloyd's of the events of 1988 and the outlook for it, given the tough competition in world insurance markets generally, this was the third major report on the insurance club in just ten years – and the lawsuits that began in the autumn of 1991 were its third serious brush with angry Names in the same period.

When someone becomes a Name at Lloyd's, he goes through a complicated vetting procedure. First he (or she) needs two sponsors each of whom must be a member of Lloyd's themselves. One must vouch for his or her being a decent sort, the other must be a director or partner of the members' agent that he is joining through and that will look after his affairs as a Name. Some members' agencies pay people to be sponsors or to introduce potential new Names to them – in which case they are supposed to tell you, and Lloyd's, about the arrangement.

The members' agent recommends which syndicates the Name should go on to for a good spread of risk, and whether and when to join more or withdraw from certain ones. Most people only have one members' agent each but you can have several if you want, in which case you have to appoint a co-ordinating agent to keep track of everything (for a fee). Members' agents also charge a management fee, and take an annual commission, generally averaging around 7.5 per cent, on the Name's net overall annual profits from all his Lloyd's syndicates. It is therefore in his interest to maximize your profits. But this can sometimes backfire.

The syndicates are run by managing agents, who also charge for their services. They appoint and pay the professional underwriters who decide what risks will be insured or reinsured; and try to make sure the syndicate has a prudent mix of 'short-tail' business on which any claims will come in quite fast and be over and done with, and 'long-tail' business against which claims could roll in years later. Lloyd's syndicates do not write long-tail life assurance though they do provide annual cover for accidental death or injury. The managing agent settles insurance claims against the syndicate, holds some premium income in reserve to invest for future claims and distributes the rest plus some of the investment income to the members' agent to pass on; and supplies the syndicate's annual report.

In return for these services, managing agents earned, in 1992, an annual fee of about 0.75 per cent of the Name's premium income, and a commission, of around 15 per cent, on the Name's profits from underwriting, investment, and reserves held for him within the syndicate. Out of this he met the syndicates' expenses, pays the underwriter, and pocketed his own profits. Thus the Name paid two lots of fees and two lots of profit commission: one to the managing agent of each syndicate on that syndicate's performance and the second to his members' agent on his aggregated profits (less losses).

Being salaried, the underwriter (who is often the same person as the managing agent) was paid regardless of whether the syndicate had a good or a bad year – and salaries had tended to be generous, along with good pension plans too. If he were also the managing agent, in a good year he got the slice of profit commission as well; two incomes for one man and very nice work if you can get it. Names who faced huge cash calls on their bad years were not best pleased to discover that the underwriters who got them into this pickle were still pocketing handsome salaries paid for by the new financially beleaguered Names themselves.

Members' agents could either be independent, freestanding organizations or, unlike the managing agents, they could link up with a Lloyd's broker. Alternatively they could be teamed up with a managing agency (but not both) – providing another potential conflict of interest if things go awry. (Lloyd's provides lists of all in each category for Names.)

Dating probably from the days when it took a ship two to three years to return from a major trading voyage, Lloyd's insurance syndicates keep each year of account 'open' for three years to meet the first rush of claims against the premiums received, before deciding it is now safe to balance the books, and paying Names their share of the profits. Then they reinsure the policies written in that year into the subsequent year's accounting period – which is still open – and pay a premium to the underwriting Names forming the later syndicate year. The premium is priced to reflect what is currently known about the risk of any further claims coming through, and paid out of the closing year's profits. In this way the liability to meet any future 'long-tail' claims relating to its policies is transferred and carried forward. This is known as 'reinsurance to close'. The rolling three-year system is why the 1988 losses could not be finally totted up until 1990 was over, and also explains why there may be fresh losses against the 1989 and 1990 years dating back to cover written, not just in 1988, but even decades earlier.

The three-year system also explains why new Names receive no profits from underwriting until three years after joining, though if their syndicate is short of money it can tap them for it from day one. Another drawback is that if a major disaster strikes two years and 363 days after 1 January 1992, it could soak up all existing profits on that year's underwriting. When a Name dies, no new underwriting is done against his assets but calls for money can still be made against his estate or his heirs until his last year of underwriting is closed. Again this is normally a three-year exposure. If a Name is unlucky enough to be on a syndicate with such grave problems against one year's underwriting that it cannot be closed – because it was impossible to work out what the risk was and therefore what the reinsurance premium paid to the same syndicate's current year should be – it is left 'open', and then the calls to meet his share of its liabilities can keep flowing in. This can go on for twenty years or more, during which the Name – or his estate – cannot leave Lloyd's, though he may have ceased any new annual underwriting long since.

Names can protect themselves to some degree by taking out 'stop-loss' reinsurance policies of their own, or estate protection policies. But these were not always cheap nor easy to come by and Names depended on their members' agents for advice about whether to buy this protection and to what degree.

To join the wider UK insurance market without losing much sleep, you could simply buy a handful of shares in Commercial Union or the Pru for as little as a few hundred pounds, and hope they will go up along with the firm's profits and pay you twice yearly dividends. Insurance groups have also been reporting some hefty losses in the early 1990s; but with them the most money you can lose is whatever you have spent on buying the shares – your original investment – and the most you ever feel you have lost is the peak value they hit if you fail to sell them at that point. Not so if you become a Name at Lloyd's. Then not just your stake money but your entire wealth is potentially at risk if things go wrong.

In 1991 with the storm clouds breaking over this financial lightning-conductor, you had to prove ownership of assets worth a minimum of £250,000 as evidence of your ability to underwrite insurance risks directly.

That had been raised from the £100,000 floor required in the 1980s, but those who suffered in the huge losses of the 1988 year grew, with hindsight, to feel that not even assets of £250,000 were enough to underpin the open-ended risk they had been taking.

To become a Name, you not only need your sponsors but you have to confirm that you own enough 'net eligible means' to meet this means test. These must be assets of which you had the outright benefit, that is, which were not already mortgaged or in some way promised to someone else. You also have to go to a 'Rota Committee' meeting at which all the risks are solemnly explained to you, in the high eighteenth-century committee room designed by Robert Adam and now housed in the top floors of the modern building. Having applied by the end of August, all the paperwork must be done by the end of November to start writing insurance in January of the new year.

There are strict rules about what you net eligible assets can be. The 1992 rules of membership state that at least 60 per cent of the £250,000 (or more) wealth demonstrated to Lloyd's had to be in the form of all or any of the following list: shares and securities traded on the UK Stock Exchange (and none of these could be more than 30 per cent of the total means you demonstrated); foreign securities listed on a local exchange; cash at a bank or building society; the surrender value of your life assurance policies; your interests in any trust funds; your national savings certificates or even your premium bonds; bank, building society, or insurance company guarantees and letters of credit; or gold bullion or gold coins adding up to not more than 30 per cent of your means test, and taken at 70 per cent of their current market value.

Ruled out as assets for the means test were your main home, shares in private companies, your share in a partnership, motor cars, yachts, furniture, the contents of your house, pictures, antiques, non-gold coins, jewellery and livestock – unless you could support the value you claimed they represented with a bank guarantee or a letter of credit, which would be accepted. After that little lot you could demonstrate having the remaining 40 per cent of the means test in freehold property, less any outstanding mortgage on it or loan against it; or via your share in any jointly owned property; and in leasehold land or property with at least fifty years of the lease to run and provided that the remaining length of the lease and your own age added up to more than one hundred years! Would-be Names from outside Britain living in countries with exchange control rules had to show means in a country that did allow assets to be moved out of it, or provide letters of credit or guarantees backing up their demonstrated wealth. There were also extra provisos for American Names from some States, to take account of local property law, and their spouses' agreement was also needed before they could sign up as Lloyd's members.

New Names had to apply in good time to qualify by the August of one year – and those leaving must resign by then – to start underwriting from the beginning of the following one. Once in, they must maintain the value of their means at the level required by the Council of Lloyd's. If their value goes down, the member must tell Lloyd's and either indicate what other qualifying assets he or she has to make up the difference, or stop underwriting. It is against the rules to wriggle out of underwriting by deliberately reducing the assets you have demonstrated for your means test, or just letting them dwindle without any effort to top up with something else to meet the means test.

Though there was no regular check that your assets were still worth what they were when you joined, the Council retained the right to double-check at any time if it thought this was necessary. Once the would-be new member had satisfied Lloyd's that he or she had the wherewithal to join, he would decide (guided by his chosen members' agent) how much business he wanted to underwrite per year.

This was the Name's premium limit. For 1992, the maximum amount of premium any individual was allowed to earn from underwriting in any one year was £2 million, and the minimum £50,000. Once new members, applying in 1991 to start writing in 1992, had agreed their premium limit, they had to keep a set ratio of it – usually 30 per cent – in funds actually held at Lloyd's so that the syndicate had instant access to cash needed to meet any large calls in future against the policies the Name underwrote.

At least 20 per cent of the premium limit had to go into a 'failsafe' deposit to be placed in trust directly with Lloyd's and the rest could be held in personal reserves looked after by your members' agent or in special reserve funds run by your agent and Lloyd's itself. This 20 per cent failsafe could be in the form of anything from a letter of credit from a bank or building society, cash in a variety of hard currencies, your building society account (subject to no more than seven days' loss of interest if withdrawn to meet calls), your national savings certificates, or shares either in London Stock Exchange listed UK companies with a market capitalization of £50 million or shares in UK listed foreign companies capitalized at over £100 million. Or you could hand over guarantees from your life assurance company or paid-up life policies (with large reputable insurers), and single premium bonds. Interest on any of these could still be paid over to you for an income stream, or retained to top up your personal reserve at Lloyd's. Getting at any capital gain on them was much trickier and subject to strict conditions.

The failsafe deposit and the rest of your funds held at Lloyd's were subject to an annual check, every 31 December, to see they were still worth the required amount. This was the annual solvency test. Fluctuating share prices, and exchange rates, could change the values of these deposits quite dramatically and if your reserves dipped below, you would be told to reduce your underwriting for the next year. If they rose, there was no problem and you might even be able to increase the amount of underwriting you did and earn more premium income.

Members agree their premium limit each year. For 1992, these fell into three broad categories, of which category 1 members were the top dogs, the people with means of £250,000 or more who had deposited at least £25,000 or built up their Lloyd's reserves over time to a maximum of £600,000. It is they who must keep at least 30 per cent of their premium limit in funds at Lloyd's. Depending on what that limit is agreed as, category 1 members could write 'lines' of insurance from a minimum £50,000, right up to the full £2 million if they have a failsafe and reserves totalling £600,000. Their premium limit could rise in increments of £25,000 a year, provided their deposits kept pace.

The next category down, category 2 members, were those whose means had dipped under £250,000 but were still more than £100,000, or people working at Lloyd's full time (or linked with Lloyd's firms) who wanted to become 'vocational' members themselves. Either way, they had to put a minimum of £25,000 into the failsafe and personal or special reserves – or more – with the actual sum worth 40 per cent of their premium limit, which was in turn restricted to between £50,000 and a maximum of £600,000.

Category 3 members' means had slid under £100,000 or they were people working in the market who as a perk were allowed to start underwriting in a more modest way. Their failsafe and reserves had to total 50 per cent of their premium limit, which again was not allowed to exceed £190,000 of premium income a year or they would be hugely overstretched given their modest asset base.

Finally, for vocational members only, there was a special category 4 membership which let them off demonstrating any personal wealth at all, but who must still put funds worth 50 per cent of their premium limit into funds at Lloyd's – and who could not write a line of more than £100,000 a year.

In Lloyd's jargon, 'vocational' members are generally known as working Names and Names drawn from outside the market-place are known as non-working Names or 'external' Names. Any Name can agree with his members' agent to increase the premium limit from 1 January each year provided he put up enough extra funds to keep his ratio in line with the new limit.

It all sounds very complicated and careful. But given that letters of credit and bank guarantees could be accepted for 60 per cent of your show of wealth and for your deposit, while a valuation of the mortgage-free part of a holiday home would do for the 40 per cent balance of the means test, it has been possible to be a Name at Lloyd's without actually physically handing over any assets. For people like farmers, with valuable land but not always a big income and few shareholdings, this made Lloyd's a most attractive way of putting their land to work twice over; once to grow crops or raise livestock, and once in the form of bank guarantees and valuations of the land for their Lloyd's show of wealth and deposits against which to write lines of insurance and earn a second income in the premiums. Those who did have shareholdings and a second home found the concept of making your assets and savings work twice over to generate two incomes equally attractive.

By and large, and particularly in the 1970s and for most of the 1980s, Names could expect enough profits from their syndicates' underwriting to meet any claims and still write them a useful annual cheque. But as the 1980s progressed the stiff competition for a larger share of an oversupplied world insurance market caught Lloyd's napping like the opium-eaters of Samuel Taylor Coleridge's acquaintance. Despite being severely undercut by the insurance companies for their syndicates' bread-and-butter business, Lloyd's managing agents made very little effort to protect their margins by cutting their in-house expenses. Instead they began the hunt for new business.

In 1982 some syndicates, including one run by marine underwriter Richard (Dick) Outhwaite and another looked after by Stephen Merrett, sought to bolster their income by reinsuring slices of others' higher risk business, chiefly old general liability policies held with Lloyd's by American companies. They charged high premiums by Lloyd's standards at the time to take on this risk, and expected claims to be a long time coming, giving their syndicate time to earn enough investment income and capital gain for their Names' reserves to meet them and still make a profit. But the move meant these larger risks stayed within the Lloyd's market instead of being reinsured outside it and this contributed to the business being underwritten at Lloyd's gradually gaining the higher and higher risk profile that came to characterize the awful underwriting results of 1988, 1989 and 1990. In retrospect, the premiums charged and the cost base had failed to reflect the true danger of the extremely high claims poised to roll in particularly from the US pollution front. Exactly the same happened with the reinsurance spiral: the premiums were too small, the claims came in too high and too fast, and Names had to be tapped to meet the difference.

One reason why the calls facing Names on their 1988 underwriting were so vast is that syndicates do not just wait until a claim is confirmed to shell out the money for it. They must also make sure they have enough cash held in reserve in each members' name to meet likely claims of which they have been notified but which are not yet confirmed: 'incurred but not reported', or IBNR in the jargon. This is important because when a company is sued by someone, for damage done by a faulty product for example, and the company disputes it, the firm's insurer may be obliged to foot the legal costs of that dispute even if no subsequent award is made against the policy.

Things went wrong on asbestosis claims for syndicates like Dick Outhwaite's during 1984 and 1985. But the real disaster for the majority of Lloyd's Names came from the wave of high-rolling catastrophes inaugurated by Britain's 1987 hurricane, coinciding with the peak in the asbestosis payouts and the arrival of these massive pollution claims from the USA. When changes in American law triggered the notification of far more and far larger potential US pollution claims than anyone could have anticipated, provisions, not only to meet these but also the legal costs of helping the insured companies to resist them, had to be made by both the primary insurers and the London reinsurers of the US employers' liability and product liability policies involved.

But Lloyd's syndicates' reserves had already been depleted by the earlier asbestosis fights and settlements, and the new flood of claims and notifications came in before the new flows of premiums could top up the reserves enough to cope with the huge potential settlements that now hove into view. With cleaning up just one US site costing $30 million, the prospect was terrifying.

Reinsurance premiums charged for general liability risks had risen steeply since 1986, and certain business was simply refused, as underwriters began to realize the threat. But it was too little, too late. Not expecting such big claims, syndicates had in the past paid out more of the premium income to Names and retained less for investment than now proved adequate. The combination of this 'under-reserving', the prompt payment of the wave of disaster claims, and the new provisions for pollution claims, soaked up money still left in the reserves and Names' other funds at Lloyd's, and the next port of call would have to be the Names' personal assets held outside Lloyd's.

There was also the issue of 'overwriting'. Names agents' are supposed to keep an eye on how much the syndicate underwriters are taking in on behalf of Names and check that individuals' premium limits are not breached. But in the general rush and tumble of the market, breaches can occur. And if the value of a Names' funds held at Lloyd's dips, he may well end up having written more premium than he should have. Syndicates that got carried away and overwrote for their Names' capacity, called the syndicate's 'Stamp', ratcheted up the risks for individual Names' considerably. When things went wrong, they had far more claims to stump up for than to which they should have been exposed.

People have always become Lloyd's Names in the hope of handsome pickings. Entrants in the mid-1980s were inspired by the near twenty-year run of profits in that market, which had yielded, on average, an annual return of 10 per cent or so on people's Lloyd's capital, and blithely overlooked the standard warnings that despite appearances this was still a risk business. Lloyd's does run a Central Fund, paid for by a small levy on all members, out of which to meet Names' obligations if one goes bust and cannot do so. But this is to protect policy-holders, not to help Lloyd's members who suddenly do not feel able to meet their calls. Its existence does not let them off the hook.

The Names are highly dependent on the skill of the individuals running their syndicates at choosing what proportion of which risks to underwrite, how much to charge, and which to avoid. Becoming a Name was effectively handing over your entire personal wealth – because of that sole trader's unlimited liability rule – to a bunch of strangers to gamble with against the probabilities of this ship sinking, that oil rig exploding, this city being rocked by an earthquake, that stately home having all its roof tiles and ancient oaks ripped out by a hurricane-force wind.

The price the underwriter charges for the cover, of which he agrees to write a share, reflects the degree of risk he anticipates of a claim being made in future. So should the amount of money the syndicate holds back in reserve on Names' behalf against each underwriting year out of which to pay the claims that do come in. Names don't mind, as they earn an extra, investment income on that money in addition to the proportion of the premium income that is paid out to them each year.

So much for the theory. When things fell apart under the treble assault of asbestosis, pollution and natural disasters in the late 1980s, the impact soon made the Stock Exchange's Black Monday crash after the weekend of the October 1987 storm seem just a breeze. Some Names harboured dark suspicions that something more than mere incompetence by underwriters had fanned their woes: favouritism for insiders, fuelled by freemasonry.

There are three masonic lodges at Lloyd's: the Lutine, Fidentia and Lloyd's lodge. Most of the big wheels at Lloyd's belonged to the Lutine lodge. A former chairman, Sir Peter Green, was said to have been Grand Master of it. If so, this did him little good in the end, for he was ultimately censured and turfed out of the club for his involvement in moving Names' money offshore in a tax wheeze from which Names did not get the full benefit, and which was exposed in the early 1980s but had been going on since the late 1960s.

Secrecy is the perfect breeding ground for abuse and even fraud, and Lloyd's has been secretive enough without adding the double jeopardy of a secret society within the Society. Worried Names understandably feared that the oathes sworn by lodge members to help each other could have sufficiently outweighed their sense of obligation towards the Names whose money provided their living, and that therefore they might not expose colleagues but try instead to resolve procedures behind a double set of closed doors without alerting the Names. One former practitioner confirmed that this was apparently the case at times during the 1950s and 1960s: a time, however, when Names at Lloyd's were mostly making good money and no one was particularly concerned. Though still pervasive, the influence of the lodges seemed to have declined in the 1980s. 'There are still rumours but I cannot believe in this modern day and age that secret societies can really run a world insurance market. If that is so, it is sad,' he said.

Names were divided about the influence of the lodges in the 1980s and 1990s. 'You might be tipped off or hear about something at the golf club; but chatter in the club's club is nasty because they swear on oath to help each other,' one said.

Another had tested the system. 'Just after school I was a freemason. One of the sets of code words was "I was taught to be cautious". I tried it out on senior officials at Lloyd's and it made no difference at all,' he said.

Whether freemasonry was to blame or not, Lloyd's had slipped badly at times in its history. When Ian Hay Davison was introduced to the market as its first independent chief executive under the 1982 Lloyd's Act, he expected to find a few rotten apples in the barrel. He later said that he found the whole barrel was rotten. Though he saved Lloyd's from further invasive legislation in the 1980s, pushing it hard to tighten up and improve its practices, feelings were so cool between him and the then Chairman that the two rarely spoke, and neither remembers the other fondly. Frozen out, and having served his purpose for the old guard of the market, Ian Hay Davison left Lloyd's for the marginally less machiavellian corporate world.

The 1982 Act allowed Lloyd's to continue regulating itself, subject to certain requirements, new outside Council members, and the independent chief executive. Thus when it was told in 1986 to look into how well Names' interests were protected in the light of changes in investor protection in the securities industry, it did so without changes in the law being made. In 1992, Lloyd's once again put itself under its own microscope hoping that it could prove that self-regulation still had the answers for this market-place. Disillusioned Names doubted it. 'Lloyd's is still all self, and no regulation,' said one.

3
True Stories

Where are all the c-c-c-customers' yachts?

(WILLIAM R. TRAVERS ON BEING SHOWN A SQUADRON OF
BROKERS' YACHTS IN A NEW YORK HARBOUR: HENRY CLEWS,
FIFTY YEARS IN WALL STREET)

The City of London is infamous for its gallows humour, if nothing else. A favourite joke in 1991 went: 'How do you lose a small fortune at Lloyd's? Start with a large one!'

Unfortunately not everyone who lost money had a fortune in the first place. They went from being comfortably off to facing a very uncomfortable, indeed, bleak, future as the calls for their money rolled in. Some could afford the bills, particularly Names who had done well in past years, and had a cushion to fall back on, made up of sizeable reserves at Lloyd's built up out of past profitable years and saving some of the distributed profits. But even some of these people now faced such monumental losses that all their investments, even their homes, were at risk if Lloyd's called in the bank guarantees issued against these assets.

They were appalled. Becoming a Name at Lloyd's is entering the world of risk capital, but many people's grasp of this point had been blunted by the record of many years' unbroken profitability enjoyed by the vast majority of Lloyd's Names – and the kudos of membership. Yet the potential rewards have been high in the past precisely because the risk is great.

In the 1970s and into the 1980s this first law of business was overlooked by many underwriters as well as Names, who were quite happy to let them set aside less in reserves, and distributed more to syndicate members than has since proved prudent. Names used the extra income to pay their children's school fees or fund expensive habits, holidays and luxuries. Few saved or invested much of the money. The last big losses had been in the late 1960s, and while the individuals who suffered then do not forget, their successors tend not to remember – nor, perhaps, to wish to be reminded. Caution was something of a dirty word in Britain in the booming mid-to-late 1980s.

The British tax regime was partly to blame for the state of affairs at Lloyd's. When top income-tax rates in the United Kingdom were 98 per cent during the 1970s, it suited the rich to lose a bit of money at Lloyd's and claim the tax relief, thereby cutting their overall tax liability – already reduced by being able to count distributions from the increased value of investments held in reserve at Lloyd's as capital gains, which attracted a lower tax rate than income anyway.

The result was that underwriters could afford to be a bit sloppy about the business they underwrote and whether the premiums they charged were high enough to reflect the degree of risk involved, as long as they kept a stream of premiums flowing in to invest a chunk against claims, and to distribute the bulk of them. 'Lloyd's had not written insurance for a profit for years,' said one former underwriter in 1992. The advent of Mrs Thatcher's government, which cut top-rate income tax to 40 per cent in the mid-1980s and set capital-gains tax relief at the same level, changed all that. Lloyd's underwriters were slow to adapt to the implications for their syndicates.

To attract the money in on the more bread-and-butter business such as motor and shipping insurance, Lloyd's underwriters also had to compete with the lower premiums being charged elsewhere in the world's increasingly oversupplied, highly competitive insurance markets. One cynic put this down to the advent of the fax machine.

Lloyd's had an innate mystique and the fax machine has taken it away. For 290 of its 300 years, Lloyd's charged very heavily, and relied on its mystique. Its underwriters are very good compared with others in the world, and they really did know how to rate risk. This was handed down, face to face. It had 50 per cent of the world's marine market, effectively a monopoly, and its underwriters grew rather arrogant. In the past, brokers would send wires, underwriters would visit places, and offer them a rate which was usually taken. Nowadays, fleets all over the world and airlines are rated by Lloyd's, and then ten minutes later a fax goes out from the broker to offices around the world with the two or three Lloyd's quotes to see what other underwriters will offer for a line – and they undercut the Lloyd's rate. Therefore there is no longer a mystique. People can see what the Lloyd's underwriters have done. And Lloyd's rising cost base meant they could not match the undercutting. The big European reinsurers – Allianz, Munich Re, UAP in Paris, Generali, Aetna, St Paul and Tokyo Marine – are all individually larger than Lloyd's and have global offices. It is no longer fashionable in a small world to have everything go to one place.

As the influx of the new money of the eighties pushed up Lloyd's own capacity to write business and while its share of its traditional arenas slipped, new syndicates sprang up to take advantage of this extra seam of wealth. Many of these, and a fair few of the older ones, looked to the developing excess-of-loss reinsurance market within Lloyd's for the business to do it. This flurry of activity also attracted new members' agents who bundled into the market in search of cushy well-paid jobs, not all of them particularly talented individuals.

The net effect of these goings-on was that the quality of service and selection of syndicates by members' agents, and the quality of the business written by certain syndicates deteriorated. Syndicates, whose underwriters failed to appreciate the greater risk involved in some of the reinsurance they were now undertaking, held back insufficient of the premium income from it to shore up their reserves for potential future claims – partly because they also failed to realize just how thick and fast notification of potential claims would come in.

In the past if they under-reserved a bit and then had to make calls against their Names' income now and again, the rich and famous were not all that bothered. Lower tax rates and the influx of Names whose wealth was largely based on a newly booming property market, rather than longer-nurtured pools of assets, changed all that, just as some of the business written began to turn bad; but many underwriters were slow to spot the difference. When the wall of disasters hit Lloyd's in 1988 their syndicates were in no state to cope.

SERIOUS MONEY

In 1978 a tall spare man whom I shall call Cyril and his (then) wife gave a dinner party. To make up the numbers they invited an acquaintance of his wife's. As dinner progressed, taking in the comfortable surroundings, he turned to Cyril and said: 'You could be a member of Lloyd's.'

'No, thanks,' quipped his host, 'I'm with the NatWest!'

'No, no, dear boy, the insurers, Lloyd's of London.' He went on to sketch the impression that Cyril need not put up any money, just be able to indicate that he did in fact have some, and that he should receive a cheque every year.

'Besides which I was being invited to join a most selective club,' Cyril commented wryly.'

This story may make Lloyd's Council members' hair stand on end, but this is the way the better-off middle classes saw membership of Lloyd's in the 1970s and 1980s. Although new Names are cautioned that they are entering a high risk market, Cyril was deaf to the warnings. 'Two things which appeal to the British middle class more than anything are greed and snob appeal,' says Cyril now. 'Flattery and greed worked their way and I was hooked. Little did I know that the charming gentleman – the dinner guest – who was guiding me towards this pit was in fact a common tout engaged on an assiduous head-hunt.'

Bitter words – but Cyril is entitled to feel grim about his decision to become a Name. By mid-1991 he faced a solvency deficiency of £716,000 for his 1988 year of underwriting, chiefly from syndicates devastated by pollution and asbestos claims. In 1978 his dinner guest had introduced him to a members' agent 'whose subordinate marched me round the corner to a friendly bank to take a charge on my family house in order to provide the necessary show of wealth for Lloyd's: not against the whole house, but part of it.'

Things did not go brilliantly on his syndicates. 'In seven years my agent lost me £140,000. I did receive a cheque for about £12,000 at one point and stayed on for the promise of things getting better – jam was always promised in sufficient quantities by one's agent and, on reflection, comparing notes with many other Names, we discover just where the low intellectual stature of the average members' agent is only matched by his lack of candour,' is Cyril's jaundiced account of his experiences.

He started on twelve syndicates, writing for premium income of £250,000 a year. The types of business underwritten by each syndicate were sufficiently varied to give him a reasonable spread of risk, yet they lost money overall. In 1986 he decided to change his agent, again on the advice of an acquaintance, 'who himself later turned out to be a commission man.' Once bitten, twice shy of acquaintances, you might think, but Cyril proved a slow learner. His new agent put him on to more and more syndicates until he ended up on over fifty and, Cyril claims, advised him that since he was on such a wide spread of syndicates he had no need of stop-loss cover.

The agent had a point – up to a point. Not all Cyril's syndicates did badly, and some were able to build up considerable reserves. But when the unprecedented damage for 1988 was totted up, his solvency deficiency was £716,000 with the net losses and cash calls that he was now expected to stump up for in his troubled syndicates working out at an horrific £400,000, 'and it could get worse next year. I'm 63 and absolutely on the floor.'

Names on Cyril's worst-hit syndicates were so shocked and angered about what had happened to them that they turned to their lawyers. Some 250 of them on just one syndicate, non-marine syndicate number 90 run by the Pulbrook managing agency, faced estimated losses of £40 million between them. It had taken on a lot of North American liability cover written in the 1940s, 1950s and 1960s; and therefore suffered badly when the US courts granted huge awards to thousands of US workers whose health had been impaired by asbestos fibres. The Names had been called upon to pay $30.5m of North American liability claims for their 1982 year.

Enough was enough and now many of them reached for their lawyers. An action committee was formed, and 308 Names finally issued joint writs. They had decided to sue their members' and managing agents for alleged negligence, and for the latters' alleged failure to make adequate business disclosures to the syndicate's reinsurers of asbestos and pollution risks – which had denied liability to meet claims under the now disputed reinsurance agreement. The rebel syndicate 90 Names also decided to sue the broker who placed the reinsurance.

Much of the risk had been placed with the ill-starred Outhwaite syndicate, whose own Names were about to take it to court. Thus one group of Names found themselves suing a reinsurance syndicate for money that, if the action succeeded, other Names would have to stump up. Some people were on both syndicates and therefore found their right hand suing their left, while the left hand was itself suing its own underwriter for damages for taking the fateful business in the first place. Writs, allegations and counter-allegations flew like confetti at a March wedding.

AN ILL WIND

When the 1987 hurricane swept across southern Britain in October, victims of its devastating force included Names at Lloyd's who soon found themselves counting the cost twice over: once in the damage done to their own homes and gardens, and again to their Lloyd's syndicates as everyone else's claims rolled in or fed through to reinsurers.

Blissfully unaware of what was going on at home, Sarah, a widow of 61, was enjoying a trip to China when the near tropical hurricane hit rural Sussex. As she drank in exotic locations, the freak storm was tearing through her well-tended gardens. The summerhouse vanished entirely. The wooden garden fence was torn up from its posts. A heavy rack full of carefully stored apples remained when the summerhouse took off, but somersaulted backwards on to the lawn. Garden tables bounced across the grass. Ridge tiles were ripped off her house roof.

When she returned, having been driven from the airport through scenes of devastation and fallen trees still strewing the countryside a full two weeks after the storm had struck, she found her kitchen full of all that had been salvaged by her son: the apple rack, the garden tables, chunks of fence. 'It was all an awful shock,' she says.

Like many other householders with storm damage she found that her own insurance policy did not cover garden fittings such as the summerhouse and fence. These had to be replaced – the fence with a stout wall this time – out of her own pocket. But, having shelled out for her repairs, she was to discover that the impact of other people's insurance claims for the UK storm damage, coinciding with one of her syndicate's sudden large provisions for US pollution claims, had soaked up all the profits due from her better Lloyd's syndicates 1988 year. Not only was a useful stream of income now drained dry, but the prospect of having to meet further substantial calls in 1992 and 1993 for her 1989 and 1990 years of underwriting, loomed threateningly.

Sarah had been made a mini-Name in 1978. Encouraged first by one of her brothers, she joined one of the syndicates he was on and which, despite one rather nasty year, had generally done well. Later, when her son went to work for a Lloyd's underwriting agency she went on to its syndicates too, and gradually increased her underwriting capacity from the original low, mini-Name base. Things continued to go well until 1988. She received regular cheques from her syndicates, built up her Lloyd's reserves, and also privately saved some of the income she had received as a Name.

This proved wise. The money was needed when her original syndicate ran into difficulties in the late 1980s with pollution claims (and subsequently shut down). In 1991 her calls to meet claims against the policies written by just this one syndicate came to £12,000. They soaked up all her other income from her still profitable syndicates, and her available Lloyd's reserve. Her own savings would be needed next to meet the future calls that were clearly in the pipeline, leaving her Lloyd's deposit intact so that she could continue underwriting and earning, she hoped, additional profits to offset any more calls falling due.

Nevertheless, she still felt 'quite positive' about her Lloyd's membership. 'One will probably have to be a bit careful, but I am lucky to have built up a bit. Thanks to good past years I have been able to put some aside and to build up my reserves at Lloyd's,' she said stoically. 'I think the losses are awful and I know people who are very badly hit, and possibly having to give up their homes, but all of us were told it could happen.'

The moral of Sarah's tale, she says, is 'don't spend all your profits, always be prepared for a bad year.' Her own brother's one bad year had taught her that. She had also taken seriously the warnings about the risks that membership brings with it. 'You do go into Lloyd's with your eyes open. It is a risk and you aren't told that it isn't.' But, she notes that Lloyd's members' and managing agents have also learned a few lessons from the débâcle. 'They are being a lot more careful with Names now, trying to predict better and to give a bit more information to people.' The agency running her good syndicates has a regular Names day now but, she adds, has always warned its members that if they want 'to get rich quick, don't come to us.'

Not everyone who has lost money at Lloyd's in this drama is able to weather the storm as well as Sarah as coped. Not all took such note of the need to play safe with their Lloyd's profits. Others had little chance to earn any.

THE WIDOW'S MITE

Like Sarah, Erica is also a widow, now in her seventies. She too had become a 'mini-Name' under the relaxed membership rules in the mid-1980s (when Lloyd's still feared it might have insufficient capacity to continue to compete with other international insurance providers), at the suggestion of her husband's investment adviser. But her story is painfully different.

In 1984 she and her husband had just retired from farming, selling up and receiving a useful sum to invest for an income to live off thereafter. They had a mentally handicapped son and thought it would be useful to have an extra income to put towards his future upkeep – the idea being that the assets put up to back Erica's Lloyd's membership would in time generate both an income from the premiums earned by her syndicates, plus an investment income on the reserved profits.

But it was not to be. Her very first year of Lloyd's membership generated a net loss of nearly £5,000 after stop-loss cover, that she had to pay for in 1988. As with Sarah, just one syndicate was to blame, already caught in the reinsurance spiral on asbestos and pollution claims from the United

States, but its losses soaked up all the profits on her other syndicates, and her stop-loss cover, and still left the net shortfall that she had to dig into her other capital to meet.

The following year was a little better. This time the 'rogue' syndicate's losses just soaked up all her profits from the others she was on. The year after that was worse than ever. Before stop-loss cover her calls exceeded £50,000, and she had to write a cheque for nearly £30,000 to meet the difference. And so it went on. Each year the calls were bigger and bigger, and by this time her troubled syndicates were also tapping their Names for additional cash to bolster up their depleted reserves against potential future claims.

In the midst of all this her husband died. Under the terms of his will Erica's daughter was entitled to another large sum which Erica met by handing over a holiday home. To meet her Lloyd's bills, Erica steadily sold shares and investments that originally had been intended to generate a reliable income for the couple and their son for the rest of their lives. Worse, she says her members' agent advised her against resigning as a member since if she did so 'she would no longer be able to recoup past losses' and, she also says, subsequently advised that she should not need a stop-loss policy for 1991 – a year on which she later feared substantial further calls. But he did reduce the amount of underwriting in her name for that year from a line of £250,000 to £100,000.

'I should never have been a Name,' she now says. 'No one worth less than £1 million should become a member of Lloyd's.'

As her capital and income fell, Erica's chief worry was how to support her son, who was already distressed by the death of his father and that of another close family friend. Having always been financially independent, she now had to rely on support from social services to keep him in the residential home he knew and was happy in. 'I was very lucky,' she says. 'I had a very kind social worker.'

She also sacked her financial adviser, resigned from Lloyd's, and turned to the Hardship Committee for help. Once taken under its wing, whatever solutions are discussed become confidential, throwing a veil over her subsequent financial predicament that neither side will lift to a stranger's gaze.

As Erica waited to hear what the Committee proposed to help her cope, her best hope was that Lloyd's could take a charge over her home, allowing her to live in it for the remainder of her own life, before selling it after her demise to meet her Lloyd's debts and the accruing interest on them. If there was anything left after that, it would revert to her estate and leave a modest mite for her son's support. Or it might not.

THE OPEN YEAR

In the mid-1970s Thomas, a businessman with a long career spent mainly overseas with a large British company, decided to take early retirement. A short secondment to a government committee had earned him recognition in the New Year's Honours List and also opened his eyes to a wider world than his old business beat, and he decided to seek a new career. The commuted pension he took with him was a tidy sum for those days, and left him feeling quite rich. His mortgage was all paid off and his family, grown up.

Looking for ways to invest some of his money, 'without putting too much cash down', he felt Lloyd's was an ideal answer. 'It was expanding at the time and seeking new and smaller investors whose total wealth was perhaps £150,000. Should they really have been taking them in, willing to commit £100,000 of that? It was too tight, in retrospect,' he now says.

At the time he trod quite warily. He took advice and came away feeling that Lloyd's was seen as 'a good bet' that would also mitigate his high tax bills. A Labour government was now in power and the top tax rate was 98 per cent. What appealed most was the scope to put up shares he owned as his Lloyd's deposit without giving up the beneficial ownership, or the dividends from them.

He took a long time to select his agent and syndicates, and became quite friendly with the boss of the underwriting agency. 'People have made bad choices of agent. It's very important to decide who you are going to let use your money and there are always bad apples in every barrel so you have to be careful,' he explains. He remains a friend of the underwriter, though both men have now lost substantial sums on some syndicates. 'I am not complaining. No one hid anything from me, and the record had been gravy all the way,' he says, ruefully. 'If you are a high taxpayer and have lots of grand-children, Lloyd's should be a good bet.'

He had ten good years. 'I kept my original investments and made a good return from Lloyd's – about 10 per cent a year, better than any other form of investment. Then nemesis. Can I blame my managing agent? In my case there is no one to blame. I just went in too deep for my wealth.'

What went wrong for Thomas was the unfolding asbestos drama in the United States. Huge claims under old liability policies either issued to US companies or reinsured by Lloyd's underwriters flooded across the Atlantic. It was the era of the US ambulance-chasing lawyer drumming up possible asbestosis victims to add them to huge lawsuits on a no-win-no-fee basis.

By the time his 1984 year was due to be closed and the results became clear in early 1987, 'Suddenly it was doom and gloom. We were summoned to a meeting. It was all laid on the table. We were told that the syndicate could not close that year and it was going to have to ask us to divi up to meet the claims on the books and various liabilities. They said it was due to changes in US law and that their auditors had told them to reserve for unsettled claims on US asbestos issues.' Insufficient monies had been set aside in the past to meet the sort of claims now gathering.

Normally a year is closed after three years inclusive (for example 1991 at the end of 1993), by which time most of the likely claims have come in. This practice probably dates back to the days of sail when it took a ship about that time to ply the world's oceans and return, but it continued to be used by Lloyd's; and by the corporate insurers for shipping and aviation risks in particular. When the Lloyd's policies written during any one year are reinsured by the same syndicate three years later, for example, 1991's in 1994, the premium comes out of the closing year's profits. This device allows Names to be paid any remaining surplus from, for example, 1991's under-writing in 1994. If a Name stops underwriting he must notify the syndicate by the August that he does not want to participate in the following year's underwriting. But until his last year is closed, he remains liable for a share of the profits or losses from that year. So 1991 Names who notified their resignation that August will not know until 1994 if they will get a cheque or a bill.

But if a year has to be left open because massive claims already notified against it cannot be met as they are still in dispute, making reinsurance-to-close an impossible burden for the current year (and new Names coming on to the syndicate), the existing Names face a bottomless pit. They cannot resign from the syndicate until all valid claims against the year are settled. And because the year cannot be reinsured to close, claims against policies written during it can still keep coming in, so there is no way of knowing what the total liability may be either for the syndicate or its members.

A nightmare indeed.

Fortunately Thomas had told his agent to spread his risk at Lloyd's across the full range of syndicates: marine, non-marine, motor and aviation insurance specialists. Profits from his other syndicates cushioned the blow in 1987, 'but still did not make enough money to cover all the asbestos losses.' He also had stop-loss cover that kicked in after a certain level of loss had been paid by him or out of his Lloyd's funds; but this sort of cover has a ceiling or limit and was gradually exhausted by the calls.

The open year itself did have some excess-of-loss reinsurance cover to claim on, but disputes broke out about whether it was valid. 'It has been a disaster and hasn't come up to snuff as the reinsurers won't pay, so the original syndicates and Names are exposed. So each year the position is that we must have more reserves and the Names are asked to stump up.' On the first year after his 1984 syndicate was left open he had a call of £7,000, which was met by his stop-loss cover. The following year brought a call for £70,000 but again his stop-loss cover (cost, £2,000) met that, and part of the following year's £30,000 call – and then ran out.

He expected a bill of £30,000 again during 1992, this time to be met out of selling other investments. He could call on his Lloyd's reserves to meet future calls because the cash he had paid so far was to build those up against anticipated claims from policy-holders. And he had no estate cover to protect his heirs from calls on his other assets in future. To buy it in 1992 would have cost him £250,000 and still left him facing potential calls limited to £12,000 a year with no indication of an end in sight.

'It is bad news for the family. I didn't realize I couldn't get out. It's just there hanging over you and you can't get an estimate of what each call could be. It all depends on what happens in the US. It's not a nice thing to have hanging over you. Yet I did lots of things right. I didn't put too many eggs in one basket. I did take out stop-loss, on the agency's advice. It's a pity I didn't take out more. I picked a decent agency. But now I'm out in the open because my stop-loss has run out and no one expected the losses to be so high or to reach the desperate state to which it would bring people.

'I still get tax relief, as a higher taxpayer. In fact, higher taxes would help me! For example if my loss one year is £50,000, with no stop-loss to mitigate it I would be entitled to £20,000 back from the Inland Revenue (40 per cent of £50,000), so it's not as bad as it might be.' (With stop-loss you do not get the tax relief.)

Turning from the uncertain future, and looking back on events, Thomas said: 'There really is no one I can blame. There had been some cowboys, and lazy careless people, more than crooks.

'But Lloyd's were wrong to encourage comfortable but not really wealthy people to become Names. To be able to write a line of £250,000 you need a few million at your back so you can ride any losses. If you are in my state you can't, and there are a lot like me. The sheer magnitude of the disasters and the size of the claims has changed. When I started in the mid-1970s a plane cost £500,000. Now its £5 million. The scale of the risk has soared.

'Lloyd's must sharpen up its professional competence. It should have realized the need to build up reserves instead of giving us all the profits earlier.

It should set ratios.

'It needs to try and get these open years closed. There should be a sinking fund to help people on the open years. It could have taken 5 per cent into a sinking fund and we would all have been better off if we had had to do that. It should also limit liability so that it doesn't extend to your estate. I would be happy if they would at least forget the charge against my estate.

'It should look at the possible redistribution of excess reserves back to Names who were on those syndicates at the time. It's not just a question of being fair to past names, but to stay in business and attract new Names, who won't join if they see how it's treated the old ones.

'I've had to start selling things and I don't know what the call will be next year. So how can you plan anything? I've got a nice house, my pension is safe – I've lost capital, not income – and I have a super family. But the uncertainty is terrible. I'm now in my seventies, and I can't relax totally.

'It's a pretty miserable end, having been careful all my life and saved up sensibly to look after my family. Have I been negligent? I can't say that I have. I'm not crippled, but I am hurt, and my story is typical. If I was starting now and heard my own story, I wouldn't join Lloyd's.'

THE WORKING NAME

John is a working Name, sponsored by his firm, and a Lloyd's broker – until 1994. In August 1991 he told his syndicates he wished to cease underwriting and hoped there would be no major disasters before midnight on New Year's Eve. But it will be 1994 before he sheds the final vestiges of his Lloyd's membership.

'The reason you become a Name is to try and absolutely maximize your personal wealth,' he says. 'I am not a suitable candidate any more. I'm just not rich enough to be putting houses on the line.

'Becoming a Name is a momentous decision. You must understand that you don't expect exceptional reward without exceptional risk. It is a danger for older people because the liability can extend to your heirs. Estate protection is always worth having because otherwise you are taking the risk for them too.'

Working Names have not had to show the same amount of capital behind them as Names who come from outside the Lloyd's industry. In the days when a 'non-working' Name had to show wealth of £100,000 a working Name could write a £50,000 line and his one-third deposit was just £17,500, capital that his employer would often provide anyway via a letter of credit, for example. For, typically, working membership was a gift from the employer, a perk, particularly in the days of high tax rates and when Lloyd's was enjoying its long run of profitable underwriting.

John became a Name in 1981, backed by a letter of credit from the Lloyd's broker for which he worked and by the close of 1991 had not made a pound from it in the ten years. 'Yet when I joined it, it was expected that after two years I would have returned the company's loan and get an effective bonus.'

He goofed. In 1982 he went on to a syndicate which subsequently had to cease trading, leaving its 1982 year open until massive potential claims were resolved or settled. As time went by all his profits from other syndicates were soaked up by its losses. At the end of 1991, the year he finally was able to resign, another two-year run-off of that year's business lay ahead of him that he knew would also bring losses. His firm will then get back its letter of credit and that, he hopes, will be that.

John is not alone within the industry in pulling out of Lloyd's under-writing membership. Many other working Names are following suit. 'I should have done it three years ago. I thought about it but felt it would be disloyal to the industry. There is still an element of mystique and tradition about Lloyd's,' he explains.

'I believe in the place passionately and in its ability to survive and become a leaner and fitter and more dynamic entity, as the unsavoury repositioning is completed.'

THE NEW BOY

Not everyone on syndicates that had to shell out for disaster-tossed 1988 lost money when the final reckoning was done, and despite all the horror stories of the end of that decade, there are still brave souls who believe this is the right time to become a Name. Brand new Names facing significant losses on 1988 were actually much better placed to cope than many long-term Names on the same syndicates. And it was the taxman who came to the rescue. Judicious use of the tax breaks available to new Names helped to ease the pain: in some cases, even assuaging all of it.

Peter, a successful and financially astute investment manager, was one of the intake of 1988 who lost £26,000 on the swings but ended a net £3,000 up on the tax roundabout. This is how.

Becoming a Lloyd's Name had not figured on his agenda until a colleague who lived overseas and wanted to become a Name asked him for help in finding a members' agent. Peter happened to live next door to one, and in the process of seeing his colleague become a Name, decided this might be a good wheeze for himself too. Unlike most of Lloyd's Names Peter enjoys the risk business and had no illusions about what he was doing with his hard-earned wealth when he signed up.

'I've always been involved in risk management, and wanted a good spread of risk. But I took care to build up my own knowledge of what I was doing and read various bits of literature, not all of it provided by my agent,' he points out. In fact he talked to two members' agents and asked for their recommendations of what sort of syndicates he should go into before plumping for one of them.

He also took care to let his agent know he wanted to avoid really high-risk syndicates, those involved in a lot of reinsurance and excess-of-loss cover, wherever possible. 'You don't always know what the underwriter is doing. Just one minute piece of business could lose all the money! But if you stick to basic business that everyone needs, for example underwriting ships or motor insurance, there is always a market for it and ultimately it should be profitable,' he reckons.

Despite all his precautions, however, Peter still got caught up in the maelstrom of 1988.

His syndicates had to pick up insurance claims on the Piper Alpha oil-rig disaster in the North Sea, on damage wreaked by Hurricane Hugo in the United States and by stormy British weather, and from the Phillips petroleum group's oil-refinery fire – a catalogue of accidents ranked by Lloyd's as catastrophes.

On top of all that, some of his syndicates faced potential claims for pollution clean-up operations in the United States, including, for example, a claim for clearing asbestos out of aircraft nose cones – and realized that their reserves would need bolstering to meet them. That meant asking the syndicates' Names to shell out extra cash in 1991. This made the biggest dent in Peter's first set of results, leaving him with an overall profit but a bill from his syndicates for a total of £26,000.

A painful introduction to Lloyd's, you might think. But Peter was fortunate. Instead of having to hand over money he actually ended up receiving £3,000 – from the taxman.

His losses were first contained and then vaporized by two things. Firstly, thanks to his refusal to get involved higher up the insurance spiral (and a members' agent who took note of this), the claims his syndicates paid out on were at the start of the insurance ladder. Most of the cost of disasters like Piper Alpha and Hurricane Hugo was passed on to the reinsurance syndicates that Peter had been at pains to avoid joining. Secondly, as a brand new Name he was able to use his beginner's tax allowances to offset all the calls on his money and reclaim interest from the Inland Revenue.

Because all Lloyd's years are open for three years, the taxman allows newcomers to offset underwriting losses on their first year of Lloyd's membership against three previous year's tax liabilities, as well as the year in which the calls are made. Thus Peter, facing losses in 1991 of £26,000 on his first year – 1988 – was able to offset them against the income tax he had paid as far back as 1984.

He was also able to offset losses against his current year's £7,000 capital-gains-tax exemption, reducing the bill to £19,000 for starters. Then he claimed the tax relief going back to his earnings in 1984, when the UK's higher rate tax was still 60 per cent (it was subsequently cut to 40 per cent). This shaved another £15,600 off the total, leaving him with a £3,400 bill – except that the Inland Revenue paid him interest on the reclaimed tax from 1984: four whole years' worth. The net effect of that was, far from having to shell out money, he ended up with his Lloyd's calls met and a £3,000 cheque from the Inland Revenue.

So his caution had paid off, and demonstrates that even in a loss-making year a canny newcomer can survive. To do it you have to grasp what you could be letting yourself in for, however.

'It is NOT an investment,' newly blooded Peter warns other potential Names. 'Don't even consider it even if you can meet the £250,000 means test unless you have at least £500,000 for comfort and you probably need to be earning £60,000 a year. It helps to be interested in insurance and probabilities as it's a numbers game at the end of the day. And it is a cyclical market so you need to be able to take the bad years as well as the good ones. Make sure that if you write, say, £25,000 of business that you can afford to pay out 10 per cent of that a year to meet any calls, as a general rule of thumb.

'Ask your members' agent questions – and go to the annual meeting if they have one and meet the underwriters on your syndicates, and the other Names. Take an active interest, because it is a business you're in. You've got to be young,' he also warns. 'Don't start when you're close to retirement age – go in while you're under 40 and come out at 60 with your profits.' At 60-plus new Names who take a bad hit early on in their Lloyd's membership may face real problems rebuilding their capital base whereas younger members stand a better chance of recovering from the financial blow.

Peter fitted the youth bill, becoming a Name in his mid-thirties. After facing losses on his 1989 year (met in the course of 1992) he looks ahead to better times as premium rates harden, hoping to start making money in the mid-1990s. 'I have no regrets,' he says. 'In fact it was better for me to be taking losses against a 60 per cent tax year than to have made a profit against a 40 per cent tax year and then be hit later by losses which you can't roll back – though I didn't plan it that way!'

GEORGIE GIRL

Georgie was one of the Names who made a profit on the 1988 year and who kept on underwriting throughout the dramas. She did it by being very fussy about what syndicates she went on; and by dint of knowing something about the industry into which she was putting her money.

She spelt out to her agent that she wanted no part of the catastrophe excess of loss reinsurance spiral; nor was she interested in general liability reinsurance; and (more to the point, perhaps) she only wanted to be on syndicates that the underwriters' bosses were on – the senior executives of the managing agency. Or, as her husband put it, only on the syndicates on to which its chairman, his wife, and his mistress went.

Whatever the reason, it paid off for Georgie.

4
Fools' Gold

Great wealth implies great loss

(LAO TZE, *THE SIMPLE WAY*)

Asbestos was the wonder fibre of the late-nineteenth century and first two-thirds of the twentieth. Then we discovered that, in our passion for the heat resistant material, we had been playing with fire indeed.

A natural mineral fibre found in certain types of rock, asbestos's ability to withstand heat and flames had been known for millennia. This property made it increasingly useful to the fast-developing industrial societies of Western Europe and, particularly, America. We went to town over it, even building our homes with asbestos compounds – but the ancient Greeks were familiar with it long before we thought of asbestos roof tiles, insulating panels, and car brake linings.

Asbestos is a fibrous silicate of magnesium and comes in six varieties, of which three were most put to work by man. The ancient Greeks gave the mineral containing the strongest type, chrysolite, its name – from the Greek for 'hair of gold', a description it earned because the veins in which the asbestos fibres lie look yellowish (and sometimes, greenish). The fibres themselves are white and silky, and can be anything from less than half an inch to six inches long. The other two most exploited varieties are amosite, a brown asbestos which has longer fibres and contains iron, and a blue asbestos called crocidolite.

The world's largest deposits of chrysolite were found in the New World, in Quebec, and also in the old Soviet Union's Ural Mountains. In due course Canada's southern Quebec boasted not only the world's largest asbestos mine but an entire town called Asbestos. The owner of the Quebec mine, the company Johns Manville, was to become famous in another sense as the asbestosis drama developed – as the recipient of massive insurance claims by asbestosis sufferers. Biggest taker of its output was Canada's neighbour the United States, which in the first half of the twentieth century rapidly became the world's main manufacturer of asbestos products.

The slippery asbestos fibres were put to a vast array of work. The longer ones, of a centimetre or more, were mixed with rougher-surfaced fibres, such as cotton, and woven into fire-retardant and chemical-resistant fabrics. Some of these were used for theatre safety curtains and other safety hangings in public buildings. Shorter fibres were put into paper, board and asbestos-cements for the building trade, and were also widely used in public buildings, such as schools. Because of its fire-proof qualities, but also for its sound-proofing, it also became fashionable to line the outside walls of houses with shingles made from a mixture of asbestos fibre and cement, instead of wooden ones, and to have asbestos roofs. Indoors, it was made into floor and acoustic ceiling tiles.

In the Second World War, firefighters on US navy ships were equipped with asbestos suits, and asbestos also went into the fabric of the ships themselves. Back on land the wonder-material was put to work in electrical equipment, insulation materials, and brake linings for the automobile indus-try. In all, asbestos fibres went into over 3,000 products before anyone realized that these life-savers could themselves be a major health hazard.

What nobody knew was that only a few short asbestos fibres lodged in the lungs can cause severe long-term damage and life-threatening diseases to the unlucky worker or passer-by who breathes the stuff in. It can take anything from eight to fifty years for the three main diseases linked to asbestos fibres to manifest themselves in breathlessness, wheezing lungs, and an overloaded heart.

The explosion of asbestos use in the first half of the century lit another, slow-burning fuse that detonated hundreds of thousands of claims for compensation for ruined health and lost lives in the latter half. Claims began to flow in during the 1970s and throughout the 1980s – and they are still coming in.

Though America, because of its rampant use of asbestos in so many products, eventually generated the most and the costliest claims, the flow actually began in Britain, first with a trickle and then a steady stream of cases in the 1960s. The stream became a roaring flood and swept across the Atlantic, where the authorities, lawmakers, and industry had been slower to react to the first signs of trouble at the asbestos 'mill', to strike in tidal waves of claims from the mid-1970s – and where the courts tended to make far higher compensation awards than the British ones.

Companies that had mined, handled, installed, or used asbestos in products were taken to court by past employees, users of the products, and those who had lived near the site involved. All sought compensation for their years of illness and reduced life expectancy. The companies naturally (and promptly) looked to their insurance policies to meet the mounting claims bill.

In most cases, the wording of their old product liability policies was regarded by the courts as indeed covering the unforeseen ill-effects of the asbestos used in their course of business, and by late 1991 the insurance industry had paid out an estimated $2 billion to America's asbestos-sufferers. Lloyd's of London syndicates were to foot half of that bill, paying $1 billion on 60,000 individual claims under policies issued in many cases as long ago as the 1940s. Two-thirds of that went to the claimants' lawyers in legal fees.

The main illness caused by asbestos is the lung disease now called asbestosis, a type of pneumoconiosis (a term for dust disease of the lungs) caused by inhaled fibres. Asbestosis seriously reduces the sufferer's quality of life and may cut its duration drastically short. It also increases the risk of lung cancer, and is linked in particular to mesothelioma – a highly fatal cancer that polishes off its victims quite fast once manifested, though it may be twenty or up to fifty years after exposure to the asbestos fibres before the tumour develops. Chief culprit here seemed to be crocidolite or blue asbestos and victims may have been exposed to the dust for only a few months, all those years before.

In asbestosis, the short asbestos fibres in the dust breathed in by factory and building workers, miners, and local residents damage the lung tissue around them. It reacts to the invasion of a few asbestos fibres by developing a form of fibrosis – growths of a fibrous tissue of its own – and gradually the affected lung membrane gets stiffer and stiffer, and the air sacs become less efficient. The sufferer grows ever shorter of breath, and later on develops a dry cough. To cope, the heart also has to work harder, which can cause heart disease in addition to the sufferer's lung problems, while the affected areas of the lung may also develop secondary infections, ranging from bronchitis and emphysema to farmer's lung.

British industry had become aware of a potential problem as early as the 1930s, leading to the Asbestos Industry Regulations 1931, which laid down rules about extracting the dust generated in making asbestos products from the air (but didn't touch on their subsequent use) and came into effect in 1933 as an addition to the old Factory and Workshop Act 1901.

The United States was slower to react, but in 1943 the US Navy Department recognized a risk to insulation workers from high levels of dust in the working atmosphere and issued a booklet setting out minimum safety standards in cutting, sawing and otherwise handling the stuff or asbestos mixes. But, overall, US industry's reluctance to peer too deeply into the problems lurking behind this wonder material, and the length of time these diseases took to develop, meant it was only in the 1970s that the incidence of asbestosis began to take on undisguisable, epidemic proportions and launched an epidemic of insurance claims against those former employers.

Yet early compensation claims had begun to appear in the United States in the 1950s when, ironically, there was also an upsurge in the use of asbestos in products. In the United Kingdom, the law was tightened in 1959 and again in 1969 to ensure that sites using asbestos protected the worker, and the visitor, more thoroughly. Though there were an increasing number of claims from sufferers from asbestos-related diseases in the UK and in the USA from the mid-1960s onwards, British lawyers reckoned the United Kingdom's early recognition of the health risks helped to prevent the surge tide of cases and claims here that was to swamp America in the late 1970s and 1980s. In the face of this knowledge, it was remarkable that Lloyd's underwriters only began to register concern about a potential problem in relation to asbestosis claims in the early 1980s . . . when the high US court awards began.

In the United States these diseases were first noticed in significant numbers among the shipyard workers who had been exposed to asbestos products when kitting out ships during the Second World War – despite the US Navy's 1943 minimum safety requirements. In 1974 Professor Irving J. Selikoff of the Mount Sinai School of Medicine in New York published his studies on asbestosis, alerting the medical – and the legal – industry to the type and extent of the problems ahead. He also concluded that being a cigarette smoker at the time of exposure to asbestos dust, multiplied your chances of developing asbestosis later, compared to the risk to non-smokers exposed to the dust; and that the already high danger of contracting run-of-the-mill lung cancer was greater still for smokers who had worked with asbestos than for smokers who had not.

The late 1970s saw the first big series of claims by workers for compensation from former employers and lawyers spotted a goldmine. They went ambulance-chasing in droves for more and more clients on a no-win, no-fee basis. Advertisements placed by law firms appeared in American papers and magazines alerting anyone with lung trouble to the possibility of it being asbestos-related . . . and to the chance of major financial compensation. Existing plaintiff's lawyers also alerted trade-union officials to the scope of compensation potentially available to past and present workers in asbestos-related industries and joined hundreds of names to 'class actions', whereby other sufferers can join existing legal suits that have already started. This keeps the cost of the action down per person, but ratchets up the victorious lawyer's take as a percentage of the much larger proceeds.

Insurance underwriters at Lloyd's, who had provided excess-of-loss cover against the old general liability policies that were now being tapped for cash for asbestosis sufferers, reported by 1992 that of all the money paid out since 1981, two-thirds was swallowed up in legal fees and only one-third went to the actual sufferers. Companies brought to court sought defence lawyers in their turn, while their insurers (who would have to foot the legal bills as well as meeting any claims awarded) took independent legal advice on whether their product liability policies really did cover the assured firms for asbestos claims.

By and large the answer was yes, so any legal disputes between insurer and assured centred instead on from what point the cover operated. Was it from when the claimant first felt ill; the manifestation of the disease? Or from when he or she was first unwittingly exposed to asbestos dust and fibres? Should the compensation be paid against policies extant since the date of diagnosis? Or simply on policies operating from the date of the insurance claim being lodged?

What depended on the answers to these questions was whether compensation awards were paid out of a series of annual policies, or met from just one year's cover. It made a huge difference to how much the primary insurer or his reinsurers picked up of the bill – and different State Supreme courts, applying different State law, naturally had differing views on all of these matters.

If first exposure were the trigger for the insurance policies to come into play, the primary insurer picked up most of the bill, calculated as so much compensation for each year covered since exposure. This left less of the total award to shunt on to the provider of each year's excess-of-loss (XOL) cover, and subsequent reinsurers. But if the trigger for cover was the manifestation of the disease, then the claim would have to be paid against that particular year's insurance policy and, under the terms of its own XOL cover for that year, the primary insurer would only have to stump up the first chunk. The rest, which could mean most of the award, would be met by whoever had provided the XOL cover. Because so many Lloyd's underwriters took out XOL cover for their old general liability risks with a very narrow band of syndicates prepared to offer it, the cost ultimately descended from a wide spread of Lloyd's Names – the 'many' to the 'fewe' on these – a total reversal of the Elizabethan principle of insurance that Lloyd's is so fond of quoting.

By and large the US courts awarded compensation against a broad spread of policy years rather than against just one particular year's cover. But the settlements were high, much higher in the case of stricken individuals than the second phase of claims, relating to the cost of stripping asbestos out of buildings and property, and the reinsurers could not escape their hefty share.

And that is how several thousand Lloyd's Names caught a nasty cold. One syndicate in particular, marine insurer number 317/661 managed by Lloyd's underwriter Dick Outhwaite, had specialized in 1982 in reinsuring a certain amount of asbestos risk that other syndicates wanted to offset. He only wrote 32 of these contracts out of the vast mass of other business done for his syndicate that year; but when the bills came in from the US settlements, the premiums earned for providing the cover were nowhere near enough to meet the claims outstanding and in the pipeline. In 1985 he announced that the syndicate could not close its 1982 year, which remained open in 1992 with claims still pouring in, and no money left to pay them; which meant regular calls on the trapped Names to stump up the wherewithal. Calls were made on individuals pro rata to their premium limit in the syndicate.

Names on the ill-fated Outhwaite syndicate – including golfer Tony Jacklin, hotelier Rocco Forte, former British Prime Minister Ted Heath and an earl, Lord Alexander of Tunis (son of the wartime Field Marshal) – faced increasingly massive calls for more and more cash to meet their ill-starred syndicate's liabilities. By May 1991, the average loss per Name was running at £84,000 per £20,000 'line' of insurances written and that October the syndicate's losses were said to total £260 million. Some high-writing individuals' share of the bill ran into hundreds of thousands of pounds each.

Personal ruin loomed, and recourse to the courts to sue the firm of RHM Outhwaite and up to 100 other firms, including Lloyd's members' agents and even their accountants, for negligence or breach of contract, soon followed.

Aware that there might be an asbestos problem for some of the older syndicates that had courted American industry, selling its general liability since the 1940s, Lloyd's and the insurance companies' London underwriting arms had established an asbestos working party in 1980, 'to co-ordinate the handling of information relating to asbestos-related liabilities'. Its deliberations were never formally released to the Lloyd's underwriting agencies, though Lloyd's has always insisted that the market 'was fully informed at the time of the existence of information which was available about these claims and was encouraged to make use of it'. Aware of the 'seriousness of the position which was developing in relation to claims proceeding through the US courts', details of the claims 'were available to the relevant insurers in the London market so that they could establish reserves for the liabilities'.

Not all busy underwriters took advantage of this take-it-or-leave-it offering. Lloyd's was severely embarrassed when a row broke out at the end of the 1980s about the alleged behaviour of some syndicates connected with members of the asbestos working party. Two of them had, Lloyd's subsequently confirmed, placed 'run-off' reinsurance contracts for their asbestos risk with one of the few providers of reinsurance for an old general liability risk at the time, Dick Outhwaite – who, it later emerged, was apparently unaware of the working party's report. Ten years later he was to tell the High Court that he had not seen it.

In 1990, Lloyd's investigated repeated allegations that working-party members had used the knowledge they had gained to rush off and cover their own syndicates' back without alerting the whole market first. Seeking the cover itself, if they could get it, to offset the risk to their Names was fair enough; doing it sneakily, using inside information and without making sure the market-place understood the risk and could price or refuse it accordingly, was not.

Lloyd's peeked under the veil and decided there was 'no evidence' that these syndicates had taken advantage of information available only to the working party so there was no need for a full inquiry. The issue of whether Outhwaite had been properly informed, however, raged on and Lloyd's did appoint a 'conciliator' to umpire the arguments and recriminations behind closed doors. This led to a number of deals and settlements with a clutch of syndicates that Outhwaite had provided with cover. But it did not avoid the danger of massive publicity about the Lloyd's handling of the asbestos problem. When the massive court case brought in October 1991 by 987 of the Outhwaite Names on the ill-starred 1982 year seeking £150m compensation, began, it was feared the syndicate's losses – already £260 million – could top the £1 billion mark in the long run. But on 3 February 1992, the judge suddenly adjourned the case for 'administrative reasons', fuelling reports that a £100 million settlement was imminent.

By late 1991 UK insurers had shelled out over $1 billion on 60,000 asbestos-related claims, and bitterly observed that most of the money went to the 'ambulance-chasing' lawyers who brought cases on behalf of clients on a no-win no-fee, contingency basis. They resolved to change this. Partly to ensure that more of the money went to the sufferers, and partly to keep their own legal costs down, insurers increasingly took to settling clear-cut claims quickly without recourse to the courts, using the thousands of past awards as a yardstick for the new payments. When the pollution battle broke, this civilized approach was not available. Feelings ran too high for such compromises.

Asbestos claims are still coming in. They will eventually tail off with the passage of time, thanks partly to a massive US programme to remove asbestos from schools and public buildings, and tough new laws about its use; but in 1992 were they not showing as strong a sign of peaking as had been hoped. The emphasis was switching, however, from personal injury claims to property damage ones. 'As far as the actual numbers of sufferers is concerned, it probably has peaked,' a rueful Dick Outhwaite said in February that year. 'But claims will still be being paid for many years.'

It may be too late to save lives already blighted by asbestosis and its attendant illnesses, and the financial fortunes of the rich and famous and not-so famous who underwrote the policies, but the authorities have acted to try and ensure there are no new sufferers from this particular ailment in the future. Insurers wonder, however, what else could pop up out of the woodwork; and general liability reinsurance is harder to come by today in Lloyd's, more expensive, and subject to more stringent terms.

Expensive though it was, the asbestos drama was to prove just a foretaste for the insurance industry of the shock to come as America turned its attention to the 'greening' of the planet – protecting and cleaning up the environment after two hundred years of industrialization without much thought about its impact on the neighbouring land, water table, flora and fauna.

In the late 1980s, through new US anti-pollution laws, supplemented by a policy of chasing the outfit with the deepest pockets for the money to clean up past damage, meant the insurance industry faced a whole new round of legal battles and massive costs – and that was just to clarify whether US companies could claim under old comprehensive liability policies for the cost of repairing decades of industrial carelessness and *laissez-faire*. The real bills, if payable, were yet to come.

Though at first sight similar issues are at stake for the insurers and their clients, the pollution cases differ from the asbestos claims in two important ways. Environmental claims are usually about the cost of cleaning up sites or neighbouring land – in other words, property damage by companies – and the money is sought by the clean-up authorities; whereas the bulk of asbestos claims was brought on behalf of named individuals seeking recompense from firms, via their insurance policies, for damaged health.

Compensating people for visibly wrecked health is a highly emotive (and politically more attractive) cause than siding with companies guilty of persistent long-term pollution of the local environment – and US State judges (who are, after all, political appointees) seemed slightly more inclined to agree with the insurers that companies which routinely polluted sites over many years were not entitled to claim afterwards, just because the law had changed, that this was the sort of accidental, sudden, or unexpected damage covered by an ancient general liability policy taken out long before pollution was an issue. Ideally they should foot the bill themselves – if they can.

But not all pollution was blatant or routine, and even where it was, the fight to prove that point is costly. It is fought, and fought ferociously by both sides each time, precisely because so much more money is at stake than in the asbestos saga. The potential clean-up costs and claims run into tens of millions of dollars per site, and cumulatively into hundreds of billions.

While the legal arguments raged, insurance syndicates at Lloyd's of London had once again to set aside enough cash to meet not only the potential repair bills that may come home to roost under the old policies, but also the additional legal costs of going on to resist the US authorities' quest for such massive sums. Once the argument about whether the policy is valid has been settled, and if the answer is 'yes', then the insurer has to join forces with the assured to do battle over whether the assured was to blame for the pollution anyway. It means the prospect of years of litigation and appeals, during which the money to meet the claims at the end of it still has to be set aside.

And that is the next chapter in the catalogue of disasters that led to so many Lloyd's Names facing more, massive, cash calls in the nineties.

5
Nemesis

The river Rhine, it is well known,
Doth wash your city of Cologne;
But tell me, Nymphs, what power divine
Shall henceforth wash the river Rhine?

(SAMUEL TAYLOR COLERIDGE, 'COLOGNE')

The 1980s saw 'a groundswell of change; a major shift of understanding of the workings of the earth, and a major shift in political and economic approach', Jonathon Porritt, Britain's leading environmental campaigner, told a meeting of top investment fund managers in the City of London in the autumn of 1991. Not all were yet convinced that they had a role to play in encouraging industry to clean up its act. The insurance industry was streets ahead of them in this regard, galvanized by bitter experience and large claims against firms' liability insurance. Few people joining Lloyd's of London at the start of the decade would have expected to become guardians and reluctant restorers of the environment.

'The polluter pays' is a simple enough prescription for repairing damage to the environment but, as many Lloyd's Names discovered to their cost, the buck rarely stops with the culprit. It gets passed to his insurer; and an expensive battle royal ensues over whether the insurer should really have to pay for the festering messes and cavalier past conduct of its client.

Tough new clean-up laws in the United States have seen corporate America falling over itself to claim that its liability insurers, past and present, should pick up the bills for its past peccadilloes. In many cases that means

Lloyd's underwriters, either as primary insurers or as providers of excess-of-loss and reinsurance cover to the US insurance companies that wrote the original cover.

In December 1980 US President Carter's parting gift to his nation was the Comprehensive Response Compensation and Liability Act, or CERCLA for short. It created the Superfund, a $1.6 billion pot of money raised through a levy on industry, mainly the oil and chemicals end, to be used for studies by the existing Environmental Protection Agency (EPA) – a legacy of Richard Nixon's administration – into how best to clean up polluted sites.

Using the fund, the EPA was able to pick badly polluted sites now crying out for rescue and repair the damage while the Superfund set about recovering the outlay from the polluter or polluters. These clean-ups of severely damaged land, rivers, lakes, and groundwater are very expensive, and the rules say that any firm that has been involved at any stage with the polluted site is jointly and severally liable for the bill. This means that if they cannot all be tracked down and made to pay between them, any single one of them may be handed the whole bill – and the Superfund's arm relentlessly pursues whoever it thinks is most likely to be able to meet the high cost of cleaning up past spills, leaks, and dumping; which includes the companies' liability insurers and their reinsurers.

This puts Lloyd's syndicates that have reinsured old US general liability policies firmly in the frame and, with the bill for cleaning up the USA estimated at anything from $65 billion to $750 billion, the echo of the alarm bells this has set ringing all over corporate America is almost as loud across the Atlantic as in the City of London, from where the sound waves ripple outwards to cause some very severe headaches for Lloyd's Names around the United Kingdom, and for some from far further afield.

There followed a frantic scramble by companies and insurers to the US courts to clarify who was covered for what, by whom, and when. These long and costly 'summary' hearings take place, all the way up to the final appeal court, before the main issues of which companies polluted what and which should now pay up are thrashed out in court with the US clean-up authorities. As one observer has put it, 'Someone is cleaning up but it's not the environment.' Step up, once again, America's lawyers.

The hearings determine whether insurers have a duty to support their clients' court battles with the environmental authorities over who has to stump up towards the bills for restoring America's polluted land, lakes and groundwater. If the cover is void, the insurers can walk away from the main fight without further costs. Every case is different, but the pattern of results has wider implications: this time for future European Community anti-pollution rules.

A draft European Commission Directive on civil liability for damage caused by waste was drawn up closely following aspects of the US model, including the idea of liability reverting to whoever was the 'holder of the waste' at the time making them the 'deemed producer' of it; joint and several liability; and the Superfund's 'deep pocket' approach to cost-collection. The Directive differed crucially from the US model by focusing on current and future pollution; pressure groups like Greenpeace immediately lobbied it to make the Directive retrospective as well, to insurers' alarm. With what one legal expert in pollution issues described as over 200 years of 'past generations' ignorance, innocence and even indolence' to clean up after in Europe, the impact on the liability insurers would be substantial. Leakage of toxic waste on one housing project alone at Lekkerkerk village in Holland was expected to cost $70 million to put right.

The European Commission was also considering setting up a clean-up fund similar to America's Superfund and also to be raised from a 'green' tax on potential polluters or, possibly, funded out of extra insurance premiums levied in co-operation with the insurance industry. And it was studying the possibility of making pollution cover compulsory for all businesses in the European Community. This particularly alarmed Lloyd's underwriters. They had no intention of being used as a sinking fund to pay for British and European industry's misdemeanours. Yet if compulsory in future, pollution cover would have to be subject to very high standards of behaviour, safety and monitoring – and would therefore come expensive. Smart insurers in Europe, notably France where 75 companies pooled together in the mid-1980s as 'Assurpol' to write pollution cover, were already offering companies highly fenced-around, high-margined Environmental Impairment insurance, while Lloyd's, freshly bleeding from its US experiences, concentrated more on how to block the European Commission's idea. Dutch and Italian insurers also formed pollution insurance pools, the former only taking on quite small risks, however. All of them covered current and future incidents; none reinsured old cover with all the lurking horror stories of the profligate past.

Under America's Comprehensive Response Compensation and Liability Act both past and present owners of sites polluted with hazardous wastes are liable for the repair bill, or 'response costs', regardless of who may have actually spilt, leaked or dumped it. So are the generators of the waste, and firms who transported the toxic wastes to the polluted sites. The Superfund's wide reach and 'deep pocket' approach, pursuing whichever of these are most likely to be able to pay up, means just one firm may find itself billed for 100 per cent of the clean-up cost, even if it was only to blame for 10 per cent or less of the damage. Not surprisingly, they are loath to pay.

By the end of 1991, the Environmental Protection Agency had spent around 70 per cent of its budget on litigation to prise clean-up costs out of reluctant companies or their insurers. In many ways this is seen as a failure on its part, since that cash could have cleaned up an estimated 400 sites instead of soaking away into lawyers' pockets (a diversion of funds and effort that the European Commission hoped to avoid or at least, reduce, in Europe's approach to the problem).

The EPA's remit goes beyond remedial action at home in the USA. Its reach, which stretches from land and water to air pollution, includes research and development work into better ways of solving complicated pollution problems. This involves helping businesses to do voluntary environmental audits and start programmes to reduce toxic air emissions, developing new ways to recycle solid waste, speeding up the removal of harmful pesticides from the food chain, experimenting with better ways to clean up oil spills, tracking the incidence of coastal pollution such as medical waste turning up on beaches, and working with other governments to help their countries – for example, regions like Poland, Mexico, Latin America and Eastern Europe – to clean up their own act. It got deeply involved in cleaning up the *Exxon Valdez* Alaskan oil spill with a biotechnology project using fertilizers to 'enhance naturally occurring microbes' that helped break up the slick. Test areas showed the length of time it took to break-up the spill was halved by this process; and the EPA has a number of other biotechnology programmes underway.

It also tries to ensure that environmental regulations are readily understandable and reasonably easy to enforce; and, to 'encourage' others to behave, it tends to concentrate on chasing the worst offenders first. Its 1990 review said:

> This means targeting long-standing violators, taking enforcement action to assure that particularly valuable ecosystems are protected, focusing on pollutants that pose the biggest ecological and human health risks, and concentrating attention on industrial sectors with serious pollution problems. Third, we need to use innovative enforcement approaches to deter violations and develop incentives for the regulated community to prevent pollution and minimize waste . . . Violators will become ineligible for federal government contracts. Enforcement actions will be publicized to maximize their deterrent value.

Tough talk. Companies that the Superfund latches on to for massive clean-up repayments immediately tend to fight amongst themselves to see who can be blamed for what at the polluted site, and be accorded the appropriate chunk of the bill. Having each scoured their respective liability policies, hoping for a sign that their insurer can be dragged into their defence case and be tapped for the huge sums of money involved in any settlements, they then shop around to see which US state is most likely to give them a sympathetic interpretation of the responsibilities of the protesting insurer. And of course they use the best (which means expensive) lawyers and expert witnesses to prove the insurers are liable. To counter this offensive, the insurers preparing for this encounter do the same.

And that is where the real fun starts. Deciding just what forty-year-old, often rather loosely worded, liability policies really cover, has proved a legal minefield – or a goldmine if you happen to be the lawyer consulted.

There are fifty different mainland US State courts, each able to make its own interpretation of the wording of old liability policies. Should a case be appealed all the way to the Federal courts, local law still applies. The companies seek to load the dice in their favour by getting their case heard in a jurisdiction with a track record of decisions in favour of the insured not the insurer. In practice, most cases come up in seven or eight main jurisdictions, reflecting either where the insurance contract was made, or which state has the greatest interest in the outcome of the suit – which tends to reflect the concentration of industry in those regions.

California, Massachusetts, Minnesota, North Carolina, and Washington States' Supreme Courts have tended to rule that older comprehensive general liability policies do cover companies for pollution claims – while Maine and New Hampshire have tended to rule that they do not. But, unlike the flood of asbestos claims still trickling through the US legal system, the complexity of pollution claims and changes in the wording of more recently written policies reduces the likelihood that a court that has supported a company in one instance will rule in favour of the next company coming along to argue its case.

So many things have to be taken into account, such as whether the company knew it had a potential problem but failed to alert its insurer at the time; whether a claim dates from the first spill or its effective discovery; if newer more tightly worded policies exclude pollution claims from their date of issue – restricting them to the older policies; and how fast the firm moved to deal with the waste properly.

Legal arguments rage around four main interpretations of policy word-ings. The first dispute is over whether, what CERCLA and the Superfund call 'response costs' – the clean-up bills – are the same as 'damages' under the wording of the insurance policies? The companies claim that the clean-up bills imposed by new laws and changes in society's attitude, long after the event, are equivalent to damages levied to repair the site. The insurers say they are restitution costs, and therefore are not covered by the policies.

The second area of disagreement asks what the definition of 'third party' is in liability policies? The companies claim that cleaning up polluted groundwater that has spread to neighbouring (or even distant) sites counts as protecting a third party and is therefore covered by third-party clauses in its insurance policies. The insurer says there must be physical damage to third-party sites and that groundwater was never intended to be covered by third-party clauses anyway. Cleaning up groundwater costs $30 million to $40 million per site, and it supplies half the USA's drinking water and 75 per cent of its irrigation – which is why no one wants to pick up the bill.

A third battleground is whether the pollution was fortuitous, in that it was neither expected nor intentional; or could it have been foreseen and prevented, and could the company have put it right sooner? This is the area of the liability insurers' strongest suit. They argue that if the company knew what it was doing might cause pollution, and did nothing about it, it cannot claim under liability policies designed to protect it from the impact of sudden, unforeseen events. The company, on the other hand, argues that provided there was no deliberate intention to inflict harm, any spills or leaks were neither 'intended' nor 'expected' and therefore are covered by the relevant clauses in the policy.

This is where the legal world stands the real world on its head. Everything hinges on whether 'sudden' means something that happened in a rush, or whether it means something you just did not know about beforehand and have only just discovered – to your surprise, of course.

If 'sudden' can be interpreted as not having a temporal context but meaning 'unexpected' and 'unintended', the companies reckon they can claim to be covered by their policies for the resultant property damage even from quite long-term leaks. A very neat semantic argument. But the insurer just appeals to common sense, and says 'sudden' means sudden, that is brief and accidental, and anyway covers only the cause of the pollution such as a cracked pipe and not the subsequent damage to the surrounding terrain. This is particularly relevant if the disputed policy has one of the partial 'pollution exclusion' clauses brought in during the 1970s to restrict cover to real accidents as people became more aware of a potential problem with long-term pollution damage.

Earlier policies do not refer to pollution at all but tend to be deemed to cover it anyway – by default – provided there was an element of happenstance about the contamination. Deliberate pollution is another matter. Policies issued since 1986 – when the Superfund legislation was also tightened up, and brought companies' bankers and other mortgage providers, or anyone who had foreclosed on a contaminated site, into the frame – tend to be more specific about excluding pollution from the liability cover available; but there can still be room for legal argument even here.

The pre-1986 partial exclusion clauses restrict cover for pollution to 'sudden and accidental', which rules out cover for steady long-term pollution resulting from the company's normal course of business. This also helps to limit claims to one policy period, and can introduce a cut-off date limiting the insurer's obligation to indemnify the insured company to just the earlier, more general policies. Companies will still argue the toss, however, claiming that they were sticking to what was known, or at any rate legal, at the time of the pollution and therefore the contamination was accidental.

If they do successfully argue that 'sudden' means 'not intended' (dumping its temporal meaning), they may be covered for the long-term damage after all. Getting the money may involve invoking several policies under which the liability cover was renewed year after year over a long period of time. But the tactic can backfire if the insurer can show that the company was aware that it had a potential pollution problem and did not disclose this when renewing its cover. If it was trying to pull the wool over the insurer's eyes, the non-disclosure may void the subsequent policies anyway. The US courts have tended to side with insurers when the pollution had been evident and severe for years with no obvious moves by the company to stem or clean up past damage.

The fourth bone of contention is how to establish the date from which any pollution cover deemed valid becomes payable by the insurer. Does it date from the first leakage, or the discovery of the pollution? The answer affects whether the company can claim under each renewed annual policy, or only against the policy operating for the year in which the damage was discovered. Another thorny question is whether it can claim cover for each spill per year – for example, on a $1 million policy, and five spills, for $5 \times \$1$ million, or does the policy cover a maximum $1m in aggregate regardless of how many 'occurrences' there were? It makes a big difference to the sums at stake for the insurers, and is particularly important, as Lloyd's Names are discovering, when working out what can or can not be passed on under excess-of-loss reinsurance contracts to the next insurer up the line.

Much also depends on the age of the policy. Those issued from the 1940s up to the early 1970s tend to give the general, comprehensive liability that may well be interpreted as therefore including pollution cover. In the 1970s and early 1980s as the 'green' movement grew, worried insurers started to bring in the partial pollution exclusion clauses now at the heart of the most complex legal arguments in the USA. After 1986 pollution was almost always totally excluded from general liability cover. Companies with a potential problem had to seek separate, specialist environmental impairment cover, which is pricey and usually involves site visits by the insurers, paid for by the company, with no guarantee of a policy being issued at the end of it.

Most cases coming to the US courts concern the pre-1986 policies with partial exclusion clauses – with insurers seeking summary judgments on whether they have a duty to pay up if the Superfund wins its case against the insured company. If the answer is yes, the insurer will find itself joining forces with the insured to fight the main battle.

These summary judgment hearings grind through the US legal system starting with the lower State court, then going to appeal at the Federal level, and thence to the State Supreme Courts – and all that just to establish whether the insured really was covered! Even if the answer is 'yes', it does not automatically mean that the main case will end up with the Superfund getting money out of the insurer. That depends on what happens in the courts hearing the Superfund's suit against the suspected polluter it has targeted.

But, with so many billions at stake at that point, the insurers and international reinsurers feel it is worth spending large sums of money up front on legal costs to establish who was indemnified for what. In the meantime, however, they must ensure they can afford to pay the bills if the worst comes to the worst. Hence the flood of calls on Names in the mid- and late-1980s to stump up enough cash to build up their syndicates' reserves against the evil hour and to meet the legal costs of trying to escape having to pay the self-same claims: a double whammy, in the short term, anyway.

The biggest example of the lot is the Shell Oil Rocky Mountain Arsenal affair. Shell Oil, the US subsidiary of Royal Dutch/Shell, was told to pay $2 billion in clean-up costs for thirty years of pollution at this remote site. It sought to claim against its insurers – and lost in the California court. The pollution was so serious, including Second World War nerve gases, so visible, and so persistent, that the courts decided there was no way it could claim the damage to lakes and wildlife was accidental and unforeseen.

The case was a watershed for the insurance industry and proved that it could resist claims from persistent polluters – making the hefty legal costs feel worthwhile. Shell Oil naturally took the case all the way to the California Appeal Court. But in London, the Lloyd's insurance community felt inspired by its lower court victory. It had been honed for battle by the experience of the 60,000 asbestosis claims that it had met so far, also as a result of changing US legislation, and from which it learned some expensive but useful lessons. To help syndicates facing the pollution problem to keep track of what was going on, an environmental claims group was formed in London, not least to follow the trail of excess-of-loss cover to see which syndicate would be liable for what proportion of which incipient claims. Lloyd's chairman David Coleridge also lent his moral support to a suggestion by Hank Greenberg, boss of the giant American Insurance Group, that to deal with the crippling cost of the clean-up of old pollution, and save insurers faced with the tab under old policies from being bankrupted (to no one's great advantage), the US industry should create a special fund financed by a 2 per cent levy on all commercial and industrial insurance-policy premiums written by insurers of US risks. This would raise an estimated $4 billion a year, with which to pay the bills for cleaning up America. The levy would effectively be paid by US industry – the polluters – in their annual premiums; and leave the Superfund, which raises its money from a levy just on the dirtier, oil and chemical industries, to concentrate on pursuing recompense for any future incidents. Simple in design, the idea inevitably led to complications, but if implemented could take the pressure off individual Lloyd's reinsurers currently having to bolster their own reserves for potential 'old year' claims. In the meantime, however, calls to the Names on the syndicates caught up in this conundrum continued to cast a nasty blight on their own futures.

The rest of the world was focusing sharply on the pollution issue too. Not only the European Commission, but the World Bank was considering the potential of a green tariff, while the General Agreement on Tariffs and Trade – GATT – revived its somnolent, twenty-year-old environmental committee in the 1990s. The air was thick with talk of encouraging, or obliging, industry to implement environmental audits, in which their manufacturing practice would be cleaned up and the most cost-effective ways of curbing waste and reducing emissions would be set in train – and without which environmental impairment insurance policies would be impossible to get, leaving the firm exposed to the full bill when the green inspectors came to call.

While British industry was slow to respond to the changing international political environment, British and American lawyers and the insurers they represented were not. The United States was beginning to realize that passing the buck for pollution to the polluters' insurers was time-consuming, wasteful of financial resources, and that a more elegant solution might be necessary.

Of the epic legal wrangles between insured and insurer, one battle-hardened US lawyer, Barry Bunshoft of California firm Hancock Rotchert & Bunshoft, said in late 1991:

> It's trench warfare out there but even World War I ended. Sometimes it takes a while to see who's winning and I think we're about five years away from having a real sense of which side is way ahead – somebody will be and I am hopeful that it's the insurance side.
>
> In cases where the insured was actively involved in waste disposal, the insurer is winning. Indiscriminate disposal of hazardous waste in the ordinary course of business is not fortuitous and liability insurers should not be called upon to indemnify polluters for decades of haphazard disposal of waste, with the lowest level of attention to this issue because there was no money in waste – companies did not put the effort into waste as they did into making profits. Companies are changing their habits, not because they are becoming model citizens but because the jigger's up and the bright lights of the Environmental Protection Agency are focused on them.

It got more complicated if the company generating the waste had hired someone else to dispose of it and a haulier to take it there. If the waste site has leaked and the operator or even the haulier no longer exists, the Superfund looks to the original creator of the waste for reparation. In turn it naturally turns to its liability cover, and in these cases the US courts have tended to say the insurers must pay, unless the policies being activated include the newer pollution exclusion clauses that rule out all cover for contamination except in the case of genuine accidents. As Bunshoft reports,

> The biggest cases are where the pollution companies were in control of their own waste disposal and the insurers are resisting them, all but to the wall, on paying claims. When there were active polluters, the insurers are unwilling to compromise. The Superfund wants the money and is not financially tuned to the moral issues of who sends it.

Lawyers investigating cases of long-term pollution by major companies say they have been:

Surprised at how much long-term evidence we have found, consistently, that while the public may have been naïve about the harm that could be caused by the chemicals, the petrochemical industry *knew*. Now they are trying to downplay that so the public doesn't know and they look OK. If they are cleaning up it is not because they've got religion, it's because they got caught.

It's very disillusioning. We are dealing with the major corporations of the world – and they act like felons.

Though himself a beneficiary of the legal battles between insured and insurer, Bunshoft deplored the cost.

It really is outrageous but the lawyers are not having the dispute, the clients are. It's more civilized to go to court than shoot it out, but it's complex – ancient history, lots of witnesses, lots of documents. There isn't a word in the English language which doesn't mean something else if you want it to – mathematics is the only absolute and you can't write an insurance policy in anything other than the language; and English is a very rich language.

Insurance is a very self-defeating industry because on one side of the business they are in claims and risk, so you have to produce a product which has value to the insured. But, some risks become so close to being certainties, and the costs are so disproportionate to the premiums received, that you ought not to write it.

Markets adjust, and over time only companies that operate to 'clean' rules will be able to get limited cover, for genuine accidents, wherever they are in the world. But in the short term, the insurance industry has a major problem to overcome. Bunshoft warns that

There is a major rift in the insurance component to the distribution of capital right now. If losses continue to be disproportionate to income, capital departs from the insurance business – and it's not a good investment. The reserves are depleted and the claims continue to be high. You get insolvencies, and a lot of them means there is no insurance. Bye bye, insurance companies. But if you are a Lloyd's Name on a syndicate stricken by the same pollution battles, it is you personally who gets to top up the depleted reserves and, if your share of the claim outstrips what you've got, it is you who goes bust.

Angry Names are blaming their underwriters. Others, at one remove from the picture, are not so sure. As Bunshoft says:

Social tolerances have changed over the years. In the past there was a higher level of social tolerance to the destruction of the environment to the greater glory of making plastic and having oil. The social tolerance has changed, but the cost should not be borne solely by these industries: it should be just another part of the tax base to which people contribute to the great cost of cleaning up past pollution. The Greenberg initiative sidesteps the main issue: of politicians having enough integrity to call a tax.

Would voters be willing to pay an extra 'green' tax to solve the problem? Will politicians, who grew up in the era of protest against society's big battalions, now be prepared to take that risk at the ballot-box? While others kick around these questions, it is a 'fewe' members of Lloyd's of London who are grimly handing over their all to pay a very substantial share of the bills for the whole of Western society's past indifference to pollution and the consequent rape of the environment by the industries of the world's largest industrial society. That's not how insurance is supposed to work; and no wonder they don't think it's fair. But no one shows any desire to help them out with the bills.

6
Apocalypse Now

If you can keep your head when all about you are losing theirs, perhaps you have misunderstood the situation.

(GRAFFITO, PARIS, 1968)

Troubles never come singly, so they say, and it was certainly true for Lloyd's of London and its corporate competitors in the London insurance market in the 1980s.

The wave of natural disasters that between 1988 and 1990 struck a world already growing concerned about global warming, holes in the ozone layer, and the greenhouse effect was almost apocalyptic in scale and multiplication. Bad weather featured for much of the eighties. Extreme cold, tornadoes, typhoons, hurricanes, heavy rains, floods and mudslides were experienced from Europe to the USA, Brazil, Japan and China. Earthquakes made their presence felt in the (then) Soviet Union, Australia, Mexico, and California.

Accidents and man-made disasters also took a heavy toll of life, limb, and the insurance markets, as the eighties gathered pace. The decade that brought us the Chernobyl nuclear power plant explosion in 1986, went on to yield the Piper Alpha North Sea oil rig disaster, and the heart-breaking Lockerbie plane crash in 1988; and peaked in 1989 with Hurricane Hugo, the San Francisco earthquake, and the *Exxon Valdez* oil spill that turned the Alaskan coast into a giant oil slick. The roll-call of tragedy and catastrophe was an extra burden for Lloyd's Names already reeling from being passed the costs of man's past exploitation of the planet – the asbestosis claims, and the battle over who should pay for cleaning up decades of industrial pollution.

For London-based insurers Britain's own, extraordinary hurricane of October 1987 was the herald of a particularly bad three years on the disasters' front. As the claims poured in, against a background of weak insurance rates and low income, the insurance companies were the first to plunge from profits into losses. In 1990 they lost nearly £5 billion which their investment income could not cover. The net result was a £1.5 billion shortfall; and this was before Lloyd's had closed its books on the disastrous 1989 and 1990 years.

There had been a foretaste of what was in store in the winter of 1983 when Hurricane Alicia brought freezing conditions to America's eastern seaboard. Claims from it were still trickling their way through the Lloyd's of London reinsurance spiral in 1988 when the next wave of natural disasters struck.

In 1985, the Japan Air Lines 747 SR crash had smashed its way into the record books as the worst single air disaster to that date, and triggered insurance claims totalling some $600 million sought from its insurers and international reinsurers. The pilot reported losing control of the aircraft after the right rear cabin door had broken; the plane smacked into Mount Osutaka killing 524 people. Just four survived the 12 August crash. Just ten days later, Britain was shocked by its own airline disaster, when a Boeing 737 caught fire on the tarmac at Manchester. Fifty-four people died in the blazing plane.

Despite being the year in which the Chernobyl nuclear power plant blew up – on 25 April – in the former Soviet Union, releasing huge quantities of radioactive dust into the atmosphere as fires raged in the reactor, 1986 brought few bad accident or insurance claims to Lloyd's door. As a result it was one of Lloyd's most profitable years ever. But it was also the lull before the storm . . . literally.

Siberian winds sweeping across Europe brought heavy snow in January 1987, kicking the year off to its coldest start on the Continent for nearly twenty-five years. In Georgia, in what was then still the Soviet Union, the melting snows brought terrible floods at the start of February. March saw the sinking of the *Herald of Free Enterprise*, the cross-Channel ferry with 543 people aboard that sailed out of the Belgian port of Zeebrugge with its bow doors open, turned over and sank with the loss of 188 lives. It was the worst peacetime shipping disaster seen in the English Channel.

But for Lloyd's, the costliest event of the year, and indeed of the decade, was 'Cat 87J' – as the UK windstorm of 16 October 1987 is listed under

Lloyd's system of recording catastrophes. Many of the bills made their way into the Lloyd's reinsurance market during 1988.

Britain was ill-prepared for the tropical severity of the storm. Hurricane-force winds, as one unfortunate weather forecaster explained the day before this one struck, do not happen in Britain, or at least only every couple of hundred years. Wrong on both counts. Not only did this one wreck homes, factories, cars, electricity supplies, telephone lines and trees in a swathe of destruction from coast to coast across southern England, killing thirteen people and plunging much of the country including the capital into chaos for days, but a second one struck in 1990.

The 1987 storm finally cost the British insurance industry (companies and Lloyd's) £2 billion – a huge sum of which reinsurance cover written in London provided £430 million. Its knock-on effects included the severity of the Stock Exchange crash on 19 October – Black Monday. As stock-markets in New York and Tokyo plunged overnight on Friday and Saturday, the London market was bereft of many of its most experienced dealers and market-makers, stuck at home in devastated Essex, with no train services and little chance of driving in (if their cars had survived the storm) because roads were blocked by fallen trees. Inexperienced dealers panicked and sent the FT-SE 100 share index into freefall. It lost 250 points, wiping some £50 billion off share values in just one day – wreaking havoc in the process with the value of many Lloyd's Names investments and their funds held at Lloyd's.

The spate of weather-borne and man-made disasters gathered momentum in 1988, building to its crescendo in 1989. Troubled 1988 brought nineteen accidents or natural disasters that each cost insurers at least £20 million, mostly far more, and one close to the £1 billion mark: Piper Alpha of which over £600 million was covered by reinsurance programmes with London insurers and Lloyd's syndicates.

Drilling for oil in the deep, chilly, inhospitable waters of the North Sea is not easy. A terrible reminder of how careful man needs to be to take every precaution when tapping the earth's resources in dangerous conditions came on 6 July when the Piper Alpha rig, owned by Occidental Petroleum, was rocked by a huge explosion. It was the region's worst disaster. In the blazing inferno that followed, 167 men lost their lives either on the rig or leaping into the sea to escape the fire only to find the waters far below also ablaze with burning oil. Helicopters and rescue ships raced to gather up the survivors from the cold North Sea whose freezing waters themselves could chill a man's life out of him in less than half an hour. The rig was a hideously tangled wreck that blazed orange, black and red and then smoked an evil black cloud into the sky for days afterwards.

Insurance claims finally totalled $1.4 billion – about £1 billion – much of it covered by insurance or reinsurance written at Lloyd's. Of the £609 million reinsured in the London market, some £376 million was reckoned to be down to Lloyd's syndicates to pay, divided between claims for the physical damage to the rig, injuries and deaths, and the cost of clearing up the wreckage afterwards. Not only that but, through the fashion run wild in the market at the time of reinsuring the reinsurance in smaller and smaller parcels of cover, time after time and creating what became known as the London Market Excess (LMX) spiral, Piper Alpha claims were reinsured so many times over that the policies totted up to over $12 billion worth of cover, which had to be reserved for until the professionals worked out which insurers really had to pick up what part of the bill. Most settlements were dealt with quickly but some took a long time to agree, in certain cases because the effects of shock on the survivors made it hard as time passed, to contact them.

The impact of Piper Alpha was felt most at Lloyd's by marine insurance syndicates; others fared better but still had some hefty claims with which to cope. Tables prepared by Chatset, an organization started by a handful of Names that has attempted to analyse and monitor the performance of Lloyd's syndicates since late 1981 (long before Lloyd's itself felt this was helpful or necessary), calculated in 1991 that the worst hit of the reinsurance syndicates – marine syndicate 255, managed by Rose Thomson Young and in 1991 an early subject of a new Loss Review procedure introduced by Lloyd's that year – lost its Names £23,000 per £10,000 of insurance written in 1988, thanks in large part to Piper Alpha claims. The best of the syndicates caught up in the reinsurance spiral, 575 (managed by J. H. Chappell Underwriting Services), managed to squeeze out a £3,124 profit for each Name per £10,000 share of the insurance written in 1988.

Piper Alpha was bad enough for Lloyd's Names, on top of the asbestos bills and the pollution battles in the USA, but there was more in store for the battered insurance market.

This was a year of storms, floods and landslides around the world. In September, Hurricane Gilbert swept violently into Jamaica, across the Caribbean and hit the Gulf of Mexico at the Yucatan Peninsular, wrecking the resorts of Cancun and Cozumel, and killing 200 people in Monterrey as four buses were swept away in the winds and floods. It was the most destructive storm seen in the Atlantic until then, and the damage from its five-day rampage was estimated at the time to be as high as $10 billion worth.

Insurance claims, recorded by watchers in the London market, were $1 billion, with those ones against Gilbert that filtered through to Lloyd's syndicates put at £170 million including at least £128 million in reinsurance claims.

Six weeks later, in late October, Hurricane Joan did its best to catch up with Gilbert. This time the Caribbean coast of Central America bore the brunt of the new hurricane's own five days of fury. Nicaragua suffered first. The powerful winds wrecked homes and left floods and mudslides in their wake as they swept on in prolonged and violent rain through Costa Rica, Panama, Colombia and Venezuela. As the first fury of the winds eased as it crossed to the Pacific Ocean, Hurricane Joan metamorphosed into Tropical Storm Miriam and lashed El Salvador with rain and wind, making 3,000 homeless as it passed. British insurers calculated the claims bill from Hurricane Joan at $800 million.

So much for nature. Human error also took its toll of 1988. For example, on 28 August, at Ramstein in West Germany, three Italian fighter planes collided above an airshow at this US base. One plane crashed on to spectators and exploded. Seventy people were killed and over 150 injured. The accident generated a £112 million insurance claim.

Human malice played a part too. This grim year closed with the terrible Lockerbie airline disaster in which Pan-Am jumbo jet, flight 103 from Frankfurt to New York via London and carrying 259 passengers flying to the USA for Christmas, many of them young American students, was blown up in mid-air by a terrorist bomb as it cruised at 31,000 feet early in the London-New York stage of its journey. It crashed on to the small Scottish town of Lockerbie, with devastating results. All the passengers died, and eleven people from Lockerbie were killed as houses were incinerated by the crashing plane and wreckage smashed into others.

Financially, this appalling event meant a $32 million insurance claim on the plane and $64 million in liability payouts in respect of the dead travellers, the people killed on the ground in Lockerbie, and wrecked homes.

Things got worse in 1989. In mid-September Hurricane Hugo crashed its way round the Caribbean and the Carolinas in the southern USA, costing insurers a total of $5 billion – about £3 billion. Seventy-one died and the trail of damage stretched from Guadeloupe, through the Virgin Islands and Puerto Rico, to Charleston. The London reinsurance market picked up at least £602 million of the claims.

On 17 October, the San Francisco earthquake rocked California. The shock, which registered 7.1 on the Richter scale, lasted just fifteen seconds, in which three-storey buildings in the city's Marina District concertina'd into one storey and a torn gas main sparked a violent fire, a mile of the upper level of the double-decker interstate highway 880 crashed on to the lower level and crushed the cars on it, killing forty-two drivers and passengers, and a span of the Oakland to San Francisco Bay Bridge collapsed. Including the Interstate 880 victims, sixty-seven people died as a result of that fifteen-second quake. Insurance claims for property damage and lost lives totalled at least $1 billion. Most of that was covered by local insurers and only a small part fed through to the London market. Reinsurance claims reaching London were subsequently put at a mere £15 million.

Three days after Christmas, Australia also had an earthquake, in Newcastle, New South Wales. It registered 5.5 on the Richter scale. Eleven died, buildings were wrecked. Total cost to insurers: £350 million.

A nasty toll of aviation accidents that year included the British Midlands 737-400 which, on 8 January, had lost power and belly-flopped on to the M1 motorway by Kegworth, just short of the runway of the East Midlands airport. One engine had caught fire and in the confusion, both were shut down. Forty-seven died, seventy-nine survived. A DC-8 plane crashed in fog near Suriname's Paramaribo airport killing 182 (thirteen lived); and at Sioux City in Iowa, USA, a DC-10 with 296 on board had a remarkable crash-landing after its turbofan tore loose and cut the hydraulic control lines. The pilot managed to steer the plane by flying it in circles to the right, trying to get to Sioux City for an emergency landing. In the event, he crash-landed just before the runway. The plane broke up and caught fire, but 185 people survived. Insurance claims were around $200 million.

Pasadena, Texas was rocked that October by an exploding petrochemical plant. That cost its insurers $1.35 billion, though a relatively small proportion – about $47 million – fed through to Lloyd's of London via property reinsurance. The accident seemed to have been caused by a leak of ethylene which set off a chain of explosions and fires that rapidly raged out of control. Twenty-two people died.

In Britain, April 1989 had brought the UK's Hillsborough football stadium disaster in Sheffield, where supporters packing in to see the match crushed the spectators already at the front against the security fence intended to stop eager fans from running on to the pitch during matches. Ninety-five people died. In August there was the tragic riverboat accident on the Thames in London when the *Marchioness*, hired for a private party, was rammed in the dark by the barge *Bowbelle* and sank. Fifty-one died.

The marine insurance market found itself awash in claims that year. The biggest, a real whale of a claim, was for the cost of cleaning up the huge *Exxon Valdez* oil spill on the Alaskan coast, estimated as ultimately likely to tot up to some $1.5 billion.

It was America's biggest ever case of oil pollution, caused when the supertanker *Exxon Valdez* ran aground, on 24 March 1989 on to Bligh Reef in Prince William Sound. At the wheel had been a fairly inexperienced seaman; allegations soon circulated that the captain had been in his cabin drinking. The tanker was carrying the equivalent of 964,000 barrels of oil; 200,000 of it poured into the sea. The tanker was refloated and towed off the reef but it was several days before the work of trying to disperse the oil spill really got under way, hampered partly by bad weather and partly by the delay in getting the right equipment up there. By 14 April when the drifting slick was finally broken up by heavy seas in the Gulf of Alaska, over 1,400 square miles of sea, and 1,100 miles of some of the (till then) most unspoilt coastline in the world, had been terribly polluted and thousands of birds and animals killed by the thick oil.

In the next six months alone, Exxon spent $1 billion on the preliminary cleaning up programme, which had to stop by September until the Alaskan winter had passed.

The incident led to the US oil industry suggesting the formation of a 'Petroleum Industry Response Organization' to deal with major spills rapidly and reduce the damage they cause. In the event, new US laws were brought in laying down that all tankers working within 200 miles of the American coast must have double hulls by the year 2015. California, motivated not just by the *Exxon Valdez* spill but by pollution of its own coastline caused by a 400,000 barrel BP tanker leak off Huntingdon Beach the following year, slapped a tax of 25 cents per barrel of oil on to the industry to create a $100 million clean-up fund. New laws also allowed the state to borrow whatever cash was needed to clean up a spill, and bill the culprit company for it. Shipowners' liability for oil spills was also increased under federal law – from just $150 per gross ton spilt to $1,200. Faced with these sort of costs for spilling oil, shipping companies whacked in orders for double-skinned tankers at once. Though fearing that trading in and out of the USA was going to become increasingly difficult for tanker owners – creating problems for a nation that still relied very heavily on imported oil – canny London-based insurance companies saw scope to write more, high-priced, liability cover for these clients.

Battered and shaken, the world insurance industry reeled into 1990: and straight into more windstorms, including the UK's second hurricane in less than three years. A hailstorm in Sydney, Australia, generated damage claims totalling £1.2bn. In the summer, Iraq invaded Kuwait and amongst other things, seized its fleet of civilian aircraft, insured for $300 million. The cost to Lloyd's syndicates worked out at around £150 million sterling. Marine and aviation losses also kept on coming in, with air accidents involving US, Indian and Chinese planes.

Britain's second bout of hurricane-force winds swept in early in the new year. The most violent reminder of the 1987 storm came on 25 January 1990, battering Britain and tearing across Europe. Holland, Belgium, France, West Germany and Denmark all felt its force. Ninety-three people were killed in the gales, forty-five of them in the United Kingdom which suffered the worst damage. The storm entered Lloyd's records as 90A; but there were more to come.

Fresh windstorms ripped through France and West Germany on 3 February. Chartres's famous cathedral lost copper tiles from its roof. Again there were deaths. More gale-force winds arrived on 26 February, wreaking new havoc not only in these two countries but across Ireland, Britain, Holland, Belgium, East Germany, Switzerland, and Italy as well. High seas added flooding to the catalogue of deaths (fifty-one) and destruction. Lloyd's recorded them as 90C (UK floods), 90D, G and H. Their combined damage, including 90A's efforts, was estimated to have cost $8 billion: nearly twice the bill for Hurricane Hugo.

Catastrophe losses for 1989 and the first two months of 1990 were estimated at between $20 billion and $25 billion, with the first two months of 1990 alone seeing worse losses than in the whole of 1987 or even 1988 – and presenting UK reinsurers with some £566 million in claims.

Britain had even joined the earthquake zone, on 2 April 1990, with a small quake of 5.2 on the Richter scale, which was centred on North Wales, did minor damage in Manchester and Liverpool and was also felt in southern England. Eastern Sicily suffered rather more, in December 1990. It was also only a small quake but nineteen died and 2,500 lost their homes to it. After such wild beginnings, the year in Europe closed for the UK and its continental neighbours with heavy falls of snow and further disruption and chaos, and loss of life.

In a long catalogue of natural disasters around the world since 1988, tornadoes, floods, and typhoons featured frequently. The earthquakes also continued. In the Philippines, the area round Manila was hit by a quake in July registering 7.7 on the Richter scale that killed an estimated 1,600 people and injured another 3,000. A six-storey school was flattened, and in mountain regions thousands of people were feared trapped in the rubble of their homes. Typhoon Ophelia had already pummelled the region in June. Next to sweep through, after battering parts of China, was Typhoon Yancy in August, and in November the Philippines were struck again, this time by Typhoon Mike which killed over 200 people, left 120,000 homeless, and destroyed sugar crops.

Aviation losses in 1990 included the hijacked Chinese Boeing 737 which crashed on landing, hitting first a parked 707 and then a fully-loaded 757 waiting on the ground and burst into flames. Some 128 people died; insurance claims were about $66 million. Indian Airlines lost an airbus that crash-landed on a golf course, killing ninety-seven of its 146 passengers and crew. Insurers received claims totalling $57 million.

At sea, disasters included Danish ferry the *Scandinavian Star* which caught fire with the loss of 159 lives, mainly from smoke inhalation. Arson was suspected. Claims totalled $24 million.

Amongst these and other major claims, 1990 was also the year that brought the 2 August invasion of Kuwait by Iraqi forces. Apart from the political turmoil, and subsequent war, this also sparked frantic financial activity as Iraqi and Kuwaiti assets in the USA were frozen, the latter to prevent Iraq stealing them. Spurred by US President Bush, Britain, Japan, and France and others followed suit. Later in the year, Lloyd's underwriters picked up a substantial share of the $300 million insurance claims for the Kuwaiti airline's seized fleet of aircraft, which were paid to the government in exile.

The year 1991 brought the Gulf War to free Kuwait; and worries in the United Kingdom about insurance claims for the cost of subsidence in houses, caused by a series of dry summers, and later fears (for the large UK insurance companies) about the impact of mortgage protection policies being called in as British home owners defaulted on their mortgages in droves as recession bit deep, interest rates soared, and house values plunged. From the United States came concern over the troubled savings and loans institutions, the 'thrifts'. Around 1,300 thrifts and banks had failed by the middle of the year and Lloyd's underwriters, who had reinsured them, feared hefty claims. There was talk of the cost to the insurance industry totalling $3 billion. Fraud was suspected in many cases, however, which would void any indemnity cover. Insurers began to wonder when the unusual number of natural disasters and manmade accidents would return to 'normal' – or was this a new norm?

It was not a good year at sea either. Lloyd's maintained that, so far, its marine account was not looking too bad for 1991 but the Institute of London

Underwriters (ILU), whose members are the large UK insurance and reinsurance companies, and foreign insurers and reinsurers drawn originally to London by the lure of Lloyd's and its attendant brokers, reported that claims against its members had totalled £4.069 billion (a £1.34 billion leap from 1990's level) against premium income of £2.21 billion – an improvement on 1990's inadequate £1.675 billion but not nearly enough beside those claims.

Though its origins lay in shipping insurance, Lloyd's had recently been losing market share to the expanding insurance companies making up the other part of the £9 billion London insurance market. They now accounted for 47 per cent of all business being written in London to Lloyd's 53 per cent – partly because the companies wrote more direct business while Lloyd's concentrated more on reinsurance – and for slightly more than half of the marine business (for similar reasons) in what was also a declining sector. After the German group, Munich Re, Lloyd's was still the biggest reinsurance provider in the world. But of the US$6.5 billion its syndicates raked in as reinsurance premiums in 1990, $1.9 billion came from inter-syndicate reinsurance generated within the club. Outside Lloyd's, Munich Re wrote $7.3 billion, and Swiss Re $4.8 billion of reinsurance that year. These three were the giants of that business.

Lloyd's also wrote 18 per cent of the world's direct marine insurance, a market worth $14.5 billion in premiums a year internationally in 1989; and 20 per cent of the world's direct aviation business – a $2.4 billion market.

Lloyd's may have been sanguine about the prospects for its 1991 marine account but watchful Chatset was not. In January 1992, it too forecast losses this time for Lloyd's marine market, anticipating a £650 million shortfall though this was an improvement upon its predictions of losses of £802 million and £750 million respectively for Lloyd's 1989 and 1990 marine underwriting years. Lloyd's hotly disputed the 1991 forecast in particular, claiming that the year showed every sign of making a modest return to profit.

The West's shipping industry had been in the doldrums for several years; marine premiums had been equally depressed as a result. During 1991 marine rates at last started to recover, but for ILU members at least, the gains were wiped out by a spate of accidents and claims. Reporting in January 1992, the ILU said 1991 yielded

> a disconcerting and ominous upward shift in the casualty graph, to the extent that the overall result was the worst seen since the mid-1980s. Moreover, losses of bulk carriers, often in unexplained circumstances and with considerable loss of life, continued in an alarming manner;

increasingly the evidence is pointing at structural failure as the main culprit.

It said 182 ships had been lost in 1991, 30 per cent in number and 40 per cent more in tonnage terms than in 1990 'including the highest-ever tonnage losses of bulk carriers'.

Retiring ILU chairman Declan MacMahon identified failure of the hull plating in bad weather or heavy seas as 'a big factor in bulker losses, but age and the method of loading cargo must also be considered in conjunction with this. In fact, it was a record year for vessels suffering structural damage.'

The ILU was deeply disturbed by this casualty rate, blaming a wave of changes within the shipping industry and recession for leaving vessels in no condition to cope with the upsurge in severe storms. As the (then) deputy chairman Peter Evans said:

Ships are ageing and breaking down and having trouble in bad weather, probably because over the last ten years there has been a slump in shipping leading to cost cutting, lower standards of maintenance and a sea change in ownership away from the old traditional shipowning family companies, which were very interested in the vessels, to financial companies with no background in shipping, who appoint managers to run the ships nice and cheaply. There is no relationship between the captain and the owner any more and that has a bad effect. Thus the health of the merchant fleet is not as good as it should be, and there are more casualties.

By the end of the year the number of ships running into trouble enabled the marine insurers to insist on higher premiums for insuring hulls, cargoes, and for liability cover. The Joint Hull Committee, representing marine insurers from the ILU and from Lloyd's, also introduced a new structural condition warranty, from January 1992, involving an age-related survey which the ILU recommended to its members should be requested as a condition of further insurance cover for tankers and bulk carriers over twelve years old, and all other vessels over fifteen – and for any other vessels 'of doubtful age' or owned by previously unknown outfits. 'Unless the physical condition of older vessels is improved, heavy losses will continue,' the ILU warned its members.

The year's crop of accidents at sea for which they had to shell out had included the 23-year-old roll-on-roll-off (ro-ro) ferry *Moby Prince*, which in April 1991 collided with the tanker *Agip Abruzzo* (aged 13) in thick fog off Leghorn (Livorno) on the north-west Italian coast. Fire broke out, gutting the ferry and killing 141 people. The worst tanker loss of 1991 was the same month. Disaster struck Italy a second time that April when the *Haven*, built in 1973, and valued at $30 million, 'exploded and caught fire off Genoa while loaded with 143,000 tons of crude oil worth $42 million'. Six of her crew were killed and thirty hurt. The *Haven* was moved to shallower waters before a series of further explosions that sank her, pumping her cargo of oil into the sea and threatening Italy's popular western beaches. The country declared a state of emergency but in the event a sixty-vessel clean-up effort succeeded in dispersing the slick.

Then 3 June brought Italy its third marine disaster in three months: this time on the other side of the country, when the cruise ship *Pegasus* caught fire at her Venice moorings. The damage cost her insurers some $45 million but the passengers and crew were all safely evacuated.

The year's worst bulker loss was the 75,330 ton (gross), 26-crew *Mineral Diamond* carrying iron ore. Valued at $25 million, she went missing, presumed sunk, that May in bad weather 1,500 miles west of the Australian port of Fremantle. Investigators feared that 'high sheer stress at the engine room forward bulkhead created by cargo loading may have contributed to her sinking.'

One of the most dramatic incidents at sea was the rescue of 565 people from the £13.6 million cruise ship *Oceanos* – built nearly forty years before, in 1953 – which ran into serious trouble in bad weather off the South African port of Durban. The ILU called the South African search and rescue service's success in plucking all but one person off the ship before she sank 'one of the most spectacular sea rescues of modern times'. Other costly losses at sea and even in port, though not always with the loss of life, that year involved instances of running aground, fires, explosions, and the horrific sinking at the end of 1991 of the ro-ro ferry *Salem Express* which, carrying returning pilgrims from Mecca, struck a coral reef in the Red Sea and sank with the loss of over 450 lives.

Marine underwriters also insure oil rigs and a clutch of other non-shipping but weather-related risks. The biggest single hit ILU members took in 1991 came when the concrete gravity base of the Sleipner A rig sank off Stavanger in Norway on 23 August 'while being ballasted down for fitting of the platform rig'. Valued at nearly £164 billion, it was the biggest energy construction loss seen 'for many years' and made waves in the Lloyd's market as well as for ILU members, though about 30 per cent of the risk had been underwritten through the Norwegian government.

Aviation underwent a major transformation in 1991. For a start, several airlines merged while others went out of business. The Gulf War hit business travel very hard as few companies dared risk their executives' lives in the air in case – with the memory of Lockerbie still fresh in people's minds – of terrorist retaliation from the Middle East. Insurers continued to provide cover for the airlines, and Lloyd's opened for business on Sundays in the early weeks of the war for the first time in history to cope with the rush of reassessed insurance risks for which cover was sought. Premium levels moved up and underwriters across the London market were determined to keep them rising to make up for three previous years of poor rates. Aviation insurers also cover even more specialist risks, like satellites, against anything going wrong with the launch or malfunctions once in orbit. Stephen Merrett of the Lloyd's agency that bears his family's name became the first scrap-metal merchant or 'totter' in space when Merrett syndicates, that had insured a wayward communications satellite worth a fortune in titanium and other precious metals, funded its remarkable recapture and return to earth. Once a claim has been paid on a lost or damaged object it belongs to the insurers and any money they can raise from its salvage is theirs to keep.

Sadly for the aviation insurers, 1991 brought a steep rise in the accident rate and therefore in claims. Reporting on 1991 two years before Lloyd's would be able to do so, the ILU listed 23 total losses of western-built jet airliners (worth between them $340 million) with the loss of 624 lives, compared to 17, killing 342 and valued at $229 million (excluding the seized Kuwaiti planes) in 1990.

The costliest had been ex-motor racing driver Nikki Lauda's airline Air Lauda's Boeing 767-300 (valued at $80 million) which crashed into the Thai jungle killing all 213 passengers. Two more serious accidents happened right at the end of the year: a $60 million Chinese Airlines Boeing 747-200 freighter came to grief; and on 27 December, the SAS McDonnell Douglas MD-81, whose pilot managed, in a remarkable piece of flying, to crash-land in forest trees saving all 129 passengers and crew (with minor injuries) when things went wrong shortly after take-off from Stockholm airport. The bill to insurers for the limp and broken hull was put at $35 million.

Natural disasters also took their toll of 1991, with several nasty ones sweeping in towards the end of the year just as everyone thought the bad run of catastrophes was over.

First came Hurricane Bob which struck the eastern coastal states of the US over 18-20 August, generating claims of around $700 million, mostly against US insurers but with some follow-through to Lloyd's. A hailstorm that struck Calgary, in Alberta, Canada on 7 September 1991 generated one of Canada's biggest ever insurance claims, at C$700 million, of which a proportion was expected to feed its way through to Lloyd's Canadian account. Then Typhoon Mireille bombarded Japan for two days from 27 September, generating its largest-ever storm damage claims, though most of these were covered by the domestic insurance market and only part of the huge, $3.75 billion repair bill was expected to find its way through to the London market-place. Even so by early 1992 Chatset was estimating that Mireille's cost to the London insurance market was in the region of $450 million.

October sparked fires that swept through the Oakland area of California on the 20th and 21st, destroying homes. Claims from that would also trigger reinsurance cover at Lloyd's.

This catalogue of disasters since the mid-1980s is far from exhaustive – if exhausting to try and take in – and only part of the insurance claims it generated came home to roost at Lloyd's or with its London-based corporate rivals. But in most cases Lloyd's share of the reinsurance claims was a substantial one; and the upsurge in the incidence of natural and man-made disasters struck many Lloyd's syndicates when their reserves had already been severely weakened.

The impact on Lloyd's syndicates' combined profits was dramatic. In the scramble to beef up the syndicates' reserves to meet the potential claims when – and in the pollution situation if – they became payable, a long run of handsome profits was abruptly and painfully halted.

The record shows this insurance market making £57 million in 1982, £35.8 million in 1983 with a massive leap to £289.8 million in 1984. This dropped back a bit in 1985, with profits of £195.55 million only to race ahead in 1986 to a record £649.46 million. It was to prove the peak. For 1987, as the tidal wave of disasters began its steady roll forward, Lloyd's profits dipped to £509.16m, shared between nearly 31,000 Names. The Names kept flocking in, to a record 32,433 members in 1988, but by now the money was pouring out. As provisions for pollution claims mounted for the 1988 year of account and premium income fell in the face of tough international competition, the high catastrophe claims against that year's underwriting sent the market sprawling.

Managing agents and auditors decided that reserves were nearly £1 billion too low to cope with the potential claims. So the calls went out to Names for cash to beef them up; and in place of a £431.5 million underwriting profit on the business actually written in 1988 Lloyd's posted losses of £509.67 million: a £1 billion turnround to disaster. Worse was to follow. An even higher loss, of £2.06 billion for 1989 was declared in the summer of

1992. Names scrambled to leave. Some 3,687 resigned by August 1991, and another 2,000 in 1992, with until 1994 and 1995 respectively to wait to hear what the bills for that year's underwriting would be. But Names stuck on syndicates with open years had no cut-off date for which to wait. Calls on their assets could continue *ad infinitum*, like a festering sore.

Amongst the wailing and gnashing of teeth, a few brave souls had decided to venture into Lloyd's membership in time for the 1992 year's underwriting. They reasoned that, by midsummer 1991, early indications already were that while 1989's results would be cataclysmically bad, 1990's would be less dreadful. With premiums now hardening at last and income in the surviving syndicates improving – helped too by a spate of mergers and acquisitions amongst Lloyd's managing and members' agents that would help to cut individual syndicates' costs and Names' expenses – they hoped 1991 would eventually see break even when its accounts were closed at the end of 1993, and anticipated that perhaps 1992, and certainly subsequent years, could be very profitable indeed. While the disillusioned 3,687 fled, 118 new Names quietly signed up as members of Lloyd's in the summer of 1991, and waited to see if the good times would indeed roll again.

7
A Day in the Life of Lloyd's

People Who Do Things exceed my endurance:
God, for a man that solicits insurance!

(DOROTHY PARKER, 'BOHEMIA')

Lloyd's of London is housed in a stunning, gleaming tangle of steel and glass that was the talk of the City as it rose in the early 1980s. It was the club's eighth home since moving out of Edward Lloyd's coffee house near the Tower of London in 1691, some twenty-two years before Mr Lloyd's demise in 1713. Each move was in search of more space for the expanding business of writing insurance. The new building, designed by British architect Richard Rogers, coped with the need to get the maximum use out of the site by hanging all the service pipes, and the lifts, on the exterior of the building and fitting electric blue service cranes on the roof. Some like the result, more conservative City folk hate it, or at least profess to, since this view seems to be required of them.

Some have dubbed it the nightmare on Lime Street – though night shows the building at its dramatic best, lit to magical effect with eerie white and blue light. Looming beside the arcaded Victorian Leadenhall Street market – where stallholders sell game, fish and cheeses, wine bars and little restaurants feed hungry insurance men by day, and the street cleaners prowl by night, sometimes to the sound of canned opera pouring out of a cassette in their vehicle's cab – the Lloyd's building seems to have landed straight out of a Spielberg movie.

So do some of its occupants at times. Nicknames abound. 'Baldy' or 'Big Ears' beaver away alongside colleagues dubbed 'Spunky von Smallhousen' or even (again) 'Nightmare'. These are the underwriters for the various syndicates who occupy the Room, the underwriting area that takes up four open-plan floors, one (more or less) at ground level and the rest hung like giant balconies around the vast central atrium. A steel and glass zigzag of moving staircases running on bright yellow rollers links these floors and disappears into the higher administrative regions that house the Council members' offices, a museum, and the eighteenth-century room designed by Robert Adam which had been removed from its Wiltshire home to be installed in an earlier Lloyd's building and now nestles in the top two floors of its twentieth-century host like a carefully candied almond cased in sculpted silver foil.

Below it, twentieth-century risks are insured following the seventeenth-century principle pre-dating Lloyd's itself that, if a loss occurs, it will be shared affordably among many people in small chunks, rather than ruining a few. That is the theory, at any rate, though something has gone awry lately.

On the ground floor the Lutine Bell presides in its ornate George V carved wooden rostrum and canopy, topped with a four-sided clock. The rostrum sits in the middle of a white marbled area of floor, studded with small black circles. The bell comes from a frigate *La Lutine* that fell into British hands in 1793 and was put to work carrying gold and silver bullion between Yarmouth and Hamburg – until she was wrecked with all hands lost in another wild October, in 1799. She was insured at Lloyd's which carried the cost. Some of her cargo was recovered over the years at various attempts. The bell was brought up in 1859 and given a new role at Lloyd's: to be rung above the din of business to herald important news: twice for good news, once for bad news of a disaster.

Under its canopy sits a man in red who calls out messages for people in the Room. Above the general buzz of business they catch their own names and look at the computer screens in front of the rostrum and overhanging other parts and floors of the underwriting area to check on their messages.

Presiding over the hubbub the Lutine Bell's polished brown pillars and canopy sit like a sedate palm grove on the white sands of its neat marble island, complete with its scarlet Robinson Crusoe, and surrounded by a sea of incessant activity. Brokers come to and fro plying their trade like little frigates themselves, docking briefly at one of the underwriter's desks – known still as 'boxes' from the old coffee house days when seating was partitioned like so many looseboxes – persuading him to underwrite a risk (or not), and casting off again in search of the next port of call.

Near the Lutine Bell is also the casualty book into which is entered each day's date and any reported disasters, or losses of ships at sea in beautiful copperplate handwriting using a real quill pen and ink. Close by is the book in use a hundred years before, open at the same date for the previous century. Beyond these is small maze of notice boards – and beyond this haven is carried on the business of insuring some of the world's riskiest projects, and some of its whackiest. A building, an oil tanker, a space satellite, a fleet of planes, a winning racehorse, the risk of having to pay a large prize if the Loch Ness Monster ever turns up, the £2 million cost of replacing a top motor-racing driver or footballer lost from the team through a disabling accident, and even a top wine-taster's palate, can all be insured here. You cannot buy long-term life cover here because Lloyd's is essentially a market for year-by-year insurance. But, impresarios can buy 'death and disgrace' cover against the star of the show being exposed for wild goings-on and having to be replaced in the line-up. Much of Britain's motor insurance is also done here, with brokers offering motorists very competitive Lloyd's policies.

THE COUNCIL

Insiders say that the reason the governing body chose Richard Rogers's ultra-modern design for their venerable market was his proposal to house their beloved Adam Room on the two upper floors of the new building, giving it full ceiling height and, to their delight, restoring to the room all its original panels: there had not been room for all of them when it had been moved from Bowood House and some had to be given house-room in the corridors of the 1958 building. Now they could be returned to their fellows.

The Council of Lloyd's made the rules that governed Lloyd's – empowered to do so by the 1982 Act – and disciplined its members. Before changes recommended in 1992 by the Rowland Task Force, it was made up of twelve working members (practitioners) of Lloyd's and eight people elected by the external Names (Mary Archer became a Council member this way), plus another eight nominated on to the Council from outside Lloyd's fief. Normally they would be chosen by Lloyd's and approved by the Governor of the Bank of England. The head of the Securities and Investments Board (SIB) is automatically a nominated Lloyd's Council member.

From within its ranks the Council would choose a chairman, and two deputies, all drawn from amongst the twelve working members; with a nominated member taking the role of chief executive and making up a third deputy chairman.

Then there was the Committee of Lloyd's, composed of the twelve working members, dealing with the day-to-day running of the market. Changes to this structure suggested by the Rowland Report, though not at first well received, were being studied in early 1992 with a degree of urgency because the incumbent chief executive, Alan Lord, was due to retire that June and no one could be appointed until a new structure – if one was ultimately to be recommended by the working party charged with this study – was determined. In the interim a triumvirate, made up of the head of market services, the head of regulation (both likely contenders for the chief executiveship if it continued in existence) and the head of finance, would hold the fort. This curious state of affairs looked set to leave Lloyd's without a chief executive for several months of what was one of the most crucial years of its life. By 1993, however, a new structure was in place.

In the meantime, the various Lloyd's groupings – underwriters' associations, agents' associations and the Lloyd's brokers' committee – had continued with the old format under which they put together a business issues committee whose chairmen and chief executives attended the main Lloyd's Committee meetings; while a host of other working parties, policy bodies and functionary bodies dealt with the aspects of running the market which the Committee devolved on to them, including studying all the Rowland proposals.

THE SYNDICATES

Marine insurance is Lloyd's oldest trade, and was practically its only one until 1880 when other forms of insurance began to appear more frequently and were developed by Lloyd's underwriters. It also pre-dates Edward Lloyd's coffee house by some 100 years. Today the marine underwriters cover hulls (the ships) and cargoes as before, but also all other kinds of transport by land and air as well as by sea, and have branched into marine structures such as oil rigs and oil and gas exploration platforms. War risks, the danger of piracy and hijacking, and insurance against ships and planes being impounded or confiscated by foreign governments are also part of the marine underwriters' portfolio.

Piper Alpha and *Exxon Valdez* claims figured large in marine underwriters' results in the late 1980s and premiums began to edge up to better – but in 1992 still insufficient – levels as the 1990s began. The marine syndicates' losses for the 1988 year worked out at £609 million when totted up in 1991.

There are also underwriters who are aviation specialists, however. Lloyd's issued the first standard cover for aircraft in 1911, and still tends to set the pace in aviation insurance rates. Cover includes the body of the aircraft (also called the hull), insurance for airline companies, airport authorities, and aircraft manufacturers who want to be covered if one of their planes crashes and the families of hundreds of victims and casualties sue them. When a plane goes down, the compensation claims for lost lives and injuries way outstrip the value of the aircraft. Premiums in this field came under heavy competitive pressure and took a dive, too, in the mid- and late-1980s, causing some anguish. In 1988, they dropped 25 per cent while claims soared over £1 billion, but aviation syndicates still made a combined £112.2 million profit on business underwritten that year. In 1989, 28 western-built jets crashed killing 1,450 people and claims running to more than $1.5 billion threatened to take this market into losses, too, by the time the tally was reckoned in mid-1992. Things improved a bit in 1990 on the crash front but premiums still dipped and aviation underwriters tightened their belts for another bumpy ride, hoping for a return to profits on the 1991 year (to be calculated in 1994). By 1993 rates were much better. But some aviation syndicates had also felt the chill wind of pollution claims blowing in from the USA.

Another category of Lloyd's underwriting is non-marine, a broad church taking in practically anything you can think of, from fire, burglary, sports stars, rock concerts; damage from natural causes such as storm, hurricane, earthquake or flood; racehorses, safari parks, hotels, factories, homes, shops and offices – and the Post Office; as well as the whackier end of the market such as the forty members of the Whiskers Club in Derbyshire who insured their beards for £20.00 each against fire and theft. Non-marine syndicates bore the brunt of claims due to catastrophe such as Hurricanes Gilbert and Hugo, the San Francisco earthquake, the Phillips Petroleum plant explosion in Texas, and a large share of the Piper Alpha accident plus some of the Lockerbie claims as well. The death of racehorse Alydar also affected these syndicates; and they were the ones who provided much of the war-risk associated with the Gulf conflict. On business written in 1988 Lloyd's non-marine syndicates lost £154 million. Though also suffering from soggy rates, the high losses and the increased difficulty of getting reinsurance cover in the 1990s, after the 1988 and 1989 years' crises, 1992 and 1993 saw catastrophe cover's premium rates improve at last.

Then there are the motor men. Lloyd's syndicates have been writing motor insurance practically since the first cars began bumbling round Britain's roads, and nowadays this market has become the largest private car insurer in the country mainly because Lloyd's-accredited brokers have extended its reach by acting as guarantors for other, retail insurance brokers wanting to deal direct with Lloyd's underwriters. This cuts out a layer of cost and makes Lloyd's motor insurance competitive with the big UK composite insurance groups. It is also the only direct link that most British citizens can have with Lloyd's. Car fleet business aside, Lloyd's reckons its underwriters insure one in five private motorists. Motor syndicates increased their profits in the otherwise fateful year of 1988, making £102 million between them.

Sometimes the cover being sought is part of an insurance 'treaty' under which a large company seeks to buy all-in-one cover for its operations around the world. Other risks may be one-off such as insuring a large art exhibition for its duration. As an experienced underwriter explains:

> The definition of insurance is that we are lending our capital to take the peaks and troughs out of disasters hitting the assured's business.
>
> Your perception of risk changes as you learn about an industry. You see losses, you learn about the unexpected – which is what our business is all about.
>
> Take a demolition contractor. It might drop something on passers-by, or have an accident on the site. You see the type of work and how they do it, and what can go wrong – and you can make a quick decision.
>
> But now this service has been devalued to just being a commodity, so they don't want to pay. But you always get what you pay for. A reasonable price, and continuity with your insurer, means you get a fair deal generally. But if the market is cheap and rates are low, you have to go with the flow. A good client won't seek the cheapest rate because he doesn't want to go to a cowboy. But the pressure remains on the good underwriters to keep their rates low and that can go wrong long-term and backfire. After a disaster, on an oil rig for example, rates will go up across the board to all the contractors who were on that site.

THE BROKER

Only insurance brokers accredited by Lloyd's may enter the underwriting Room to place cover with Lloyd's syndicates. In just one day a busy Lloyd's reinsurance broker in London can find him (or her) self discussing subjects as diverse as insuring the employees of Argentina's national telephone company against personal injury at work, and cover for people stationed in the wilds of the North Sea on the rigs of Norway's biggest offshore oil company.

While they work in the South American sunshine or battle against North Sea winds to extract black gold from the sea bed, he sallys out from his office in the south-eastern side of the City of London, just a stroll away from the towering high-tech Lloyd's building. At mid-morning he may pop into the neighbouring offices of underwriters with whom he has already made appointments or with whom he has a regular weekly date to discuss matters such as renewing a clients' annual cover or amending existing cover to take account of a new acquisition in an overseas country.

The people he calls upon may not be Lloyd's underwriters but employees of the big UK and international insurance and reinsurance groups, who maintain offices close by Lloyd's itself and are increasingly taking on classes of business that corporate insurers in the past have had neither the stomach nor the underwriting muscle to do. Now they may underwrite a hundred per cent of some of these risks, and certainly a part of them. The bigger the risk, the wider it will be spread within the total insurance market including Lloyd's. They sit, several to a room, at neat desks with ever ringing telephones while the hopeful broker perches opposite and runs through what the existing arrangement is, what has changed, what the claims record is like to date.

The thoughtful underwriter may ask for additional information, especially on the claims record, before he will agree to extend the cover, or increase, reduce or drop altogether the share of the risk he is prepared to underwrite and name his price. For this reason little chats about the insurance required may take place some weeks ahead of the renewal date to allow time for queries to be answered.

After these sessions are over, the broker will touch base with his own office and then head off to the Lloyd's building to try his luck there. Rising up through the steel and glass building on the shiny moving staircases, he hops off at the right floor for the man or woman he's after. Each floor is brimming with people and the 'boxes' or desk-cum-offices that the insurance underwriters occupy from mid-morning to late afternoon.

On a busy day there may be a queue for the best underwriters in particular fields. The broker explains his or her mission, the client, and the type of cover sought. Out of his bulging leather file he will produce any further information he requests about the company. If agreement is reached, it is time to stamp and sign the 'slip' or sheet of paper giving a résumé of the cover. The slip is a large sheet of paper folded back on itself several times. When unfolded the left-hand section is a form for administrative use, naming the client, its country of origin, the type of cover and gross premium it must pay when all the cover is arranged.

Next comes a typed list of details giving more information about the type and form of cover, the assured, the duration of cover sought, to what value, and for what parts of the world it is needed. Any special conditions will be listed here, too, the premium recorded, and the latest financial information about the client, how many employees it has and in how many locations may also be noted.

The next folds of the slip are blank for the underwriters' stamps. Having decided this is a reasonable risk the underwriter will indicate what percentage of the cover he will provide; and date, initial and stamp the slip. The completed slip provides the broker with a binding, working record of what the cover is for and who has underwritten what proportion. Each stamp has a ship's anchor logo next to the underwriting syndicate's initials on the right, above a row of boxes where the underwriter's own reference number is filled in, underscored by a heavy line for dates or signatures. Many underwriters have evolved instantly recognizable flourishes of their own with which to sign and date the slip, often in the space to the left of the anchor sign. By each stamp the underwriter clearly writes the percentage of the risk he is taking – two, five, ten, or perhaps even a hundred per cent.

The first underwriter to take a chunk of the risk is the lead underwriter. Armed with his stamp on the slip, the broker is off to the next box on his agenda and so on until one hundred per cent of the risk has been broked. On a busy day he may have to wait in line for the underwriter he wants to see. Everyone is scrupulously polite. The men call each other sir. The broker uses his best sales technique to woo the underwriter. He or she may lay on the charm or dazzle with technical information about the client, but if the underwriter is unimpressed or does not touch that particular type of risk, the broker may find himself swiftly sent on his way. Or he may be skilfully pumped for gossip before being disappointed in business. An underwriter who does not want to do the business may suggest another who has been known to look at this type of risk.

No sooner has one broker, satisfied or refused, gone on his way than another perches on the stool, puts his bulging leather slip-case on the desk and begins his story. If it is a renewal of cover that has proved trouble-free before with no new aspects to worry about, it may only take a few seconds of brusque inquiry for the underwriter to say OK and reach for his stamp. If it is new business that the underwriter grills the broker about before reaching a decision, or the broker has several different slips for different clients, or for different types of cover for the same client, it could take half an hour or longer.

Once the broker has gone round all the boxes he needs to call at, he will return to his own office to complete the day's work. This may involve calling clients around the world who, because of the time zone are now getting into their own business stride for the day, and want to hear how he has got on, or discuss what they have in mind next. Complications, and queries, can be gone into, and reports made back to superiors about what has or has not been achieved that day.

THE UNDERWRITER

Underwriters are the kings and princelings of Lloyd's. Courted by the brokers who wish to place business with them, they have the power to grant wishes, dash hopes, do it kindly and make a broker feel like a splendid chap, or cruelly and make them feel a complete fool. These are the men and women who take the risks for the syndicates' money and every day they have to weigh up the chances of accident or mishap for particular companies in a myriad industries in every corner of the globe – and try to decide whether to underwrite it and what to charge for so doing.

They start their day in the managing agency's office and make their way to the Lloyd's building by mid-morning to install themselves in their boxes and see what the brokers have to put to them that day.

Underwriters, like their syndicates, will tend to specialize within broad categories. One may be a shipping man through and through, another an expert on product liability, another on aviation or motor cover. The brokers seek them out according to the business their client is in and the type of cover it wants.

The underwriters' boxes, designed by the Italian business Tecno, are reminiscent of a flip-top school desk. Flat surfaced, their middle sections lift up to house the box's telephone handset, and notes and papers accumulated during the day. Each box has its own computer screens. Underwriters have taken advantage of computer technology to record all their underwriting and the claims records of each risk for instant recall at the touch of a keyboard. The keyboards themselves can be stored on sliding surfaces housed under the flat surface to keep clutter to a minimum. The lead underwriter and his team sit, two or three to a side, facing each other across the box. At either end of the box are stools or chairs for the brokers to perch on during their visits. It is not just the risks to be insured that are discussed. A good underwriter pumps the visiting broker for news and gossip about the client, the broker's own firm, other events in the market, other people's willingness or unwillingness to write this sort of business. Just as in the coffee house days, information is valuable when you are putting fortunes at risk. The stream of gossip carries on in the lunchrooms, inside and outside the Lloyd's building.

One day in the life of a Lloyd's underwriter saw cover being sought just at one box for such diverse things as:

■ A waste management company seeking employer's indemnity cover. More information was requested.

■ Cover for a film being shot in Hong Kong is refused because it was a one-off project with no scope for a stream of premium income for annual renewals.

■ A stevedore company is refused cover because that underwriter wanted to charge more than the broker knew his client would pay.

■ An oil storage company seeking product liability cover is 100 per cent underwritten for that risk.

■ A resort company running marine parks in the Caribbean with water skiing is refused cover because it had had hurricane damage claims before, and attracts lots of American guests. Americans tend to sue for pots of money if they get hurt. Staff could also sue for a small fortune if something went wrong. The broker is advised – slightly tongue-in-cheek – to try a marine underwriter instead of a specialist in indemnity.

■ A South African provider of professional indemnity for accountants and solicitors, seeking reinsurance at Lloyd's, gets a mixed reaction. The underwriter feels that accountants have rather too high a claims record as a profession but sends the broker away for more information.

■ A maker of insulation looking for a change of insurer in hopes of cheaper premiums has its claims record gone over with a fine toothcomb and then is rejected.

■ A company involved in biochemicals and pharmaceutical products with quite a bit of turnover in the USA is turned down, after much haggling, because this kind of business can attract very high claims especially in the USA where settlements tend to be much higher than in Europe. (Premiums for product indemnity are calculated using a group's sales turnover as a yardstick, while premiums for employer's liability will reflect the number of staff and the wage bill – and of course, in all cases, the number of previous claims, how much for, and what was finally agreed.)

■ A Japanese pharmaceutical company does get cover, however. The syndicate has underwritten it before and the underwriter knows a lot about the company. To underwrite this type of business he needs to keep up to some degree with what is going on in the medical world, at least where the company's drugs are concerned, in case there are reports surfacing of problems and side-effects.

■ An American company bought out by its employees is seeking excess-of-loss cover. The Lloyd's underwriter says no, because of the unpredictability of the type of awards US courts might make if there was a claim. A big award could trigger the excess-of-loss policy and could be very expensive for the syndicate. The risk outweighs the benefit of having the premium up front.

■ A broker is seeking excess-of-loss cover on another large Japanese pharmaceutical company's primary insurance for product liability claims. The broker is grilled but eventually is told the syndicate will underwrite 20 per cent of the risk. It makes drugs for the nervous system, heart and digestive systems for the domestic Japanese market and the agreement he has just signed specifically excludes any cover for Canada and the USA.

■ Excess-of-loss cover is also needed for a big German electronics company on third party and product liability. Its products go to other manufacturers not to the public direct and the underwriter wants to know more about who buys the equipment and particularly seeks details about its North American manufacturing subsidiaries. He says he'll think about it and sends one of his team off to photocopy the details for him to mull over again later on. German insurers tend to issue ten-year policies, whereas Lloyd's syndicates write annual cover and he fears that he could end up with a big claim against just one year's premium income and then lose the insured back to a German group offering a ten-year deal. That could leave his syndicate with a thumping loss. What the underwriter is interested in is writing cover for clients that the broker will bring back to him year after year, for a steady stream of premium income for the syndicate, and which do not have a catalogue of inherent problems that are highly likely to lead to a lot of claims – for industrial diseases, for example. The group's financial strength is also important. 'You don't want to underwrite for a company that is financially not solid in case it goes bust and you can't get the premium,' he points out.

■ A Swiss hotel group is seeking personal accident cover for its staff and their dependants world-wide, including funeral costs. After humming and hawing a bit the underwriter takes 5 per cent of the risk.

■ A broker who had been sent off to find out more about his client's risk the previous day returns with satisfactory answers and gets the slip stamped.

That was just the morning's business. The afternoon brought:

■ An up-market travel firm providing trekking and adventure holidays seeking cover for its clients. But it wants to raise the total cover in the event of a fatal mishap to $5 million and the underwriter is not keen on that especially as the group has US clients. In the end he refuses the business.

■ A small building and heating contractor wanting to renew its product liability cover fares better. He underwrites 25 per cent of it and, having checked the claims record, also takes 15 per cent of the reinsurance risk. The same broker has a stream of items to put to him, for the same client, and since the underwriter knows the company quite well now, he agrees to cover a slice of the excess-of-loss cover against the employer's liability, and primary cover for its design and consultancy staff as well.

■ Next comes a broker seeking employee liability cover for a foundation contractor using pile-driving equipment. It has a terrible accident and claims record and wants to find a cheaper insurer than its current one which has whacked up the premiums. The Lloyd's underwriter says he would want a five-year bank guarantee to see that the firm can meet the first layer of claims, and insists that it must start up a loss fund too, and then he would provide cover over and above those sums. It is still expensive and the broker goes off to refer back to this client and see what it thinks about the proposal.

■ A gas terminals company wants to bring two different types of cover together into one policy. A Lloyd's broker seeks professional indemnity cover. The underwriter says he does not do Lloyd's brokers! An investment management group wants similar cover and directors' liability cover. VISA, the credit card umbrella, wants reinsurance for travel accident cover granted to holders from a particular, small country. It recently had to pay out quite a lot after a nasty accident concerning several people from that country, but the deal is so small the underwriter is not interested in it. A large French food group wants employee cover, but is turned away because the food packaging industry has a bad record for accidents.

Things are quietening down now and the underwriting team decides to call it a day at Lloyd's and go back to the office to tidy up the day's business. Others are doing the same. Files are gathered up, blue overcoats are put on, and a steady stream of people is filling the moving staircases and pouring out of the building. Tomorrow is another day.

8
The Day of Reckoning

| *Lloyd's has got a Clint Eastwood*
syndrome – lots of men with no Names

(TOM TICKELL, FINANCIAL JOURNALIST, *DAILY TELEGRAPH*)

In the hothouse of financial boom when salaries and house values were soaring, particularly in the south-east of England, it had been easy for new Lloyd's Names not to dwell on the danger of making losses; and to dismiss the spectre of their unlimited liability to meet claims against the insurance cover written by their syndicates. In the previous two decades, premiums and investment income had – across the market if not in every syndicate – comfortably outstripped claims, and existing Names were used to receiving a cheque for their share of the profits each year. Newcomers had expected this agreeable state of affairs to continue once they too joined the gravy train.

By 1991 many of them had been sadly disabused of this assumption. Essex housewives, the owner of a vineyard in the Isle of Wight, property developers, farmers, peers of the realm, sports and show biz stars and even a group of Canadian dentists from Ontario who had been put into one of the unlucky syndicates were among the 30 per cent of Lloyd's 26,500 Names who in 1991 carried 70 per cent of the 1988 underwriting year's £509 million loss.

Calls on individuals ranged from more than half a million pounds a person to a few thousand. Once-enthusiastic Names, who had joined in mid-1987 in time for the 1988 year and waited until the end of 1990 for their first year of underwriting to be reinsured to close, had hoped for their first cheques to arrive in the course of 1991. Instead, they faced the prospect of 'calls' for £50,000, £60,000, or £70,000 a year. Many, including working Names whose firms had paid their deposits, could not meet demands of that sort. There were special tax breaks for new Names who lose money on their first year of underwriting but help from the taxman after that was limited. Dreams of wealth had turned sour overnight.

Unable to wake from the nightmare, many Names began to ask some very pointed questions about how they came to be in it. Why did the loss-making syndicates, stuffed with such a large percentage of the 'bad' business, appear to have mostly 'non-working' Names, many of them new Names, on board – while most of the 'working' Names employed within the Lloyd's insurance market were on syndicates that had not taken on so much of this ill-starred business? Did being on the inside track mean they could get themselves, family and friends on to the better syndicates leaving the rest to the newer outside Names?

There was an element of truth to this in that the older syndicates were heavily subscribed already and therefore harder to get on to. Many new members' agents drawn to Lloyd's in the 1980s were inexperienced in the ways of insurance and its risks and simply found it easier, and more attractive, to channel incoming Names towards the hungrier syndicates willing to undertake the higher risk business in return for higher premiums and thereby, higher profits (and higher profit commissions) – they all hoped.

The business they were writing so avidly included the excess-of-loss (XOL) cover that was to spread like wildfire through parts of the market as the fashion grew. Underwriters thought they saw easy pickings from taking on this XOL business, and then offloading most of the risk by reinsuring a chunk of their syndicates' exposure by taking out XOL cover for them too. It meant they could count most of the difference between the premium they received, and what their own XOL cover cost, as a profit straightaway. New syndicates were attracted to the higher risk business because it was a growing market with room for newcomers, whereas stiff competition world-wide had affected the more traditional areas of Lloyd's business and kept rates low.

Older, mostly non-marine, syndicates were also drawn to writing XOL cover on catastrophe business for the extra premium income during leaner times in their normal field. In addition, established marine syndicates were casting about for extra income and moving into areas of underwriting where, unfortunately, they lacked sufficient expertise to evaluate the risks they were taking on. There was a tendency during the period of weak marine insurance rates for them to be pressured by brokers into underwriting package deals for the broker's big clients seeking all-in-one cover for their international operations. This meant that specialist syndicates were taking on rather more types of risk than they had in the past, without really being knowledgeable enough to evaluate the extra risk and adjust the premium accordingly.

Had these risks been broken out and placed with underwriters in the appropriate field, premiums per item would have been higher – and since brokers were also seeking the best financial deal as well as the most convenient for their clients, this did not always appeal to them. Now that they were no longer allowed to own managing agents, a split insisted upon by parliament in the 1982 Lloyd's Act in the wake of deliberate fraud by a few, the brokers had less incentive to think twice about the appropriateness of the business they were placing for the particular syndicate that underwrote it.

This trend for syndicates to underestimate and therefore underprice the risks they were taking on was exacerbated by the practice of letting the junior underwriter in the box cut his teeth on the small proportion of related but not strictly marine business that these syndicates had long written as a modest sideline, while the shipping expert concentrated on the main business in hand. Thus as the 1980s progressed, marine syndicates in particular increased their syndicate's non-marine business for additional premiums that were in reality inadequate.

Older syndicates who agreed to underwrite special risks like run-off policies for other syndicates' US general liability exposure were attracted to this new source of business precisely because higher premiums could be charged. The syndicates could then distribute higher profits while also, they thought, having more money available to build up their reserves to meet any claims. This attracted the Names they wanted to boost these syndicates' capacity to underwrite more business, closing what was not, sadly, a virtuous circle but all too soon a vicious one.

Given the way members' agents had been remunerated at the time – with a slice of the syndicate managing agents' fees and profit commission, until 1990 – the higher profit distribution also meant more income for the members' agent and, again, appealed to the newer ones trying to get established. They were all too often neither experienced enough nor sufficiently motivated to wonder whether the syndicate was under-reserving. It looked as if everyone would be making good money, so why worry? Ironically, the new syndicates eager to hoover up most of the new external members also attracted many of the new, younger working Names who were equally in a hurry to make good profits out of the privilege of Lloyd's membership.

What few people foresaw was the size, number, and speed with which claims against this cover would pour in.

The cover many of these syndicates were writing for extra dosh in the late 1980s was chiefly 'excess-of-loss' reinsurance against potential catastrophes. Few could have anticipated the explosion in the number of catastrophes from late 1987 that would turn this business so sour so fast and so profoundly. Most insurance cover involves an agreement that the insured will pick up so much of the tab if something goes wrong but looks to his insurer for anything over that sum. In case a real catastrophe occurs, triggering a very high claim from the insured, syndicates and insurance companies will themselves buy excess-of-loss cover. They will agree to pay the first £1 million, for example, of the claim and the reinsurer will pick up the rest of the tab. Except that he, too, reinsures part of the risk, agreeing for example to pay the next £5 million and passing on any claims exceeding that. Thus a claim in excess of £11 million (£1 million from the primary insurer + the next £5 million from the first reinsurer + the second £5 million from the second reinsurer = £11 million) is divided between three different syndicates. This is called retrocession.

The premiums for this cover started out quite healthy but with each further layer of reinsurance premiums shrank. This was because reinsurer number one kept part of the premium he was paid by the primary insurer and paid part of it to reinsurer number two. Each time another slice of the risk was repackaged and passed on the slice of premium that came with it was smaller because so many other people had taken their cut out of it first. It was terrific business for the brokers that placed and re-placed each slice of the business for the syndicates. They too got a cut each time it went round, in their brokerage, charged as a percentage of the underwriters' premium. Brokers fuelling this process earned millions of pounds – each – in annual profit-related salaries during this period.

Excess-of-loss cover parcelled out in this way within the wider London market is known as London Market Excess (LMX). Excess was the word. In the 1980s with its traditional business drying up as the shipping industry went into a world-wide slump and insurance premiums came under pressure for a host of reasons, more and more Lloyd's underwriters decided to boost their syndicates' premium income by writing a chunk of this business. The LMX market went crazy. Syndicates not only wrote reinsurance and then passed on a slice to other syndicates, but then took another slice of the reinsurance on the same risk as it passed round again further along the process. Instead of being passed on, the same risk was being re-underwritten, for an additional but smaller premium every time. And as more and more Lloyd's syndicates joined in the game of pass-the-parcel, more of the risk remained within the Lloyd's market-place instead of being more widely spread across the whole London market. It was rather like passing a radioactive parcel from hand to hand. Everybody who touched it got burned in the end. At first everyone had wanted to join the party, but the game finally proved very dangerous indeed, and not only for the person holding the parcel when the music stopped.

The whole shaky edifice became known as the LMX spiral. When the unprecedented number of hugely costly catastrophe claims described in Chapter 6, 'Apocalypse Now', hit the London market, every Lloyd's syndicate that had insured, and then passed on a reinsured part of one of these policies, was soon making reserves to meet their whole liability in case the next syndicate along the spiral refused to pay up. Thus cover for the Piper Alpha disaster, a catastrophe that ultimately cost around £1 billion, had spawned an LMX spiral of reinsurance that stacked up to $12 billion of potential payouts depending on which reinsurer had to pay what. In the end, the insurance market cannot pay out more than what is actually claimed, but until the payout trail could be followed through all the twists and turns of the spiral, in and out of Lloyd's and back again, and through any disputes *en route*, each syndicate with a slice of the business had to make reserves to meet the sums they had underwritten. If they had taken on several different layers of the reinsurance, the higher up the spiral this took them and the greater the potential losses were against the tiny premiums received at that point.

Thus, though no one syndicate consciously double-counted its own exposure, each catastrophe that struck actually ended up being reserved for several times over while the bills came in and were sorted out. For the Names who had to stump up the ante in thousands of pounds of cash to sit on deposit at Lloyd's or put additional assets at their syndicates' disposal while the issues were resolved, the LMX spiral proved a crazy and terrifying creation.

Before the music stopped, however, the extra premiums charged by the syndicates prepared to underwrite these types of cover, and the conversantly larger profit earned at the time, had meant fat pickings for the brokers, in particular, but also for the managing agents, the underwriters they paid, and still left room for bigger distributions to their Names and – therefore – for a larger slice, in the form of profit commission, for the members' agents too. The excitement blinded everyone to the danger that was facing the Names.

Names accepted their annual cheques and their fate, relying on the expertise of their agents to look after them.

There was another twist to the tale, too. An unfriendly Inland Revenue; deeply suspicious of Lloyd's and its workings ever since the scandals of the late 1970s. Then, not only were fraudsters exposed, but almost the whole market had devised a wheeze to maximize Names' investment income on their Lloyd's deposits and reserves by moving vast sums of money offshore (without telling the Names) where the investment income would be tax-free.

The crooks had abused this abuse, siphoning off the extra money earned this way and leaving their Names none the wiser; while the rest had repatriated most of the gains to the Names' benefit (less the hefty offshore management fees they levied, of course) one way or another. When the crookery came to light the lid was lifted on the whole process and the Inland Revenue was livid – and wanted 'its' money back. Lloyd's subsequently paid it £40 million to settle the unwitting Names' tax liabilities.

As a result the Inland Revenue took a very sideways look at anything Lloyd's did thereafter, and had refused to grant the London insurance industry similar status to its powerful German corporate rivals, who were permitted income-tax relief against money set aside in additional reserves as an extra rainy day fund to meet any unexpectedly high claims suddenly coming in. The Revenue did allow tax relief on normal reserves against anticipated claims but drew the line at relief on 'what if' reserves. The result was that neither Names, who would not wish to pay income tax on money that was not actually received in income but stashed away at Lloyd's, nor managing and members' agents, whose profit commissions would suffer if less was paid out to Names each year, had any great incentive to be prudent and make extra 'what if' reserves. So, most syndicates did not. This was to prove a costly mistake, and not one that the Inland Revenue can entirely be blamed for, much as Lloyd's likes to point the finger now. Short-sightedness and a degree of greed in the Lloyd's fraternity were just as much at fault.

As for the Lloyd's brokers who cheerfully fed the LMX spiral, churning policies by reinsuring slices of them and then reinsuring chunks of the slices, and so on again and again: they had nothing to gain from ending the game of pass-the-parcel. Taking a profit commission from the brokerage charged on the premium levied by their syndicate clients each time they placed a slice of the business, turned brokers on performance bonuses into the City of London's top earners. Biggest earner of them all was Bill Brown of Walsham Brothers, described in the independent *Digest of Lloyd's News* as 'the main spinner of the spiral', who was paid £9.7 million pounds in salary and bonuses in 1989 and achieved near legendary status while trying to maintain a low public profile. By 1991 his income, including dividends, was put at £17 million for that year. In contrast, losers on the turns of the LMX spiral were Names looked after by underwriters Bryan 'Nodding Donkey' Spencer, of 985 syndicate, and 'Time Bomb' Terry Green whose Names lost a cool £26 million as the spiral unravelled. Winners – at least for the time being – included 'Money in the Bank' Frank Barber whose 990 syndicate was one of Lloyd's most exclusive and hard-to-join.

The LMX spiral had been a remarkable gravy train for the drivers, and for a while the passengers too had benefited; when the 1988, 1989 and 1990 catastrophes just kept on happening, the trip turned into a nightmare as the spiral span out of control into a dizzying ride to ruin. By 1991 LMX business had contracted sharply, if not collapsed in on itself. It shot up in cost, and fewer and fewer syndicates were prepared to write as much of it. The problem had self-corrected but the whole insane period left many Lloyd's Names high and dry. Given that most Names will be on anything from a dozen to fifty or more syndicates, many who had been trapped in open years dating back to asbestos problems subsequently found themselves also facing calls on their assets to beef up the reserves of syndicates caught in the collapsing coils of the LMX 'catastrophe' spiral. Those who, on top of all that, were also on syndicates that from the spring of 1991 began to panic about the US 'Who pays?' pollution situation, and to make calls for cash to jack up reserves against potential claims from that source, were reeling by midsummer that year from blows raining in from every side.

It was the top-up reserving for these two additional sources of loss that sent the Lloyd's market's 'global' result for 1988 spinning into its £509 million loss – and so many Names into financial hardship as they struggled to meet the accumulating calls. The LMX spiral helped to quadruple that for 1989.

The LMX spiral grew up before changes were made in 1990 to the way members' agents were paid. Before then, the managing agent charged the Name a fee of about 1 per cent of the Name's allocated premium; and a high profit commission, of 20 per cent on average or more on some syndicates. The members' agent was paid by the managing agent, who would give him around one-third of the fee and one-third of the profit commission. The higher the syndicate's distributed profit, the more the members' agent also got. Lloyd's tradition of *uberrimae fidei* was severely tested by the LMX spiral which set temptation in the way of members' agents to put their own short-term good before considering the long-term risk to the Names flocking on to the riskier new syndicates.

Clearly unsatisfactory, the system of remunerating members' agents was in fact changed in 1990 to the one described earlier in Chapter 2, 'What's in a Name?' and a host of other new rules and guidelines came in for managing and members' agents, even before the sweeping improvements called for by the Rowland Task Force in its swingeing January 1992 critique of the ways into which the market had fallen.

Only in November 1990 were members' agents given a code of practice by the Council of Lloyd's that 'encouraged' (but did not force) them to provide qualitative as well as quantitative information to Names about syndicates' performance, though some of the better agencies were already trying to do this, using computer technology. That month managing agents were also told for the first time to give written statements of their policy on expenses, to provide members' agents with quarterly figures on premiums and claims received by each syndicate, and to give uniformly comparable statistics on how much the syndicate had made or lost per £10,000 'line' of insurance written.

Out of the fees and profit commissions charged by the managing agents after the 1990 rule changes, they still paid themselves a basic salary, and a performance-related bonus. In May 1991 the Council of Lloyd's decided that the managing agents should publish their annual income, letting Names see how much they and their underwriters were earning; but even then there was no hard and fast requirement to give the breakdown between the various types of income, pension benefits, et cetera.

This was self-regulation with an equally velvet hand inside the velvet glove.

As all the past rewards and built-up reserves of Lloyd's membership were outstripped by calls on Names' assets, for the rich and famous, who had risked part of their wealth underwriting business at Lloyd's, the bills were at worst an inconvenience. For the less rich and for people who had just joined the market in the euphoria of the get-rich-quick, if-you've-got-it-flaunt-it 1980s and were hoping for their first cheques, it spelt ruin.

Other events had also moved against them. The Black Monday stock-market crash and a later, 1989 mini-crash had eroded the value of their investments (and therefore any Lloyd's deposits or reserves that held these shares) just as the calls began to come in to meet their syndicates' steadily mounting obligations.

UK share prices did recover to new highs in late 1991 but remained very volatile. Meanwhile a very serious economic recession had hit the United

States and the United Kingdom and left people whose main claim to wealth had been based on valuable homes, farmland, commercial and residential property or country estates suddenly sitting on assets that might now only fetch half their previous perceived worth. Not only would they raise less to meet any calls but, if these assets were part of their Lloyd's deposit, the Name also had either to put more cash or assets into the deposit to top that up, or had to reduce the underwriting he did the following year to match his reduced wealth. Just as once he had made his assets work twice to earn two incomes, he now faced the prospect of a double drain on them, making it harder to trade his way out of trouble on future underwriting (if he was willing to try).

By the time of David Coleridge's speech to the annual general meeting of Lloyd's members in June 1991, reporting on the final results of the 1988 year, news of a big overall loss was expected.

Names also knew that there could be even worse losses to be reported in due course for the 1989 and 1990 years. But when he announced that Lloyd's syndicates had gone from making combined profits of £509.1 million for their members in its 1987 year of account to losing an unheard of £509.7 million in 1988 – an unprecedented £1 billion swing from the black to the red – there was uproar.

That summer around 6,000 individuals faced calls for money from their syndicates to meet anticipated insurance claims from a mixture of catastrophe and pollution worries. Asbestos claims were also still coming in, not having abated as hoped, but mainly concerned those stuck on open years such as the 1982 Outhwaite syndicate, where there was now talk of claims of up to £1 billion facing the Names.

As the shocked and angry Names on the worst-hit syndicates once again demanded explanations of what had happened to them, familiar allegations once again resounded – of scandal, of incompetent insurance underwriting, of failure to keep reserves high enough, of conflicts of interest that meant members' agents had let Names down, and of some insurance syndicates being stuffed with reinsured claims by unscrupulous rivals offloading their own potential risk without disclosing the full extent of that risk.

For some individuals the nightmare was made worse by this being their first, and bitter, taste of what they had thought of as 'investing' at Lloyd's. Old hands at least understood the risks better – though none had expected them to come home to roost like this. The last time people lost serious money at Lloyd's had been in the late 1960s and the lessons of that had been lost on most Names and Lloyd's practitioners who had joined the market from the mid-1970s onwards.

People from all walks of life were hit by 1988's losses, from the high-rollers to the mini- and working Names who had been allowed to join during the 1980s period of expansion.

Working Names had been sponsored by their employers – including Lloyd's brokers – who would even put up the necessary bank deposits to qualify the person for membership. Thus people of quite modest means who were sometimes only peripherally connected with the business of Lloyd's, such as a broker's secretary, had become Names in the glory days. It had seemed an easy way to reward staff, who saw their annual cheque from their syndicate as akin to an annual bonus – until the calls began to come in.

They also coincided with Lloyd's putting up its minimum wealth qualification, from £100,000 to £250,000. Existing Names could either raise their Lloyd's deposit to write the higher premium limit this also conveyed, or become category 2 members whose deposit and Lloyd's funds now had to be 40 per cent, instead of 30 per cent, of their shown wealth. So they had to stump up more assets just to stand still even before they met the calls to beef up each of their syndicate's reserves. The combination was painful.

As Names built up their reserves at Lloyd's they had two options. There was the normal reserve that the managing agents saw they built up as a cushion for meeting future claims promptly. And there was the special reserve into which they could put an extra slice of their profits each year if they so chose (up to the limit that the Inland Revenue will accept). High taxpayers liked the facility, such as it was, as they could set aside some of one year's profits without incurring the top rate tax they would have had to pay on it if it were distributed to them as income for that year. As tax rates fell under the Tories in the 1980s, however, the tax advantages became less great than in the highly taxed 1970s and again there was less incentive to beef up one's special reserves. Which was a pity, because when calls are made against the Name's assets, the special reserve is tapped first of all.

Losses are a double-edged sword for the moderate earner since though they can be offset against tax, this has to be against tax that he or she has actually paid. It is no good having tax losses and too small a total income to claim for all of them.

The burning question for Names in the summer of 1991 was whether the Lloyd's system had tempted some of the newer, more go-getting members' agents to push more of the Names they acted for into the riskier syndicates, without weighing up fully whether this was really to the Names' longer term advantage. Had the managing agents who let their underwriters do so much of this business been incompetent in distributing so much of the premiums and consequently under-reserving for the risk, been careless or negligent? Had members' agents who paid intermediaries for introductions to Names been sloppy about who they accepted as Names? Should they have put new applicants who just scraped through the means test on to such high-risk syndicates? Had the members' agents been negligent, or worse?

The newly impoverished 1988 Names harboured the worst suspicions about how they had come to be on the worst syndicates, and they reached for their lawyers in droves. Threats of writs against managing agents and members' agents, and then the writs themselves, were soon flying. Groups of financially distressed Names formed to plan their campaigns to discover what had actually happened. They broke roughly into three camps: those investing in the syndicates that had reinsured older asbestosis and pollution cover in the early 1980s, and who now suspected the original insurers of not having made full disclosure about the size of the likely claims to come; those accusing their agents of incompetence in their choice of too many high-risk syndicates for their clients in the mid- to late-1980s; and those who felt the governing body of the Corporation of Lloyd's, the Council, had failed to regulate the market adequately under the terms of the Lloyd's Act of 1982.

Many turned to the law because they were simply unable to meet the calls for their money when the claims rolled in. Others sought the help of the Hardship Committee that had been set up to try and help sufferers to find ways of raising money, under the cool and analytic eye of external Council member and Cambridge academic (and novelist's wife), Dr Mary Archer. In exchange for its assistance, Names were expected not to go to litigation, and to keep the terms of their assistance confidential.

In June 1991, the Council of Lloyd's reduced the trigger point, at which any independent study of how a syndicate came to lose money would be conducted, to the level where losses exceeded 100 per cent of its stamp capacity (the total of its Names' premium income limits), rather than 150 per cent. By November six troubled syndicate years were in loss review.

As well as the Hardship Committee, a host of other schemes was also launched, with Lloyd's blessing, to help Names meet their cash calls. They varied from allowing Lloyd's Names to raise life-insurance linked mortgages on their second homes, to a tie-up with art auction house Sotheby's to help them hand over works of art. This was fine provided you had a second home, and an art collection, of course. If like many of the Names of '88 you had not got, or no longer had the wherewithal, it was off to the Hardship Committee for you, to try and avert the risk of bankruptcy, if you could not meet your liabilities.

Names who had lost a lot of money they could ill afford blamed the Council and Corporation of Lloyd's for not running a tight enough ship. The old Lloyd's hands somewhat arrogantly took the view that if you get seasick you shouldn't sail.

Whatever his private sympathies may have been (having lost money on syndicates himself), publicly the chairman of Lloyd's David Coleridge indicated forcefully that he had no sympathy with mewlers and pukers. When you join Lloyd's you are warned that you are sailing into the waters of unlimited liability and are expected to be able to take financial squalls without bleating, he intimated.

This was not good PR. There had not been widespread, big losses at Lloyd's since the late 1960s, and now there were allegations that the newer Names had been shunted into highly unsuitable syndicates before they had even gained their sea-legs. Many should never have been allowed to become Names. Though they had met the basic wealth criterion, this had also been almost the sum total of their assets and they simply did not have enough leeway to be able to sustain substantial losses without real hardship.

Lloyd's has never run a fund to bail out Names in trouble; but it does operate a Central Fund raised from a small annual levy on all Names out of which to meet the liabilities of Names who default for whatever reason. This protects the insured person or business and makes sure their legitimate claims are paid. The Name is not let off the hook, however, for the Fund will then seek to recoup the money from him.

In 1991 Lloyd's also created CentreWrite, also financed by a small levy, designed to offer reinsurance-to-close to syndicates with open years which it would then run off over time. This embryo fund concentrated initially on fairly small syndicates but was encouraged in January 1992 by the Rowland Task Force to switch its emphasis to reinsuring individuals' positions rather than whole syndicates in future, thereby helping more people to draw a line under their commitments. The Task Force also suggested the fund should be considerably larger.

A clutch of other run-off funds exist, meeting claims on syndicates that had hit trouble in the past, such as the PCW syndicates whose claims are paid by Lioncover, the fund created via the settlement negotiated between Lloyd's and PCW Names defrauded by Peter Cameron-Webb and Peter Dixon.

Into this picture steps the Hardship Committee, created once Lloyd's realized that the reinsurance spiral and catastrophe losses were going to leave a great many Names in real financial difficulty. But, the committee has no resources to pay Names' Lloyd's calls for them. What it does have is a brief to help them find ways of paying, up front, or in stages, or in deferred arrangements that last the Name's whole lifetime.

First, there was a working party; then the committee that it recommended be created and which worked out its system more or less as it went along. Between its 1989 inception and early 1992, some 300 people had applied to it and 90 cases were resolved. The others remained pending while details of their position were thrashed out. Of the 90, a third had their applications turned down: they were not hard up enough for the drastic measures involved. A third had accepted the Committee's tailored proposals; and a third were still (in February 1992) mulling over the committee's suggestions. Half a dozen had rejected its proposals and gone back to square one.

Money paid in stages to the Hardship Committee goes to the Central Fund to meet the claims as they come in, though an interim, holding fund also helped retired Names who needed to draw an income from the capital they handed over. Dr Archer stressed:

> We aim to get what we can for Lloyd's but not to drive a Name who fully discloses into penury or bankruptcy. The Central Fund picks up the rest of the shortfall. But the committee is not a benevolent fund, it does not have a penny-ha'penny to its name and cannot take over the loss but just defers it, either indefinitely or for a fixed time, to give Names time to pay.

Applicants are sent a long and detailed questionnaire to fill in giving information not just about their own income, assets and other obligations (such as dependent relatives) but also their spouse's. This has caused some anger. Lloyd's cannot ask the spouse to contribute to the Name's call, but the Hardship Committee studies the Name's ability to pay in the light of his or her wider circumstances and is loath to offer deferred terms to someone who can actually afford to pay up faster because their other half is comfortably off and able to keep the family. Dr Archer explained that:

> We are empowered to make arrangements with Names who would suffer severe financial hardship, with their families, if they were to meet their cash calls in full. To accept that is the case, we have to know the family circumstances. While the Name might be severely financially embarrassed but the spouse has a luxurious home and a large income, we can't accept that lands the individual in hardship. It is not a question of attacking the spouse's assets but of mitigation of losses and avoiding severe financial loss for the family.

It can also help a Name: we can take into consideration the Name's dependants, such as handicapped children or elderly parents [when it comes to assessing what they can, or cannot, afford to pay and when].

But we are less friendly where we discover 'distancing' of assets: transfers of assets from a Name to the spouse [to avoid using them to meet cash calls] which we require to be returned before we will agree to help. The bankruptcy laws are very helpful here. We can go back five years; but intent is everything. If they didn't know there would be cash calls and it was in good faith, it's OK.

Applicants have varied from having trouble facing calls of £10,000 right up to calls of £250,000-plus. Once a Name has filled out the lengthy declaration of his or her financial position, and their spouse's, it has to be verified by a non-Lloyd's accountant and signed as accepted by the members' agent as well. Dr Archer explained in 1992:

Once the financial position is clear, our staff prepare a factual report on the individual and a menu of possible arrangements which might be made. The committee's main job is to decide on what course of action to offer and why. In general we are able to help a Name who is willing but unable to meet his cash calls and therefore is prepared to make a frank disclosure. If it is accepted by the committee that the cash call is substantial compared to his net worth, including income and capital, we can offer a legally binding agreement which might make a partial recovery, put a charge on an asset, for example the home, or take some assets such as shares, where the income on them still goes to the Name.

Because the cash calls are to bolster reserves against anticipated future claims – known in the industry as 'incurred but not reported' or IBNR for short – shares and other securities can be held by the interim fund created to hold hardship cases' assets, without depriving them of the income from them. Dr Archer added that:

For retired Names we can take over some of their capital but continue to make part of the income available to the Name. What they hand over goes into a sort of suspense account, not the Central Fund, and earns interest that can make an income available to the Name. For younger ones able to earn, it is less vital. For example, we could take an attachment on their income . . . Income is a fairly good indicator of liquidity and ability to pay.

Other options may be taking a charge on the house 'which would be called in after the deaths of the Name and the spouse'. The house will then be sold to discharge the debt and rolled-up interest, and any money left over after that would revert to the Name's estate. If a hardship case wants to move house at some point, perhaps after the children have grown up and moved out, 'Lloyd's would transfer the charge and take a hand in the value of the new home.' The Name could then use the sale of the old house to unlock capital to pay off the debt. Early deals involved a mixture of immediate payment of part of the calls – say 25 per cent – by handing over any liquid assets plus the Name's Lloyd's deposit, plus a longer term arrangement for the balance. In assessing how to tailor a repayment programme for stricken Names, the committee took into account their Lloyd's premium income limit, the means shown when they passed the Lloyd's wealth test, their age, gender, whether they were a working or external Name, and their family circumstances. Many of them were fairly recent Names, people who joined in the big expansion of Lloyd's membership in the 1980s. Others were long-standing members 'who have come to grief on excess-of-loss syndicates'.

Some were retired, others were still working but generally they have modest incomes. On the whole people needing help tend to be older, with smaller premium income limits and smaller means; and those who passed the means test with a bank guarantee against the value of their home and do not have other assets to sell to meet calls, 'whereas a more wealthy Name might do that for convenience but also have more liquid assets.'

Lloyd's does not officially allow a Name's private home to be shown directly as part of his means test,

> But they do allow a bank guarantee on the house, passing the risk to the bank; but if we draw down on the guarantee, the Name could lose his home – and the Hardship Committee has discretion not to do that if the Name would be dispossessed of his modest and only home.

But what is modest?

> We don't want hard-hit Names to be thrown out on to the streets. The property-market slump has not helped. Some Names may be philosophically willing to sell a big house that is mortgage-free and go downmarket and can't – which is frustrating.

The committee gave them anything from six months' to two years' grace but interest is charged on the delayed debt, at the Judgement Debt Rate used by the courts as a measure and normally two points above the London Interbank Rate, LIBOR. In 1992 Dr Archer reported:

A lot of cash – around £800 million or more – has been called this year. On the open year problem, we are mindful of future deterioration and our arrangements offered to Names take that into account. They are also subject to periodic review. This is a long-term, perhaps a lifetime, commitment.

At that time any inheritance that came a Hardship Name's way could disappear at periodic-review time into meeting their deferred cash calls – though benefactors could avoid that by steering legacies to the next generation, the grandchildren. As more people ran into trouble, slightly less punitive rules about this were introduced, in 1993 (see chapter 15). So was simpler and more readable documentation; and brokers were persuaded to contribute charitable funds towards Hardship cases.

The year before, Dr Archer warned that:

A condition of application is that they cease underwriting: we can't help people trade out of trouble, just help them to pay their residual losses. Therefore they will not be there to participate in any recovering of the over-reserving via future profits.

The experience she garnered from chairing the Hardship Committee will be put to good use for present and future Names. She was swiftly appointed to the working party set up in the wake of the Task Force report to examine ways of improving Names' liquidity, and generally tighten up on the wealth checks that should protect their financial health better in future.

Attacked on so many counts, and though it had instructed the Task Force to study its warts and all and to 'think the unthinkable', in public Lloyd's was very much on the defensive in early 1992. It did itself few favours by sounding so unsympathetic to individuals' plight. The Hardship Committee's demand for vast amounts of information about people's means and their spouses' means also caused upset to some. The outward effect was to make Lloyd's seem both dismissive and harsh towards the very people who had provided the livings of all those who worked in and oversaw the market – and very good livings too.

David Coleridge's somewhat intemperate criticism of one campaigning Name, the former MP Tom Benyon who had formed the breakaway Society of Names composed of rebellious and litigating, loss-making Lloyd's members, led to Lloyd's having to pay Mr Benyon damages following a libel suit.

It was not Lloyd's only embarrassing brush with the courts over this multi-million, and soon to be billion, pound fiasco. Names caught up in a tangle of bad underwriting, 'overwriting' and losses, in a syndicate run by the Oakeley Vaughan agency, were furious when they realized that earlier the agency's principals had been disciplined secretly by Lloyd's without informing Names and then had been allowed to carry on operating. Had the Names known of the disciplinary action, they argued, they would never have stayed with the syndicate, which subsequently collapsed in 1983 under the weight of impending claims, losing them a small fortune. After years of wrangling, thirty-three particularly incensed Oakeley Vaughan Names issued writs against the insurance market. Past rows had led eventually to settlements organized by Lloyd's before things got to court, once it realized that Names' determination and the damage from bad publicity outweighed the benefits of refusing to finance a rescue. But this was to be the first time in its long history that Lloyd's was dragged across the threshold of the Law Courts by its own members, though it dug its heels in every inch of the way, and threw as much sand in the works as it legally could. The motto, on Lloyd's coat of arms, of *Fidentia* – implying a confident and assured future – had never sounded so hollow.

9
Where Legal Eagles Dare

| *The market is a place set apart where men may deceive each other*

(ANACHARSIS: DIOGENES LAERTIUS, *ANACHARSIS*, SEC. 5)

S hake a cupboard hard enough in the Lloyd's building and a skeleton is sure to fall out. In March 1981 the leadership of Lloyd's instigated a discreet inquiry into the operations of underwriting syndicates managed by Lloyd's broker and underwriting agency, Oakeley Vaughan, after a complaint about irregularities in the conduct of aviation insurance. This was still in the days when brokers could own underwriting agencies; but only just. The Lloyd's Bill, which would become the 1982 Lloyd's Act and ban such cross-ownership, was in mid-progress.

The complainant was Lloyd's broker Christopher Moran who had employed two former Oakeley Vaughan staffers. He produced evidence to the Lloyd's Chairman that the underwriting agency side had been 'netting' premiums.

Oakeley Vaughan had been massively 'overwriting'. Overwriting is when a syndicate writes more risks and receives more premiums than it is supposed to, based on the aggregate of its Names' premium limits (the syndicate's 'stamp'). If the quality of the insurance business taken on was good and few claims resulted, this could let the syndicate make extra profits by breaking the rules. But if the business written was poor and the claims poured in, then the Names were in dire trouble. The syndicate had taken on more liability to pay claims than they ever had assets to back them.

To disguise its overwriting from the Lloyd's authorities, in the form of the Lloyd's Policy Signing Office (LPSO) which officially signs and seals all the policies underwritten and initiated by Lloyd's syndicates, the Oakeley Vaughan underwriting agency had been declaring the premiums earned net of expenses, brokerage et cetera, instead of the gross ones. This mattered because the gross premium more accurately reflects the degree of risk borne by the Names which is why premium limits are set at the gross, not the net, level. The extra money netted off was subsequently thought to have been tucked away out of the LPSO's sight somewhere in the broking arm.

Moran was able to supply enough evidence in the form of Oakeley Vaughan slips and other paperwork to persuade the chairman of Lloyd's that there were grounds to instigate 'an informal inquiry' into his allegations. After a preliminary check with the help of an accountant from Ernst & Whinney rejoicing in the name of Mr R. (for Richard) Nice, and conversations with the underwriter for Oakeley Vaughan syndicates 862 and 423, the investigation was upgraded to a formal committee of inquiry chaired by Henry Chester. The Chester committee felt that to get to the bottom of the problem it should extend its reach from looking into Oakeley Vaughan Underwriting to its broking operation as well. This was blocked by the directors.

Oakeley Vaughan was chaired by the late Charles St George, whose chief passion was owning racehorses – winning the St Leger with his colt Michelozzo in 1989. In the search for famous Names to join 'his' syndicates he had attracted jockey Lester Piggott aboard; and boxer Henry Cooper and tennis star Virginia Wade. But he left the day-to-day running of the business to others including his son. His brother Edward, a London barrister, was chairman of the Port Authority in Freeport in the Bahamas (which despite its name is a private company) where he spent most of his time, and a director of the Oakeley Vaughan broking arm.

The St Georges insisted that throwing the broking arm open to investigation as well would prove too disruptive as they were in the midst of trying to sell this business ahead of the divestment rule soon to become law. Instead, the inquirers were welcome to lots of long chats with the directors. Anxious to avoid a public scandal in the midst of the Bill's passage, Lloyd's accepted this compromise at first, but had second thoughts after reading the Chester Report which found a mass of irregularities, a senior staff member with 'a drink problem' – who got most of the blame for wordings on insurance slips that had 'misled' the Lloyd's Policy Signing Office about what premiums were being received – and generally flaky accounting procedures. Nobody seemed particularly well-equipped to do their job, either through lack of training or some other incapacity. The result was chaos. Some transactions had been credited and other sums debited to syndicates in advance of their actual occurrence. Credit was taken by Oakeley Vaughan for maximum brokerage when sometimes there was a delay in returning 'pendulum swing' brokerage due back to the syndicate on risks subject to a certain type of indemnity.

The Chester team found that syndicate 862 was owed some £129,250 in returnable brokerage at 31 March 1978, for which internal debit notes had been first issued by the broking arm, and then cancelled. Oakeley Vaughan took another full year to return the money to the underwriting syndicate.

The Chester Report concluded, largely based on a written assurance from Charles St George to this effect, that no individual had benefited from any of this toing and froing of funds; but it did find that everyone had failed to carry out their duties one way or another. The Chester committee had also 'encountered a number of further matters' which seemed worthy of detailed inquiry, it reported, mainly related to the crediting of brokerage and accounting habits (or lack of them).

Further inquiries duly followed that summer. Again they were on 'a semi-informal basis' (whatever that may mean). Oakeley Vaughan was invited to provide 'comprehensive answers' to a 'detailed questionnaire' prepared by Lloyd's.

It was issued on 24 June; the answers received on 3 July and discussions followed. 'No individual member of the board appears to have had specific responsibility for the accounts and there is no formal record of detailed discussions by the board concerning the figures,' the inquisitors reported. The directors had instigated some reforms and stopped 'netting' premiums but, they went on:

> There appears to have been very little attention paid by the board to the on-going solvency position of the company; with regard to internal controls, it seems apparent the board paid little attention to this area, particularly identification of outstanding debts and credit control.

Profits and reserves 'were overstated which enabled the company to pass the various Lloyd's solvency tests'. Nor, from the correspondence seen, had the auditors queried the practices that allowed this to happen.

By this stage Edward St George had become chairman of the broking arm and a new finance director was in place. He blamed his nephew James (whatever happened to nepotism?) and the deputy managing director of the underwriting side, Michael Whitelock, for the chaos and over-optimistic accounting in the syndicates' books.

Once again the investigators had been denied a look at the books of the main company and had to rely on what Edward St George and his staff told them in a series of meetings. But they were clear that profits for the 1977 and 1978 years had been overstated and that Oakeley Vaughan would in truth have failed the Lloyd's solvency tests for 1977, 1978, 1979 and 1980. The deficit in 1978 would have been £150,000. The investigators found no direct evidence that the 'adjustments' made to the figures were deliberately designed to make the balance sheet look better 'but it is considered relevant that every contract where the pendulum swing was applied subsequently saw the brokerage reduced.' The investigators expressed 'surprise' that the sums involved 'escaped the notice of the directors and auditors'. They also found that profits for the year to March 1980 had been inflated by overestimating the benefits of some business. The result 'enabled the company to pass Lloyd's Solvency Test 3 which showed a surplus of only £267'. It had just scraped through.

Shareholders in the Oakeley Vaughan parent company stumped up £150,000 to support the firm, including £89,125 put in by Edward St George, who announced his retreat from the United Kingdom and plan to sell or otherwise merge the company to another Lloyd's broker.

Formal inquiries should now be made of the auditors to find out how much they were aware, or should have been, of the effects of all the financial juggling that had been going on, the investigation said.

Ernst & Whinney were supposed to carry out just such a formal inquiry, but not long after a private afternoon meeting with Edward St George and the then Lloyd's Chairman Sir Peter Green, its investigation was suddenly halted by Lloyd's with no formal explanation. Charles St George had recently called in the same accountant, Peter Benzikie of Josolyne Layton-Bennett & Co., to mount an internal inquiry for Oakeley Vaughan, as had acted for certain offshore interests of Sir Peter Green's business, Janson Green. Five years later, in 1986, Sir Peter was himself hauled before the Lloyd's Committee and Council chiefly for having arranged for funds to meet reinsurance claims to be placed with an offshore Cayman Island insurance company of which he was a director and shareholder. The move avoided UK taxes on the investment income but unfortunately Sir Peter's offshore company failed to return the full benefits to the Names, whose money it really was. The practice of moving monies offshore to avoid high UK tax rates had become common at Lloyd's but, as so often happens within clubs, what had become custom and practice or merely seemed a jolly good wheeze at the time was not necessarily good or even lawful practice, while the secrecy involved laid the system wide open to abuse. Sir Peter was roundly censured by the Council in January 1987, for discreditable conduct, negligence and various sins of omission, and fined £32,500. Angry Oakeley Vaughan Names subsequently became deeply embroiled in a bitter battle with Lloyd's to lift the veil of secrecy that hung over what had been going on in these syndicates, to which they had entrusted their money, in the late 1970s and early 1980s.

For whatever reason, the Ernst & Whinney investigation was shelved. Instead of a massive formal investigation, on 29 September 1981, up went a notice in the market announcing that three Oakeley Vaughan executives had been extensively disciplined. Underwriter Barrymore Bowen, James St George (son and nephew of the senior St Georges) and Michael Whitelock, 'have been guilty of acts of defaults discreditable to them as underwriters or otherwise in connection with the business of insurance in that they have failed to comply with established procedures in conducting insurance business at Lloyd's,' it said. The committee suspended them forthwith from carrying on insurance business as members of the society for two years and banned them from being a director or a partner 'in any broking or underwriting company or firm which subscribes to Lloyd's'. This was regarded in the market as severe action.

The financial press reported the news. But Names on the Oakeley Vaughan syndicates were never formally told of the disciplinary action, nor of the Chester Report. When as a result of the bans, four of the five syndicates were moved for the new underwriting year from January 1982 to a new underwriting agency (under the auspices of Robert Napier), they were told by Oakeley Vaughan itself that this was in order to comply with the upcoming new Act's requirement that Lloyd's brokers divest themselves of their underwriting arms. The Act in fact took effect from the following January.

In the event, the change of management did the Names little good anyway. So appalling was the quality of the previous underwriting undertaken on their behalf, that potential claims outstripped the syndicates' assets. Syndicate 862 was already in dire straits, costing Names losses of up to £50,000 apiece. Its 1982 year had to be left open, and run off (wound down) over time as the claims came in. Now the other four began to crack under the weight of their potential liabilities. Many of the 250 Names concerned, now facing calls to top up their deposits, decided to leave their deposits as they were and just reduce or cease underwriting for the coming year. This meant there was not enough capital available to the syndicates to support their continuing operation, and Napier decided the remaining four should go into 'run off' as well.

The poor business overwritten in the past had been reinsured into the 1982 year, but now the merry-go-round was grinding to a painful halt. Names were stuck on the run-off syndicates until all claims that came in over the following years were met. They faced years of being bombarded with fresh calls for money to meet the syndicates' outstanding liabilities. Not surprisingly they wanted to know how things had come to this pass. Getting the answers was if anything harder than getting blood from a stone. Eventually they had to turn to the High Court to try and get the Chester Report out of Lloyd's. In 1988 the Court ruled that the Oakeley Vaughan Names at least were entitled to see it. When they read the contents, they were horrified. Had they known in 1981 what the leadership of Lloyd's knew and had kept quiet about, many of them would never have stayed on the syndicates into 1982 and subsequently been trapped on them, they argued.

Now they found that the overwriting was of such magnitude that by April 1982, syndicates had written businesses up to their overall premium limit, but had just kept on going. The poor quality of the over-the-top business being written had exacerbated the syndicate's underwriting losses by as much as 130 per cent, Names calculated. They felt Lloyd's had failed them by not alerting them at all to the problem unearthed by the Chester Report (let alone while there was still time to resign from the syndicates) and they wanted redress. Since this was not forthcoming, it meant suing the Corporation of Lloyd's. It was not the first suit against Lloyd's but it was the first one that was not settled by the Corporation just before it came to court. Thus, for the first time in its history, Lloyd's found itself preparing to defend its conduct in a public courtroom.

Action had been started against Oakeley Vaughan Underwriting itself, but it was in liquidation and the liquidator rapidly ran out of money, while the syndicates' 'Errors and Omissions' cover, under which Names might have been able to collect, was exhausted – so there was little point in pursuing that line of action. One Name, architect David Becker, did get satisfaction pursuing a lone action against Charles St George who, he claimed in court, had privately agreed to indemnify him personally against any net underwriting losses. He had joined Lloyd's for cachet not cash, Becker said, wooed on to the Oakeley Vaughan syndicates by Mr St George. His action to have his £120,000 loss met by Charles St George was eventually settled out of court in February 1990. 'I got what I came for,' he said afterwards.

Other dissident Names decided to concentrate on getting redress from Lloyd's itself. They turned to the law firm best known at the time for expertise in insurance matters, Elborne Mitchell – a very 'Lloyd's establishment' firm, however. To their surprise, the senior partner left the firm part-way through their case and popped up representing the interests of Charles St George. Astounded, they turned instead to Michael Freeman & Co., who took up the cudgels vigorously on their behalf, seeking £8 million compensation. Forty-four Names clubbed together to fund the mounting, potentially £1 million cost of their legal action somehow.

In contrast, Lloyd's report and accounts for 1990 show it spent £8.45 million in that one year on 'legal and professional fees and related costs'; before millions in additional legal fees and expenses incurred overseas on a variety of general business and other matters. The Oakeley Vaughan 44 were tiny Davids beside this Goliath, but potentially as lethal, for by now this Goliath was fighting on several other fronts for his survival.

The change of lawyer (and extension of pleadings) meant the dissidents were dangerously close to running out of time under rules which prevent old sores being brought to court more than six years after the original dispute. Since time was precious, action concentrated on the main writ, headed by the name of Lady Ashmore, that had been issued first. There were sixteen supplemental writs, issued by others among the 44 fighting fund members, which sat on the sidelines for the time being.

The meat of the Names' allegations was that Lloyd's had failed to protect members' interests properly and was negligent. Under the 1982 Lloyd's Act, the Corporation of Lloyd's had gained immunity from prosecution by Names. But the Oakeley Vaughan case turned on events that pre-dated the 1982 Act, when Lloyd's had no such immunity. This made the lawsuit quite different from the disputes Names had with Lloyd's and its practitioners, as other syndicates ran into trouble in the 1980s. Their problems post-dated the 1982 Act, so they could not sue Lloyd's itself and had to be content with suing the underwriters, members' and managing agents by whom they felt let down, or worse, and possibly their auditors as well. But the Oakeley Vaughan Names could go for the main jugular, and did.

The case finally began before Mr Justice Gatehouse in April 1991. By then, the plaintiffs wanted to extend their pleadings to bring in the 1983 underwriting year to the case. This was allowed. Lloyd's promptly threw a spanner in the works. That June, it applied successfully for a trial of a preliminary issue: its lawyers argued that since it did not believe it had owed the Names a duty of care at the time of the Oakeley Vaughan affair, it wanted that issue resolved first.

Naturally if the court said Lloyd's did not have a duty of care to Names, then there was no case of negligence for it to answer. Thus it wanted a hearing to determine this fact before the Chester Report was unpacked in court. The judge agreed that this issue should be considered first.

In the midst of all this, Lloyd's chairman David Coleridge told Names at the June annual general meeting, in an answer to a question from a member about whether Lloyd's had a duty of care: 'The answer to the first is of course yes. The Council does have a duty of care to see that the society is properly regulated. It does not have a duty to underwrite on behalf of the members.'

The Names promptly counteracted Lloyd's legal move by appealing to a higher court, saying the question of duty of care should remain part and parcel of the main trial, not be taken off into the sidings for separate consideration. Lloyd's itself came out with a statement to the effect that the question answered by Coleridge had not been about a *legal duty* of care. Into this Alice-in-Wonderland world of semantics, the legal profession's summer break brought a pause for breath. Then, on 20 September after the summer recess the Appeal Court agreed with the Names. Lloyd's lawyer David Johnson QC promptly wrote to the Appeal Court asking it to reconsider; and was told on 20 November that this invitation was 'inappropriate and unprecedented'.

On 5 December Lloyd's application to the same Court for leave to appeal to the House of Lords was refused; but, undaunted, Lloyd's petitioned the House for permission anyway and on 30 January was granted it by three Law Lords. The hearing on the question of whether or not it owed the Oakeley Vaughan Names a legal duty of care was heard by five Law Lords in late February. On 27 February Lloyd's won its appeal to have the duty-of-care issue resolved in a preliminary hearing before the Names' grievances were addressed. Nearly half a year had gone by in which the Names had got not one step further in their main case, with costs ratcheting up all the time. One or two cynically wondered if Lloyd's was trying to drain them dry, beaching their case for ever.

Names involved in the Oakeley Vaughan litigation hailed from all over the world: Australia, the USA, Canada, Switzerland, France, and Ireland as well as Britain, some of them British nationals living abroad, others not. By early 1992 they had paid fortunes into the Oakeley Vaughan open year syndicates to fund their liabilities. Of the five syndicates, 551 was the worst hit. On every line of insurance worth £20,000 in premium income written by a Name, the loss had ratcheted up to £101,000. Syndicate 423 Names writing lines of £5,000 each had lost £17,000 per line. On 420, each £10,000 line of premium income had turned into an £18,000 loss. Ironically 862, the first to go into run-off, and 168 were less painful engines of loss by this stage.

Tim Powell, a sports promoter and power-boat fiend, had stumped up the best part of £1 million, selling his large Chelsea home and moving to a smaller and far less central house in the London borough of Wandsworth (swapping his 071 central London telephone code for an 081 outer London one but at least gaining the benefit of the lowest poll-tax charge in Britain at the time). Sports promotion all but gave way to the campaign for justice from Lloyd's.

Another litigant had paid over £200,000 in calls by February 1992 but, looking at lost interest on the money and legal fees, counted the total cost at nearer £300,000 and rising.

Shane Alexander, son of Britain's famous Field Marshall, had by early 1992 faced calls of more than £100,000 from Oakeley Vaughan syndicates, which soaked up all his Lloyd's deposit and reserves and left him having to raise cash to meet the balance. Being a career soldier's son, and a second generation earl, he did not have rolling acres to sell. He said, his plight suddenly reminiscent of one from the pages of Charles Dickens's great novel of nineteenth-century law and injustice, *Bleak House*:

> I only live in a modest house; I am not rolling in money. I have now borrowed money to pay for cash calls and fund the legal costs and, at the present high interest rates, there is a risk of going bankrupt before this ever comes to court. This is the horrifying and frightening aspect of the English legal system.

Meanwhile Charles St George went on to higher – or perhaps lower – things. He died in May 1992. Absorbed as they were in the case and their cause, Oakeley Vaughan Names were not alone in their obsession. Their cause, and that of other groups of dissident Names, received a dramatic shot in the arm when, on 11 February 1992, a leading Lloyd's underwriting agency and eighty members' agents caved in and agreed a £116 million settlement to another lawsuit brought in 1991 by angry Names: the Outhwaite case.

The change of heart came as the Lloyd's defendants realized they could lose the lawsuit. To avoid case law establishing liability on the part of Lloyd's underwriters and agents, Lloyd's chairman David Coleridge urged the defendants to negotiate a settlement. His intervention held out hope to other litigants that they, too, might wrest an out-of-court deal from their erstwhile agents. Suddenly Names flocked to join the dissident associations and fight alongside them.

10
Things Fall Apart

| *He heapeth up riches, and knoweth not who shall gather them*

(PSALMS, XXXIX.6.)

The most significant of 1991 campaigns for justice was the Outhwaite litigation. Syndicate 317/661 was a marine syndicate, one of the largest at Lloyd's, and managed by the RHM Outhwaite underwriting agency whose leading light was Dick Outhwaite. He had a good reputation and had steadily made money for his Names – until 1982 when things fell spectacularly apart. For that year the syndicate lost a fortune on asbestosis claims from the USA and could not be reinsured to close. As the claims kept coming in, the losses mounted, and calls upon Names to prop up the reserves went out year after year. By the end of 1991, the cumulative loss was £260 million and showed every sign of rising year-by-year for the rest of the decade.

This attrition finally generated a £160 million lawsuit for damages, brought by 987 of the 1,614 Names stuck on the open 1982 year. When it opened in October 1991, the Names' QC Sir Anthony Boswood told the judge, Mr Justice Saville, that 'never in the commercial history of the City of London has so much of other people's money been lost by the single-handed negligence of one man.'

Yet Dick Outhwaite's record up to 1981 had attracted over 1,600 Names including such luminaries as the golfer Tony Jacklin, actress Susan Hampshire, tennis player Buster Mottram, Lord Alexander (unlucky again), former Prime Minister Edward Heath, hotelier Rocco Forte, publisher Lord Weidenfeld, publishing magnate Robert Maxwell (before his own bizarre demise on 5 November 1991) and a host of well-to-do businessmen such as Anthony Tennant, property developer John Ritblat, Sir Patrick Sheehy of BAT, and Rupert Hambro of the City banking family. Members of Lloyd's flocked to be on an Outhwaite syndicate. What had gone wrong?

In the early 1980s concern began to mount amongst Lloyd's underwriters about the potential claims from asbestosis sufferers in the USA against past years' general liability cover. The premium from these had been pocketed, partially put into reserves and largely paid out to Names, long since. The cover had been reinsured, year after year, into each syndicate's new underwriting period.

Worried that the reinsurance premiums the syndicates had paid into their new manifestation each year had been too low to build a sufficient buffer against the outbreak of US asbestos claims now feared, some underwriters cast around for external reinsurance against these long-tail risks just in case. Not that external, however, for they found it within Lloyd's. Dick Outhwaite was one of the underwriters who was prepared to make a market in this particular business. He had already turned his attention, in 1974 when he left the Merrett Group to set up his own agency, to providing some cover for run-off syndicates: ones that had ceased underwriting for one reason or another – such as the retirement of an underwriter and gradual dwindling of new Names wanting to join subsequently – but which still had old years to reinsure and administer.

Though his expertise was primarily in marine insurance, Lloyd's share of that market was dwindling as the insurance companies grew larger, and as fewer and fewer of the world's ships were built in the United Kingdom or sailed under the British flag. As marine insurers continued to cast about for extra sources of premium income, Dick Outhwaite believed adding a service of writing run-off policies for syndicates seeking reinsurance for their US long-tail liability risks was a good answer for his syndicate. Premiums that could be charged were far higher than shipping cover yielded just then. Described by one broker as a man who 'cannot ever refuse a challenge – he always believed there was a rate for any risk,' Dick Outhwaite thought he could balance premiums and liabilities in this field and again come out on top for his Names and himself.

Observers later commented that, going through a costly divorce at the time, any additional cash flow through to his salary would have been welcome for personal reasons. He said later:

> It was not a question of making a lot of money in a hurry. I have always been interested in making as much as possible for Names, and every policy I wrote was because we thought we'd make a lot of money on it – though we knew it was a risk – but there was no question of a get-rich-quick plan. Our run-off policies never exceeded 10 per cent of premium income in any one year.

By an odd coincidence, fallen stars of the market Outhwaite – who remained in the fold, still making money for all his Names bar the unlucky class of '82 – and 'Goldfinger' Ian Posgate, who was censured for his links with an earlier Lloyd's scandal, the Howden affair, and told he was no longer welcome in the market (and subsequently played a role in the unseating of former chairman Sir Peter Green), were both regarded as infinitely cleverer men by their first mentors than were the sons who went on to inherit the mantle at their fathers' respective firms. Sir Peter Green's father Toby had fostered Posgate's early career; while Stephen Merrett's father Roy had given more support to Outhwaite's early underwriting career at the Merrett agency than to his son's. Ironically, Merrett's agency was to pick up most of the bill for the Outhwaite settlement: it had written the sued agencies' Errors and Omissions Policies from which the money came.

Lloyd's was a market riven by undercurrents of jealousy, club gossip and sometimes the settling of scores. The gossips and many Names suspected that Dick Outhwaite was in some degree legged over by brokers with little love for him who placed reinsurance business from other syndicates with him; that the Lloyd's rule of *uberrimae fidei* was ignored and that Outhwaite was not always told everything the broker and his client knew about the increasing risk and size of asbestosis claims that might come in. He is certain that, in most cases, full information was provided but nursed nagging doubts, though no evidence, about certain others. His own judgement in writing these risks also came under heavy fire in court. In 1992, he said:

> It is impossible to say now absolutely what people thought. In 1981 or so, asbestosis appeared. The first inklings were around 1978. By 1980–1 it was clear that there would be liabilities arising from it but it was not known how big they would be. Therefore old syndicates, which suddenly had to establish asbestos reserves – which have to come out of today's premium and was difficult and embarrassing at the time – and

had to say to their underwriting members that they had some liability, looked for some sort of commercial reinsurance to take the sting out of it, to give comfort that if things got worse they were protected. Asbestosis itself was not necessarily the spearhead as it was not seen as a terrible risk until around 1985 when the scale began to be appreciated. The effect in 1980–1 was to make people realize other things could become a problem too.

Thus the market for excess-of-loss reinsurance for decades of old year risk developed.

> Once one person gets the idea and a broker places it, the broker is quite likely to go to another underwriter and say, 'Do you want this too?' And the broker will take it to the guy who underwrote the first one.
> I wrote a number of these, and as many as I thought appropriate and then I stopped writing them, as did others who stopped writing at the end of 1982. It stopped either because the underwriters interested in taking out a reinsurance policy had done it, or because those prepared to underwrite it had done as much as they wanted.

While the reinsurance spiral developed to gargantuan proportions in the catastrophe excess-of-loss market, it stopped in the field of asbestosis after only a couple of turns. For Names on Outhwaite's syndicate in 1982, some thirty-two high-risk reinsurance contracts he signed during a few brief months that year were to prove almost as deadly as the disease they covered. They included cover for the huge Johns Manville asbestos plant in America, but its biggest single exposure turned out to be to the Shell Rocky Mountain pollution clean-up case. Twenty-six of the policies took on claims without limit beyond the excess level agreed with the original insurer. At the time they were not regarded as very different from the run-off policies written since 1974, nor were they all seen as particularly relating to asbestos. But the results were disastrous.

By the time the 1982 underwriting year was due to close, after the end of 1984, it was already clear that syndicate 317/661 had serious problems stemming from these reinsured general liability policies dating back as far as the 1940s. A long-tail Lloyd's policy never dies; the liabilities that can be assigned to it live on via the reinsurance-to-close process. Asbestosis awards to individual sufferers against companies under these old policies and the number of class actions (where many many people join forces to sue) they attracted to the US courts were massive, and the firms' London reinsurers were getting most of the bills.

As 1985 dawned, the explosion of high awards and the difficulty of knowing where and when they would end meant Outhwaite could not close his 1982 year for syndicate 317/661. For the Names stuck on it, this meant no new premium income was being earned, since it had not been reinsured into 1983, while calls for them to stump up cash to meet the influx of bills multiplied. With so many cases as precedents, more and more claims that looked genuine were simply paid by insurers and their London reinsurers, rather than incurring additional hefty legal costs disputing the case. 'It costs the insurance industry less and the sufferer gets the money faster without paying legal fees out of it either,' said one underwriter.

The number of asbestos settlements were quite small in 1981, another reason why few alarm bells rang at RHM Outhwaite then. But as they rose in the early- to mid-1980s, insurers found that two-thirds of the payments against claims they made were being absorbed in the claimants' legal fees with only a third on average going to the asbestosis sufferer. And by the time they realized the extent of the potential liabilities if claims continued to grow as fast, syndicates like Outhwaite's were unable to get any reinsurance of their own to spread the risk a little wider. 'No one was prepared to do it,' Dick Outhwaite found. Having realized claims could escalate, he needed to increase syndicate 317/661's reserves but the premium income coming in to the new, 1985 year was not enough to cover the increase in reserves needed. The 1982 year stayed open; and calls went out in 1985 to the Names who had been underwriting that year to provide the ante 'and they have gone on ever since.'

In May 1990, for example, they were asked to find another £76 million by 23 July, after which they would be charged interest on any overdue amounts at 2 per cent over base rate. By the end of 1988 the open year had lost 412 per cent of its Names' premium income limit of which by May 1990, including the £76 million call of that date, 228 per cent had been called in. In 1989, the open year lost another £26 million against incoming claims. That year, there was an attempt to construct a rescue plan for the trapped and increasingly strapped 1982 Names, negotiated by former Lord Chancellor Lord Havers who had been appointed non-executive chairman of RHM Outhwaite in September 1988. His plan was to cap the losses of the 1,614 stricken Outhwaite Names then facing a cash call of 150 per cent of their premium limit: a demand for money totalling £142 million or £38,000 for every £20,000 line of insurance they had written under Outhwaite's star, and which they knew could rise to anything between £340 million and £1 billion *in toto*.

The Havers plan involved a borrowing facility from the Midland Bank. It would underwrite a financial reinsurance policy, via a Bermudan subsidiary, for which Names would pay a multi-million premium – borrowed if necessary from the bank – towards immediate claims. The invested premium money would grow during the duration of the run-off of the 1982 year, generating more with which to meet claims, and Lloyd's of London would provide additional help towards future ones with a £300 million contribution to the pool from the Central Fund. Except that it refused to. Though Names on the ill-starred PCW syndicates had been bailed out eventually in a special deal with a large contribution from the Central Fund after years of wrangling, it was because there had been fraud, not because of poor underwriting, the Council said; and therefore did not set a precedent for the Havers plan – which, thus torpedo'd, foundered.

A great deal of work also went into curbing the potential losses by negotiating deals with a host of the reinsured syndicates. Disputes had broken out over two issues: whether the reinsurance contracts were valid – if not all the material facts had been made available at the time of underwriting, they were not – and whether claims fell within the scope of the contracts anyway.

This was unseemly squabbling and did Lloyd's reputation little good so, despite its affirmation that no one on the working party had pulled a fast one, the Council appointed Mark Littman QC to act as conciliator. As a result by May 1990, sixteen contracts with Outhwaite were either renegotiated, settled or, in one case, commuted. Even so the stranded Outhwaite Names' losses had mounted to £260 million and further hefty cash calls towards losses clocked up during 1989 were scheduled for July 1991 and July 1993. Even with the benefit of Time and Distance policies – which allow syndicates to pay a very expensive premium up front that is invested to fund meeting large claims arising in future – the syndicate's cash flow projections anticipated the run-off process for the 1982 open year continuing until '2010+'.

The year 1990 brought little respite. Though foreign exchange gains reduced the annual loss, Names were still required to stump up enough money to cover both it and half the previous year's £26 million loss. They were more convinced than ever that the total cost to them of Dick Outhwaite's foray into asbestos reinsurance could eventually top £1 billion. Even shared between 1,600 people, 500 of them working Names at Lloyd's, this was a terrifying prospect: a potential average loss of £625,000 per head though some individuals would be in for far more. The 10 per cent of premium income they had received a year till 1982, even if they had saved all of it up, would not cover that.

Left high and dry, most of the external Names decided to sue. They felt Outhwaite had been negligent in taking on the risk and that their members' agents should never have steered them on to a syndicate that was writing such business. Asbestosis had been known to be a problem for several years; why had Lloyd's underwriters been so slow on the uptake? Why did a marine syndicate stray so far from its normal business without doing more research into new risks? Some 987 Names including 100 US Names banded together to take the legal action, far more than the small team of dissidents in the Oakeley Vaughan débâcle. They spread the net wide. Writs were issued in 1991 against RHM Outhwaite (Underwriting Agents Ltd), alleging reckless and negligent underwriting, and 81 members' agents who had put them on this syndicate, also for alleged negligence. If the Names won, the defendants would look to their Errors and Omissions insurers for the wherewithal to meet any awards.

The case came to court on 7 October 1991. Names faced losses of 500 per cent of each line they had written. Their legal bill by that stage had racked up to £2 million and could reach £2.5 million if they lost. Anthony Boswood QC, acting for the Names, accused Dick Outhwaite of 'wilful negligence' in failing to realize the extent of the possible claims. Outhwaite, a witness for the defence of his firm, denied the charges. 'People underestimated what the liabilities were, but not deliberately. They made a genuine assessment and it proved hopelessly inadequate. It is happening again with environmental pollution,' he said afterwards.

Having got to court, with a mountain of documents, the civil case ground on for months, through the autumn of 1991 and into February 1992. At this point, whatever the outcome of that state of the fight, all parties assumed it would then go to appeal. Then, suddenly on 3 February, the judge adjourned the hearings. A £100 million settlement was rumoured to be imminent: broked by Lloyd's chairman David Coleridge himself – anxious to avoid an embarrassing defeat for the home team.

RHM Outhwaite's defence had rested largely on Dick Outhwaite having trusted the syndicates he was reinsuring to tell him all they knew about the risk, as they were supposed to, rather than researching it hugely himself. He admitted not knowing a great deal about the North American liability market at first hand, but insisted that what he had done accorded with the market's perception of the situation at the time, and that everything his syndicates did was in accordance with Lloyd's custom and practice. When challenged as to whether his approach to underwriting amounted to little more than gambling, he argued that insuring any new and therefore unknown quantity (such as the first oil rig or satellite, or the first big hurricane in the United Kingdom) always involved an element of guesswork.

Outhwaite's methods and his system of reserving money for future claims were attacked by expert witness for the Names, Ulrich von Eichen who had recently retired from the massive German insurance group the Munich Re, and had a much more cautious and methodical approach to insurance underwriting and sounded appalled by the more entrepreneurial, Lloyd's style. His strong performance in court went a long way to convincing many experts that the Names would win; while Dick Hazell, the expert witness for Outhwaite's side, actually said that Dick Outhwaite had been 'imprudent in some respects' – and that poor record-keeping was endemic at Lloyd's at the time. 'If Mr Outhwaite was living in a cocoon, we all were,' Hazell said. This only strengthened the Names' suit.

Outhwaite also revealed that he had not seen the results of the Lloyd's Asbestos Working Party researches when he took on these risks. This apparent omission caused Lloyd's quite a headache. The working party had been set up in 1980 by Lloyd's and corporate insurers to co-ordinate the handling of information about the growing threat from asbestos-related liabilities to old policies. Dark suspicions were later harboured that working party members had quietly ensured that their syndicates reinsured their own liabilities, having realized the extent of the potential claims.

Finally, in 1989, members' agent John Donner, with a lot of Names on the stricken syndicate, complained to Lloyd's that the working party report had been misused in this way. This was what led Lloyd's to set up the four-man team to investigate the allegation, and which concluded that it was groundless – a view endorsed by the Council in April 1990 and described at length earlier in Chapter 4 'Fools' Gold'. Two working party members had arranged run-off policies for their syndicates, but, said Lloyd's, there was no evidence of their underwriters taking advantage of the information not available to the rest of the market.

'On the contrary the market was fully informed at the time of the existence of information which was available about these claims and was encouraged to make use of it,' it said. Lloyd's had also issued guidelines to syndicates in early 1982 about reserving for asbestos risks. Donner was concerned, too, about the role of Lloyd's brokers running around drumming up reinsurance business for these risks and placing them with a limited number of perhaps not sufficiently informed underwriters. The Council of Lloyd's verdict:

It was natural and proper for brokers to advise their clients on what was available and no evidence has been produced or found that suggests that there was any misconduct on the part of any broker in the placing of such policies.

Nor did it find any evidence of non-disclosure or misconduct by members of the Lloyd's community. It also reminded its critics that the Corporation did not act as a nanny that would just pick up the pieces if something went wrong and redistribute them around the rest of the market, if this was unfair on Names in other syndicates.

Lloyd's Olympian calm about the asbestos allegations was seriously shaken in the summer of 1991 when suddenly it emerged, in an answer to a Parliamentary question in the House of Commons, that the Serious Fraud Office (SFO), which investigates suspected frauds exceeding £2 million apiece, was now running its eye over the background to the Outhwaite losses. This caused much ruffling of feathers within the citadel at Lloyd's. An SFO investigation into losses on asbestosis reinsurance at Outhwaite would imply its own checks into John Donner's complaint had failed, and could even imply a cover-up.

In the end, after the SFO's initial inquiries, Attorney General Sir Patrick Mayhew told the House of Commons, in answer to a question by MP John Bowis, that the SFO had concluded that no fraud investigation was warranted. Lloyd's then chief executive Alan Lord was delighted. It confirmed, he said, 'Lloyd's impeccable record of investigating alleged wrong-doing within the community.' The headlines in the meantime had been colourful, however, and the Names' civil case was about to fan them again with long accounts of the Names' £260 million losses to date as the hearings began that October.

Not everyone sued over the Outhwaite affair. About 600 ignored every chance of joining the litigants – most of them working Names who felt it was 'bad form' to sue fellow Lloyd's practitioners, and who had believed the Lloyd's establishment's constant repetitions that the suit would take years, cost a fortune, and end with the plaintiffs losing. Some Names traded out of their losses, staying with Dick Outhwaite's other, still profitable, syndicates. One told the *Sunday Times* in October 1991 that, by staying in, he had earned enough money since 1982 to offset his calls of £80,000 thus far on the 1982 open year. His experience added fuel to Lloyd's frequently repeated argument at the time, that this was the best course for the struggling Names it was refusing to bail out. Those who had obediently remained aloof from the legal fray, regretted it when the settlement came, however.

■

'Errors and Omissions [E&O] insurers only respond when a writ is served; either with an offer or a fight,' said one member of the Outhwaite 1988 Names' Association. The £116 million that the E&O providers finally agreed to pay out in settlement of the Outhwaite contest was for the 987 litigants. The other 627 Names on the syndicate's ill-starred 1982 year, most of them working – who had not participated in the legal battle got nothing. Moreover, it was too late to start their own action if they were time-barred under the UK limit on how long after the disputed event a legal case can be brought to court. The Outhwaite litigants had been granted two standstill agreements to save them from becoming time-barred, as it was, and there was little scope for any new action to be brought. This was bitter payment for loyalty to Lloyd's and a stiff upper lip. These were the people who had taken to heart Coleridge's and others' remarks about taking losses on the chin, and not mewling and puking when the weather got rough. So much for that advice. After von Eichen's stalwart performance in court and Dick Hazell's weak one, it is said that the defendants' Counsel warned his clients that they could lose the case; the Judge's tone and own cross-examination of witnesses did not bode well. There may have been some disagreement on this between the solicitors and Counsel, but the fear of a swingeing judgment against the Lloyd's practitioners and for the Names sent the Lloyd's establishment into action.

Lloyd's Chairman David Coleridge called the battling Names' Association's chairman Peter Nutting – himself a pillar of the British establishment, being an old Etonian, a magistrate, former Irish guardsman and even a Lloyd's Council member – and the defendants' Errors and Omissions insurer Stephen Merrett to his office. Merrett was reportedly told that, for the sake of Lloyd's – to avoid creating a precedent in case law that could trigger a flood of claims and lawsuits, not to mention a lengthy process of appeal and continuing poor publicity about past practices at Lloyd's – the club wished him to negotiate a compromise settlement with Nutting and his litigious Names.

The court case was duly adjourned, on 3 February. Despite having been told by his peers to settle, 'Merrett is a tough negotiator' says one Outhwaite Name and Nutting did not get the full £160 million he went into the talks seeking for his Names. He did get them a good deal, however. The £116 million settlement announced on 11 February was 'in respect of past losses, interest, compensation for the risk of future deterioration' and a contribution for the legal and other professional costs incurred by the Names.

The breakdown was 'approximately £61 million . . . compensation for cash calls made or paid to date, £19 million represents interest, £34 million represents compensation for the risk of future deterioration and £2 million is a contribution towards the association's costs,' Nutting told his Names in a letter that went out to all the plaintiffs. There was no admission of liability on the part of the members' agents and managing agents involved in the lawsuit. This was a 'no fault' deal. The figures included an element of discount reflecting the fact that the settlement called a halt to what would have been a long legal process during which costs (and calls) would have continued to ratchet up.

Nutting and his team advised the Names to accept. 'Money on the table, and a bird in the hand is worth two in the bush,' one Name on the association's committee said of the weekend decision to recommend the terms. A special general meeting of the association was called for 4 March to ratify the deal: and Peter Nutting flew off on a well-earned holiday to Barbados, hours after announcing the February breakthrough. The winning Names would share in the settlement pro rata, according to what their losses were up to that point. Once the settlement was ratified, they were promised that anyone who had written a £30,000 line in the 1982 year, for example, would receive a £135,000 cheque by Easter 1992. Names duly approved the deal.

Syndicates paying out under past E&O cover written for the Outhwaite defendants for 1982 had, by 1992, largely made provision for a payout in the event of the case going against them or being settled, so Names on those syndicates were unlikely to face sudden calls for money to recompense the Outhwaite Names. The E&O syndicates themselves were also likely to have some reinsurance under which to claim, but there was no question here of another reinsurance spiral. The buck really did seem to stop.

Errors and Omissions cover is similar to the professional indemnity cover that accountants, doctors, lawyers and architects must have to protect their clients from mistakes made by that practitioner. But as signs of trouble grew it became harder and harder, and more costly, to get at the end of the 1980s. (Insurance is about the unexpected, and, though Lloyd's denies it, this trend suggested E&O writers expected lots of negligence claims against members' and managing agents.)

Things reached such a pitch that many members' agents could no longer afford the hefty premiums demanded when they could find someone to write them the cover, and it was to prevent wholesale breaches of the requirement for E&O protection, that in April 1991 Lloyd's had waived the rule for members' agents – but not for the managing agents whose underwriters conducted the syndicates' business. This was an ironic state of affairs, as odd as British Rail chairman Bob Reid's suggestion in the winter of 1991–2 that since the service was so erratic on the 'misery' line into the City's Fenchurch Street station – a stone's threw away from Lloyd's – it might be better to dispense with a timetable altogether. A society of insurance providers that could not, or would not, organize cover for its own team? This sounds like an admission of failure in the home patch. 'Lloyd's will have to reconsider that. It is neither professional nor tenable that a professional body should operate without E&O cover,' said one unimpressed Name.

The Outhwaite settlement covered only losses on past claims and those known to be in the pipeline – 'incurred but not reported' in the jargon. The 1982 year remained open, and the prospect of further claims coming in, causing fresh losses and further calls, remained. To reduce Names' exposure to the uncertain future, Peter Nutting and the association's office started to negotiate terms for stop-loss cover, that each Name could purchase with part of his or her share of the settlement. This would not eliminate each Name's unlimited liability but it would provide a deep layer of protection against future calls. Other pitfalls lay in wait for the money, however.

The Outhwaite settlement had ramifications for thousands of other Lloyd's Names. For a start, news of such an apparently satisfactory deal, and the fact that only parties to the litigation benefited, had Names leaping off the sidelines in scores to join the various groups and associations already in existence and pursuing or contemplating legal action of their own. The secretary of one group found her membership count rising by the day. Others reported a similar influx. News of the deal gave tremendous hope to already battling Names from other syndicates that they too would get recompense one day, as Lloyd's sought not only to avoid case law against its practices getting on to the record, but also to put an end to public wrangling and discontent that would put off new entrants to Lloyd's membership.

But even in their triumph, Outhwaite's Names had words of caution for other litigants. Said one of the Outhwaite Association's inner circle:

> Each case is unique. If you are well-organized with a strong chairman like Peter Nutting, well-financed and have a very good Counsel like Anthony Boswood, and good lawyers and a good chance of winning, it is certainly worth having a crack at it. But you must present your case on the facts. And the expert witness, von Eichen, was superb. The combination adds up to a very good case. But with a weak chairman, a weak lawyer, a weak Counsel and a weak expert witness you could still lose.

Shortly before the Outhwaite settlement, a much smaller deal had been struck for people belonging to the Warrilow 1984 Names Association. This was a less gratifying achievement, organized by law firm Elborne Mitchell – the firm fired by Oakeley Vaughan and which was acting for a number of members' agents in disputes between Names and their agents. Names on Warrilow Syndicate 553's 1984 year disputed the underwriter's decision to close and reinsure the 1983 year into 1984 account; alleging negligence. Losses subsequently hit £80 million. Writs had been issued in May 1991; but in the event the settlement agreed yielded only £4 million, including £1.5 million in legal costs, for the plaintiffs.

By early 1992, all 74 Lloyd's members' agents had been caught up to some degree in litigation or the threat of litigation by Names they had placed on syndicates whose combined losses were then approaching £1.5 billion. Legal costs on that lot were estimated at some £25 million. Some were suffering from the impact of asbestosis claims and reserving for looming pollution claims; most of them were syndicates caught up in the LMX spiral and sent reeling.

By the end of 1991 a dozen different associations and action groups had been formed by Names following the example of the Oakeley Vaughan and Outhwaite Names and forming up to fight their corner. Some 5,000 Names – out of 17,000 trapped on open years (though not all of them had ceased underwriting in subsequent years) – joined the various bodies to see what they could do about their respective positions and take legal advice.

Working hard to find a solution for those trapped on syndicates impaled on the reinsurance spiral was lawyer Michael Freeman. He did not concentrate just on the members' agents of Names belonging already to a dissident association or group but on all those on the syndicates painfully entangled in the LMX spiral: 7,200 people. This was to avoid non-litigating Names being left out in the cold like the 627 Outhwaite Names who had not joined in that association's legal action. As the 987 more fortunate Outhwaite Names celebrated their reprieve from penury, he was planning to seek an injunction preventing all Lloyd's members' agents with Names on these troubled syndicates from passing papers to Lloyd's that would allow it to draw-down on the Names' funds held at Lloyd's for the money to meet their unpaid cash calls.

Syndicates' premiums are held in trust funds, out of which claims are met and profits paid. Lloyd's American Trust Fund (LATF) is the home, for legal and administrative reasons, of all US dollar premiums received by syndicates. This was, overall, in surplus even though some syndicates facing high claims were in deficit on their US business.

Chief LMX sufferers were Gooda Walker 164, 290, 298 and 299; Feltrim 540 and 847, Devonshire 216 and 833, and Rose Thomson Young 255. To allow some LMX syndicates in difficulties generally to avoid making hefty cash calls on their membership for new funds, the trustees – astonishingly – had apparently allowed some managing agents, notably Gooda Walker, to borrow money from the cash-rich Lloyd's American Trust Fund to pay accumulating claims from all over the place. The syndicates expected to make enough money on subsequent underwriting to repay the borrowing. But they did not, and the calls had to go out anyway – to repay an estimated $100 million worth of this debt.

No way, said the Names' legal advisers. We think the borrowing was illegal: and why should Names have to repay an illegal debt acquired by the managing agent? Freeman also advised Names that since members' agents had merely passed on calls, not checked them in any way, the agents had failed to act in Names' interests as they were pledged to do and therefore the calls need not be paid, as yet – particularly while syndicates were in loss review, implying that there was indeed cause for investigation into what lay behind such large demands for fresh funds.

When they refused to pay up, Lloyd's instructed Names' members' agents to meet the syndicates' calls out of their Names' reserves. (The Central Fund will pay claims on behalf of Names in default, but always pursues each name for the money.) Michael Freeman promptly wrote to all the members' agents involved, reminding them that they were supposed to be acting for their clients, the Names who instructed them, not for Lloyd's. The agents were on the horns of a dilemma. Lloyd's can exert tremendous pressure to toe its line. To prevent them passing the necessary information to Lloyd's that would allow a draw-down of the Names' monies, Freeman decided to go for court injunctions. To save cost, he aimed for five injunctions per agent: a warning shot across their bows. 'The trustees – Citibank – and Lloyd's are a party to the deed,' he said, of the American Trust Fund. 'No one can understand why they did it: the fund is to meet all dollar claims on the syndicate on a Name-by-Name basis.' His argument was that borrowing from the American Trust Fund, to allow syndicates to meet other claims instead of mounting a cash call at the time, was equivalent to him as a lawyer using one client's money to repay another: strictly against the law.

On 24 February the first of between 400 and 600 writs went out, seeking injunctions stopping all draw-downs of Names' funds at Lloyd's. On 3

March, Lloyd's was granted permission to have the hearings moved from the Court of Chancery, which deals with trusts to the Queen's Bench division on the grounds that the dispute had more to do with the law of contract than trust law. Most of the Names involved were on LMX syndicates. Meanwhile some members' agents agreed to halt draw-downs provided Names would meet their costs and any damages if the hearings failed.

The LMX syndicates were also the chief subjects of the new loss review process set in train by Lloyd's in 1991. This was designed to investigate the causes of unusually high calls or losses cumulatively exceeding 100 per cent of a syndicate's 'stamp' for any open underwriting year. There were half a dozen loss review cases in progress by early 1992. Though the first, set up in July 1991, had been asked to report within three months, the investigations took far longer than Lloyd's had anticipated, amid mounting rumours that widespread mismanagement and malpractice had been unearthed. The loss review committees were not empowered to apportion blame or censure – Lloyd's was anxious not to provide fuel for litigants – but to 'ascertain the commercial facts and report on them to the Council of Lloyd's'. The resultant report would also go to the Names involved and their members' agents. There was nothing to stop the investigators from being highly critical, however; and by February 1992 the belief was growing that the results of the first review – into syndicates 540/542 and 847 managed by Feltrim Underwriting Agencies Ltd – would not appear until April and when they did, would produce 'a very damning report indeed.' Such conjecture was fuelled by the loss review committee's October progress statement confirming that 'the assimilation and analysis of material it has gathered, together with the non-availability of witnesses and necessity to interview some of them on more than one occasion, had resulted in a longer process than had been expected.'

In November 1990 three syndicates managed by the Feltrim agency had shut up shop. They were marine syndicates 540 and 542 and non-marine syndicate 847. All had been heavily involved in the LMX spiral and between them faced catastrophe losses that by October 1991 were estimated on a 'worst case' basis to be as high as £320 million on the 1988 and 1989 years' underwriting. Some 4,000 Names were affected and, it was rumoured, up to half of those could face bankruptcy.

Many felt Feltrim's underwriter Patrick Fagan had taken on far too much risk. An *ad hoc* action committee called a meeting at the Westminster Central Hall in London on 8 May 1991 which 1,400 of the Names, from all over the world, attended. They came from America, Canada, South Africa, Greece and Singapore as well as Britain. Colin Hook, the chairman of the

Feltrim Names action committee called for an independent inquiry into the Feltrim losses and for a new approach within Lloyd's to handling disputes between Names and underwriters. He was to get satisfaction, of a sort, within a month. On 2 May the Council of Lloyd's had already approved in principle the plan to set up a loss review system and on 8 June, having in the interim seen syndicate results for the gruesome 1988 year, it decided to lower the trigger from losses of 150 per cent of 'stamp' capacity (premium income limit) to 100 per cent. The by-law applied equally to syndicates in run-off if the cumulative losses went through that point. Cash calls that also breached 100 per cent of stamp (singly or cumulatively) would trigger a review, too. Feltrim's troubled syndicates were the first candidates.

Sir Patrick Neill QC, the top lawyer who had conducted the Neill Report into Lloyd's protection of Names in the mid-1980s, was appointed to lead this first review procedure. Syndicate 540 Names faced losses on the 1987 year's underwriting of between 200 and 250 per cent of stamp, of which 75 per cent had been called for from Names by May 1991. Syndicate 542 Names, caught up in the Piper Alpha LMX spiral in 1988, were looking at losses of 125 per cent for that year and up to 300 per cent of stamp for 1989, thanks to the additional impacts of Hurricane Hugo and *Exxon Valdez*. Syndicate 847's 1987 year of underwriting promised to yield losses of between 100 and 125 per cent of stamp capacity. It was breaking even on 1988's business and then plunged back into loss for 1989 where the tally could be another 283 per cent of its stamp. By May 1991, only 29 per cent of its 1987 year's losses had been called and the rest was yet to come. Names wanted the underwriter's actions looked at, as well as the brokers' and the members' agents' conduct, and the role of the syndicate's auditors.

Despite the £500 joining fee to cover the cost of its activities, the Feltrim Names Association had nearly 1,000 members in January 1992. Plans for legal action went on hold until the Names saw the Neill Report, heard any recommendations, and took legal advice on the content. Some 500 pages of submissions had gone to the review team. While its deliberations continued into 1992, Names received letters from their members' agents advising them of a fresh call for their money. Failure to pay would mean the agents would start drawing down the Names' funds at Lloyd's. Colin Hook wrote to Lloyd's chairman David Coleridge asking him to let the Names off paying at least until after the Neill review team reported. Coleridge refused on the grounds that it was not Lloyd's that authorized such draw-downs. It merely responds to invitations from the members' agents to do so in regard to Names. But Hook drew courage from the fact that the agents' threat, to draw-down deposits and other securities held for Names, stemmed from warnings to them from the Lloyd's Underwriting Agents Association that if they failed to persuade Names to meet calls, then their own finances might come under scrutiny. Saying this contradicted Lloyd's stance, he wrote to Names suggesting they point out the anomaly to their members' agents and see what happened next. Feltrim was also under Michael Freeman's eagle eye as he prepared his injunctions to stop members' agents releasing Names' funds to meet calls from LMX syndicates.

Feltrim Names Association chairman Colin Hook felt vastly encouraged by the Outhwaite settlement. He also received a sudden influx of new members joining the 1,000 already aboard, out of 2,087 Feltrim Names facing losses on their open years (not 4,000, as widely reported; syndicates 540/542 and 847 had around 2,000 Names each but many were the same people writing lines on both syndicates). In the week of the Outhwaite deal, he said:

> We are seeing, perhaps, the start of a trend. There are two precedents, the settlement of Warrilow, and the better settlement of Outhwaite. It would not surprise me, though there is not much love lost between the plaintiffs and Lloyd's, if there is a settlement on Oakeley Vaughan where the sums are small in relation to everything else.
>
> More far-sighted Lloyd's people are saying that if Lloyd's have to survive, we have to prevent all these old years going into litigation that could last five years. I have been hearing for three months that there are people beginning to say, 'We must organize a settlement', because the consequence of litigation is to scare off the basic business of Lloyd's and to scare off new capital.
>
> There is a mutuality of interest between the working Names who want to save it because they believe in it, and those who are looking for a settlement, because a surviving Lloyd's will pay them out.

Though the Feltrim Association was waiting for the Neill loss review committee to report before pressing ahead with any litigation, the game plan was to study its findings and their legal implications, present a report on that to the association's May annual general meeting, and seek the membership's authority to issue a writ against appropriate parties such as the underwriters, managing and members' agents, and even their auditors. Lloyd's itself might yet be in the frame. Armed with this authority, the association would then go to Lloyd's and invite it to broker an agreement and arrange a settlement. 'If they won't, we'll nuke 'em,' was how one player put it. Legal battle would commence.

Feltrim had no back year asbestosis or pollution problems. What it did have was a chronic hangover from the PCW affair. Syndicate 540's previous manager had been involved in that and, as part of the settlement, 540's liabilities up to 1983 were also transferred to the PCW run-off agency in 1986. However, so were £24 million of its reserves leaving it with just £4 million in the kitty as a back-up to its underwriting since 1984. Names who were not underwriting before 1 January 1984 were not told of the transfer. The result was that the syndicate was seriously under-reserved for its capacity and the business it subsequently wrote. It was overwriting on a massive scale. Hook said later:

> For an excess-of-loss syndicate, you would be restricted to writing £5 million of business to £5 million of assets: a ratio of one-to-one. But Feltrim was writing £20 million of business on £4 million of reserves: a five-to-one ratio. This was an LMX syndicate, a high-risk business, now made thoroughly dangerous.

On top of this, in 1983 syndicates 847 and 540 had agreed a joint reinsurance programme, which led to chaos when Hurricane Alicia 'blasted through the top of 847's cover'. The liability for claims under the programme was eventually transferred to yet another run-off agency which proceeded to get into a wrangle with the first one about who would pay which claims. In the light of these complications, the run-off agency set up to handle PCW-related claims recommended that syndicates 540 and 847 should be closed down completely; but Lloyd's rejected this advice because of the difficulty of splitting out their 1983 liabilities. The two syndicates continued to underwrite new business and, Names later alleged, the 540 underwriter was told at the end of 1986 not to alert Names to the £24 million asset transfer. Said one:

> 540 was a pimple on the PCW problem at the time and overlooked, at best. The auditors have a duty to report to the Names. Yet Arthur Andersen [540's auditors] never told the Names the statistical record of the syndicate. The report and accounts were not adequate. I feel Lloyd's is 15 to 20 years behind the rest of the City in its accounting standards, which conflicts with everything else we have had to do in the City.
>
> And what were the members' agents up to? They were well-dressed and from good schools but they had an IQ of 10, no degree, and no professional qualification. Many of them are also undercapitalized – they just don't have the capability.

There were suspicions, too that Feltrim underwriter Patrick Fagan had taken on a lot of very poor quality reinsurance risk, dumped on him by pushy brokers as it went round the LMX spiral. 'Why was Fagan's nickname "Dustbin"?' wondered one Name aloud later on. 'Lloyd's makes a great deal of fuss but never quite goes far enough; self-regulation doesn't seem to work . . . People are protecting their own – yet it's the non-working Names who put up the capital.'

Within three weeks of the Feltrim loss review committee being appointed in 1991, two more families of syndicates followed suit. Kieran Poynter, a partner in accountancy group Price Waterhouse, was appointed to head a committee to look into massive losses in four syndicates run by managing agency Gooda Walker; and Tim Boatman, a partner at Coopers & Lybrand Deloitte, was put in charge of a team checking the cause of losses at three syndicates from the Rose Thomson Young stable: 255, 345 and 1101.

Around 4,500 Names were thought to be affected by the four Gooda syndicates caught up in the LMX spiral for the 1988, 1989 and 1990 years. Their losses were estimated in October 1991 to be running at £250 million. One of the difficulties facing would-be action groups was that members' agents, in possible danger of being sued by angry Names, were loath to give out lists of everyone who was on each syndicate. Thus Names had to be contacted by fellow-sufferers by word-of-mouth or alerted through the pages of newspapers or the independent newsletter, the *Digest of Lloyd's News*.

By early 1992, the Gooda Walker action group had nearly 900 members, who each paid a £300 joining fee. It was chaired by engineer Alfred Doll-Steinberg. Gooda's syndicate 298 had a particularly complicated situation. Its underwriter Stan Andrews had left after writing an excess-of-loss policy for syndicate 255 run by Rose Thomson Young (RTY). Itself in difficulties thanks to the LMX spiral, RTY 255 had cross-infected syndicate 298 in the pass-the-parcel LMX game. With RTY and Gooda both in loss review as of 29 July 1991, like Feltrim Names, the Gooda action group held back from any decisions about seeking damages and compensation while awaiting the conclusions of the Gooda loss review team led by Kieran Poynter.

The LMX spiral left Names in a delicate situation, and not just financially. If a reinsurance policy were disputed between one stricken syndicate that had written it, and the equally destitute syndicate that had placed it, Names on one syndicate were effectively in dispute with Names on the other. Given how widely spread most Names' underwriting activity was, a Name could find him- or herself on both these syndicates. Thus an RTY Name on 255 who was also on Gooda 298 would be in conflict with himself. If

298 honoured the reinsurance policy, 255's loss was reduced but 298's rose. If 298 did not have to honour it for some reason, the reverse was true. Either way, the Name unlucky enough to be on both syndicates would lose – unless there were a series of E&O settlements like Outhwaite's.

Feltrim Names and Rose Thomson Young Names had one advantage over others on loss-making syndicates. Because it was primarily the Piper Alpha spiral that had knocked them sideways, and any remaining claims should be quantifiable by spring 1993, they would then be in a position to know what their final exposure was likely to be. Names on the Pulbrook syndicate 90, open since 1982, were not so lucky, dogged with calls against asbestos and feared pollution claims. They formed another association and started looking into possible negligence in connection with a run-off policy placed with syndicate 661. In early 1992, members of 90's 300-strong Names association were considering lodging individual claims against Pulbrook and various members' agents.

Rather like Lewis Carroll's oysters, the loss review announcements came in thick and fast. September 1991 saw syndicate 421, managed by Stephen Merrett's underwriting agency, join Feltrim, Gooda and Rose Thomson Young on the list. About 50 worried Merrett Names (out of a membership of around 340) also formed a steering committee to look into the losses. This time a partner at KPMG Peat Marwick McLintock, Roger Whewell, was the accountant heading the formal loss review.

November saw two pure, personal stop-loss syndicates, laid low by everyone else's losses being passed on to them, go into loss review under the aegis of Michael Lickiss, senior partner of accountants Grant Thornton. They were syndicates 134 and 184 run by PSL Services, previously called Mackinnon, Hayter & Co. Their Names, too, were busy taking legal advice about what action lay open to them. They were angry because the 1982 year had been reinsured to close when syndicates, against whose losses they would have to pay out, had themselves had to be left open. 'We say 134 and 184 should not have been closed because there was no way to calculate the reinsurance,' explained Michael Freeman, the LMX crusader.

Also under the new microscope were syndicates 216 and 833 (subjects too of the Bohling 216 Action Group formed by around 200 of the 1,200-plus Names affected by their losses). The two syndicates had been run by the Devonshire Underwriting Agencies, looked after by underwriter Christopher Bohling. After he retired in June 1991 the syndicates were acquired by the Castle Underwriting Agency. They were suffering the classic post-catastrophe symptoms of the time, high claims on low premium income, on a mixture of storm and hurricane damage (Hugo), shipping and cargo losses, and reinsurance losses. On 27 February a loss-review committee was appointed under Anthony Blake of Lloyd's-approved audit group Neville Russell to investigate losses of over £90 million on Devonshire syndicates.

While the loss review subjects waited to see what the reports would dredge up, legal action was also planned or pending in several other instances. About 300 Names from Poland syndicates 105 and 108 – led (like the Warrilow group) by Tom Benyon – fired out writs in autumn 1991 alleging negligence, misrepresentation and breach of contracts against their managing agent and 44 members' agents in connection with losses of £110 million on two open years: 1985 and 1986, victims of the continuing epidemic of asbestosis claims and reserves for feared US pollution clean-up bills. They claimed to have been misled when they joined or stayed on board in the course of those years, having been told the agency had eliminated its US long-tail exposure. Names picking up the tab included the veteran holiday camps boss Sir Fred Pontin, Tesco supermarkets' retired supremo Sir Leslie Porter, and the Confederation of British Industry's economist David Wrigglesworth.

A second Merrett syndicate, 418, also had problems; and a ginger group going – headed by Canadian Ken Lavery – representing distressed North American Names. Marine syndicate 418 had, like Outhwaite's, written run-off policies in 1982 but had reinsured that year to close into 1985. However, by 1987 potential claims from the reinsured policies, mainly on pollution risks, were building up to such a size that the 1985 year could not be closed. Names who had joined, since 1982, in a marketing drive embarked on by the syndicate in 1983–5 and which had netted 2,089 new members, an 83 per cent increase, were incensed to be landed with losses on contracts pre-dating their signing up. They felt they had been recruited at least partly to spread the burden of the pollution claims that Merrett's had realized would be a considerable strain on the 1982 syndicate's membership of 1,959 Names. By late 1990, the cumulative losses were running at £65 million and around 49 per cent of the syndicate's premium limit whereas, Lavery reckoned, had 1982 been left open, the loss would have been 111 per cent of its stamp or £40,830 per Name. British Names trapped on the 1985 open year included David Coleridge himself, his wife and son; as well as Foreign Office Minister Tristan Garel-Jones, glass-maker Sir Anthony Pilkington, former hotelier Sir Reo Stakis, property magnate John Ritblat, and Roger Seelig the former merchant banker caught up in the Guinness share support scandal (who won some respite from his troubles when his trial on the charges relating to that affair was halted in early 1992). Lavery also discovered that Canadian Names signed up by Merrett's might not legally be members of the syndicate at all: 418 was not registered under the Ontario Securities Commission regulations. 'They argue they were not selling securities; but that is in retrospect. They probably didn't think about it,' said Lavery. If not really members, the Canadians on 418 would not be liable for its losses. 'The establishment of Lloyd's are a dumb lot,' was Lavery's own verdict.

There were various attempts by Canadian and American Names on a range of syndicates, including loss review subjects Feltrim and Gooda Walker, to sue Lloyd's and/or Lloyd's practitioners in the North American courts, and to resist cash calls. In Denver, Names were told that, under the terms of the agreements they had signed as Lloyd's members, the local courts did not have jurisdiction and that Britain was the proper place to take legal action for redress. However, Names in Chicago, New York and Canada had better luck. A Toronto judge ruled that Names could seek injunctions there against four local banks to prevent them paying out on letters of credit held by Lloyd's, though not against three others. A similar ruling was made in Chicago. The most serious of these attempts, in Lloyd's demonology, was the series of complaints filed in New York by law firm Proskauer, Rose & Goetz alleging violations of the USA's Racketeer Influenced and Corrupt Organizations legislation (RICO), normally used to target drug barons and the mafiosi and under which punitive damages, set at a multiple of the basic award, are payable. The Federal Bureau of Investigation was also now taking an interest.

The New York writs were fired out with a scattergun approach: against almost 400 defendants including 216 Lloyd's syndicates (the first time syndicates had been sued directly), 16 members' agents, 42 managing agents, and 59 individuals, including Task Force head David Rowland of broker Sedgwick, Stephen Merrett, and a recent Lloyd's chairman Murray Lawrence. The suit depended heavily on whether or not Lloyd's had been acting illegally in allowing Lloyd's agents (representatives) in America to recruit US Names to 'invest' at Lloyd's without being registered with the Securities and Exchange Commission (SEC). Lloyd's had had an agreement since 1988 with the SEC that it was exempt from SEC approval under the Commission's regulation D; and went into a huddle with SEC officials in Washington in early 1992 to discuss the agreement again. If recruiting in the US had been done illegally, all US Names might be able to walk away from their syndicates' calls, and reclaim past ones – at massive cost to Lloyd's.

Several months after the issue was originally raised, the SEC had still made no public statement and when asked, intimated that it would only have something to say if there were changes in the deed of arrangement with Lloyd's. Once again, Lloyd's was fighting a rearguard action.

Into the midst of all this insurgence and counter-insurgence came the Rowland Task Force report. Published in mid-January 1992 it came up with firm proposals to reform the Lloyd's market and tighten up procedures at home, floated a few radical ideas, and kicked the debate into the future. But the past refused to go away. The report offered no solutions to the open year problems facing the Names trapped on them, nor any way out of the calls falling due in 1992. It did propose a cap (but a permeable one) on future calls upon Names, however, in the form of a 'high-level' compulsory stop-loss scheme funded by the entire market; and the stress it laid on the need to return Names' interests to the forefront of market thinking, if Lloyd's were ever to attract the new members and the financial capacity it needed to survive into the next century, probably helped to make Lloyd's hierarchy realize the value of, if not a new climate of reconciliation, at least clearing the decks of the worst snarl-ups and set the scene for the ice-breaking Outhwaite settlement.

11
America the Brave

| *When sorrows come, they come not single spies*
But in battalions

(SHAKESPEARE, *HAMLET*, ACT IV, SCENE 5, L.78)

While trouble brewed at home for Lloyd's, North American Names, sick of the bitter results that membership of the British club had brought them, decided to go into action. In Canada and the USA, legal battles were soon underway. In the USA a Senate investigation was also launched, as was a separate inquiry by Congress. The country that had already yielded some of Lloyd's worst claims and losses, on asbestosis and pollution counts, had decided to give the old crock a thorough going-over. Central issues were the legality of Lloyd's canvassing for Names in the first place; and whether, having invited them aboard, it had policed the marketplace sufficiently to protect them and the newer syndicates they joined, or turned a blind eye to the practice of older syndicates offloading their dodgier risks on to a bunch of greenhorns.

In Canada, where Lloyd's had around 500 members, a group of Names in Ontario – mostly recruited in Lloyd's 1986–8 search for new blood – banded together in an action group that quickly earned the sobriquet of 'the Medics' in the British press: composed of two doctors and fifteen dentists, several accountants and lawyers, sixteen businessmen, two investment counsellors, nine retired people and eleven couples where husband and wife were both Names. The Medics embarked on legal action.

Most of them belonged to a grouping called LIMIT: Lloyd's International Members in Trouble which, though small, drew members from as far afield as Norway and Australia as well as the United States and Canada, and provided a support group and a conduit for information for Names bewildered by the demands for money that kept arriving. As one Ontario Name said:

> One of the problems at Lloyd's is its philosophy of divide and conquer: you can't find out who else is a Name. It makes people feel very fearful and alone. People here on Gooda Walker syndicates have just had another C$100,000 cash call – just a letter in the mail.

In mid-February 1992 the Medics numbered seventy-three, with more members joining each day, spurred on by news of the Outhwaite settlement in Britain. Seventy of them had already embarked on legal action in Canada, each one individually fighting along the same lines. All the Medics were on one or other, or several, of the Feltrim and Gooda Walker syndicates, introduced on to them by the Lime Street underwriting agency, so the legal fight targeted those syndicates first.

Unlike the US Names who went on the attack primarily seeking compensation for their losses, stress and strain, the Canadian Names concentrated on proving that their contracts with Lloyd's were void, on the grounds that membership was misrepresented to them, and on fending off the calls for their money in the meantime. This involved stopping Lloyd's from cashing the letters of credit that had formed part of their original Lloyd's deposit. Said one of their co-ordinators:

> Ours is a defensive posture. We allege that the whole thing was fraud, and misrepresented to us.
>
> Joining Lloyd's was presented to us – people who did not know a great deal about insurance – as a passive investment. Let the agent in the UK look after it, and Lloyd's will supervise, was what we were told – and we had faith in the name of Lloyd's, not the Lime Street agency but Lloyd's.
>
> My membership card says 'Lloyd's' on it, not Lime Street, and it was in Lloyd's that we put our trust. We knew the 300-year-old history; it was like the monarchy. That was our mistake. Lloyd's failed us and it should not be allowed to regulate itself any more.

Our letters of credit were collateralized against our homes, so now we could lose them. Many of us are older people who have retired or are close to it and do not have time to recoup. We have already had one nervous breakdown in our group.

There was a lot of misrepresentation by individual syndicates. For example, 540 did not indicate in its accounts that it was writing LMX business, which is a market category. It said XOL, not LMX and there is a difference. That is misrepresentation, and we charge that Lloyd's was responsible, because its responsibility was to regulate.

The insiders knew which syndicates to stay off. Two per cent of insiders are on Gooda Walker and these syndicates, full of external Names, were reinsuring syndicates of insiders so that they stayed safe. It's not right, and we feel we've really been wronged.

The Medics' first move in the legal fight was to try to stop seven Canadian banks, holding the letters of credit collectively worth C$25 million that had formed part of their Lloyd's deposits, from paying out against them to meet calls that the Names could not or would not pay; and also to stop Lloyd's from trying to draw-down these letters of credit. The pivotal legal precedent they turned to was an earlier Canadian Supreme Court ruling (the Angelica Whiteware case) that it was possible to get an injunction against a Canadian bank to prevent it from paying out on a letter of credit in the event of fraud or fraudulent misrepresentation. As the Medics' group secretary said:

We were looking for an injunction against seven Canadian banks not to pay out on letters of credit, and an injunction against Lloyd's to prevent it calling the money, all on the grounds of fraud and fraudulent misrepresentation. Lloyd's and the banks challenged us on the issue of jurisdiction because of the contract Names had signed on joining, saying all disputes would be handled in the UK. We say if we had known Lloyd's operated like *this* we would not have signed the contract and therefore we want it voided *ab initio*. That is our suit but first the issue of jurisdiction had to be settled.

So we went to court on 26 September 1991 on jurisdiction. The judge, in the Ontario Court General Division, ruled that we could go ahead and apply in Ontario for an injunction against four of the seven – the four main chartered banks of Canada: Toronto Dominion, Royal Bank of Canada, Canadian Imperial Bank of Commerce, and Scotia Bank. This was a big loss for Lloyd's.

It was encouraging news for the forty-four Medics of the seventy whose letters of credit were held by these four banks.

The judge allowed the Names to seek the injunctions in Ontario because these would have equal force in London where these four banks all had branches where the Canadian letters of credit could have been cashed. The other three banks, however, had no direct outlets of their own in London but arrangements with other banks, in some cases their parent banks. In theory the Medics' letters of credit could be cashed at the London outlet of the correspondent bank which would then have to pursue the Canadian issuers of the letters of credit to reimburse them as innocent third parties to the dispute. So the Ontario judge ruled that injunctions to prevent these letters of credit being cashed would have to be sought in Britain.

The three banks concerned were Citibank, Hong Kong Bank of Canada, and CT Credit Corporation. Citibank in Canada dealt in London with the Citibank parent, as did CT Credit Corporation, while the Hong Kong Bank of Canada used the Hong Kong and Shanghai Banking Corporation. So, the Medics' representative said:

> The action against these three banks and Lloyd's would have to proceed in the UK. But in Canada, plaintiffs have an automatic right of appeal, which we exercised, while the four banks which lost the jurisdiction case have to seek leave to appeal from a judge, which they have done. We expected they would get leave but in February the judge adjourned the case while the Names developed a proposal with their lawyers for international arbitration. This would bypass the question of jurisdiction, and let us get on to the meat of the case. The banks would stand back and not pay out on the letters of credit and let Lloyd's and us fight it out. The arbitration could be in the UK, the Hague, or Bermuda and we'd use our own lawyers. If Lloyd's answer is 'no' to this plan we would still appeal on the ruling about the other three banks.
>
> You cannot get a letter of credit issued in favour of Lloyd's in Canada now until this is settled. The banks want it settled too.

In March 1992, Lloyd's rejected the plan, however, and the battle moved back into the two areas of jurisdiction, Canada and Britain.

Canadian Names faced losses far in excess of their letters of credit. As one Medic said:

> I would say they are middle-class people, not extremely wealthy, for the most part. Lots of us are in Hamilton but from as far away as northern Ontario, one in the West, some east of Toronto. The vast majority

joined Lloyd's in 1986–8 and some in the 1970s and no one who is included in our legal action has made a net profit out of all those years of underwriting.

In 1992, a typical Medic whose first year of underwriting was 1988 – that ill-starred year – with a premium limit of £250,000, faced calls for C$400,000 so far on a letter of credit for £70,000. As one Medic reports:

I have already been asked for cash of almost double my underwriting limit and we still aren't hearing the truth of what the total losses might be. They let bad news about 1990 calls go past the year end so that people could pass the solvency test and keep underwriting. We were probably still underwriting while insolvent but they didn't tell us until 1991.

Publicity about the Canadian Names' fight spread to the United States where the Senate, the country's senior ruling body, had decided to investigate Lloyd's and its conduct in the USA. The Senate permanent subcommittee on investigations set to work under the direction of Senator Sam Nunn. An investigator was sent north from Washington DC with a team of people to spend two exhaustive days with the Medics going over their experiences and legal actions. There was also an investigation under way under the aegis of a Congress house committee under Congressman Dingle. 'Lloyd's is not a huge part of the US market but it has a niche role in offering insurance that is not offered by US companies and investigators are concerned as to whether it is solvent,' said one Name, 'and the US government and courts take very seriously the protection of Americans.'

Its niche role had already got Lloyd's into hot water in the United States. A large anti-trust suit was grinding on against Lloyd's in California, relating to a change in the way that it wrote insurance to avoid long-tail liabilities which had led to some organizations, such as playgroups, finding it hard to get cover. They had accused Lloyd's of abusing a monopoly position within its special niche.

The parallel Senate and Congress inquiries were quite separate from the Securities and Exchange Commission's own deliberations into whether Lloyd's was indeed exempt from registering with it as a purveyor of invest-ments. The issue was whether or not the funds raised and kept there – the syndicates' US capital base – counted as securities. If they did, this could also make the syndicates issuers of securities, in which case 'they will not be eligible to escape the SEC.' The problem for Lloyd's was that the syndicates had never sought exemption from the Securities Act: only the members' agents looking after Names had done so.

When New York law firm Proskauer, Rose & Goetz took up the cudgels on behalf of 100 US Names – facing losses of 'well over $30 million and still rising' – it therefore added the names of 216 Lloyd's syndicates to its list of targets alongside the 42 managing agents, 16 members' agents and 59 individuals in its sights. Like the Canadian suits, the New York litigation was not a class action (whereby groups of interested parties can join an on-going action) but a series of separate claims in which, though based on the same general approach to the issues, individual plaintiffs selected different targets: listing their own syndicates, managing and members' agents. More and more US Names began to inquire about mounting their own legal actions, again encouraged by news of the Outhwaite settlement in Britain. Meanwhile, lawyers in Texas were considering launching a class action on behalf of Names there; but their New York counterparts thought the plaintiff-by-plaintiff approach more appropriate to the circumstances.

Lawyer Dale Schreiber added the syndicates to the New York legal action because he regarded them as having a legal personality of their own; Lloyd's first move in reaction to the New York suits was to argue this was not the case. Ignoring for the time being the question of whether the New York courts had jurisdiction to hear actions concerning Lloyd's of London, the insurance club sought to have the syndicates dismissed from the suit. The plaintiffs argued that the syndicates had acted as issuers of securities in the USA by raising and retaining money there, and therefore did have a juridical personality that could be brought to book alongside the managing and members' agents. (Lloyd's tack also raised the interesting question of whether, having not challenged the jurisdiction of the New York court at once, it could subsequently play that card.)

Counsel for the syndicates served a Valentine's Day motion that they should be struck out of the action and both sides settled back to wait for Judge Morris Lasker's decision, which could be delivered with or without him explaining his reasoning.

Close observers of the US scene did not expect the SEC to come up with any dramatic new rulings on the thorny question of whether Lloyd's and its practitioners and syndicates were exempt from registering with it, until after the various investigations, and any court findings resulting from Names' legal action against Lloyd's practitioners. 'It will await court decisions to define the issues and then respond,' said one observer.

'This is the first time in the Securities Act filings on behalf of Names that syndicates have been named, and it presents a lot of practical problems for Lloyd's,' US lawyer Dale Schreiber commented. 'It is the syndicate's name that appears on the policies so, if it is sued, doesn't Lloyd's have to tell the insured?' he wondered in 1992.

Underlying all the outcry was the suspicion that Lloyd's syndicates had gone on their American recruitment drive specifically to boost their membership and capital base enough to reduce the impact per existing Name of the losses they knew were building up. If this were true, the US Names had indeed been sucked into membership on false pretences. There was also the whole question of the way Lloyd's had administered the market-place, and whether indeed it had favoured insiders' interests to the detriment of external Names. It was not Lloyd's system of a club of separate syndicates that was under attack in the US court cases: but the way it operated that system. As Dale Schreiber said:

> The notion of allowing returns to be based on the performance of a finite number of insurance risks is not a bad idea – but it was used at Lloyd's without adequate disclosure for the purposes of investment decisions. The use of separate performance centres is fine. General Motors has separate classes of stock depending on different centres of performance.

Lloyd's detractors claimed that its syndicates

> haven't even tried to comply with the law; they made no pretence of our standards [of securities trading in the US]. If they do have to start filing with the SEC that will involve disclosure of balance sheets and operating statements. Will they be willing? Or can't they do it because it would mean disclosing information they don't want to publish? If so they won't be able to roll over their capital and will have to return it to the Names.

That would involve 'about $1 billion and would be a devastating blow to Lloyd's: and if there are losses, Lloyd's becomes the insurer of them,' argued one lawyer.

Another area that the litigants were curious about was the nature of the syndicates' interests in the trust funds that contained the US Names' Lloyd's deposits. Later, the New York court decided that the syndicates could not be sued; and that in any case jurisdiction lay in the UK. But in early 1992 Lloyd's was facing a threatening prospect.

If Lloyd's had not after all been properly exempt from SEC registration some Names' membership might be void, and therefore free from all claims and calls, lawyers thought. But the New York litigants were chasing a different avenue: compensation under the rules designed to make sure anyone taking an investment decision had the proper information they needed to take that decision. Inadequate disclosure was the second line of their legal argument under the Securities Act alongside the question of failure to register with the SEC.

Remedy and damages for inadequate disclosure would be set by the authorities. An altogether more alarming prospect for Lloyd's, however, was the third line of attack presented for Judge Lasker's consideration: Names also alleged that America's anti-racketeering laws had been breached by a persistent and knowing violation of the securities laws by the way Lloyd's representatives courted new Names in the USA – and any damages awarded under that Act would be punitive damages, in which the basic award made by the courts would then be multiplied by three.

The Racketeer Influenced and Corrupt Organizations Act was created to use against gangsters, the mob and fraudsters; not at all the sort of company the chaps at Lloyd's considered that they kept. Now they would have to explain how their club's recent behaviour differed from criminal cultures' conduct: a most embarrassing predicament and a very galling prospect. 'All this will take some time to hear,' said one observer at the start of 1992. 'I expect that ultimately Lloyd's will have to settle. This is just the foreplay at the beginning of the case.'

It was foreplay that was viewed with increasing anxiety by some of Lloyd's brighter practitioners. By February 1992 the insurance club was under fire in the UK and US courts. The Canadian suits were awaiting Lloyd's response to the international arbitration proposal. This was also a route open to the market to proffer to head off the New York litigation if it so chose, though Lloyd's own lawyers felt confident of spiking the US action by getting a ruling on jurisdiction that would oblige plaintiffs to switch their attack to the British courts in line with decisions already made by courts in Denver and Illinois. In Britain, MPs from the left and the right were hurling insults and accusations at the market. Worried Lloyd's insiders were reported to have privately made overtures to the Bank of England, inquiring whether plans could be laid to help the club cope with a 'cash crunch' if Names' refusals to meet calls and success at blocking draw-downs of their assets left the Central Fund running out of money to meet claims. An incensed Lloyd's hierarchy denied categorically that it had held any such talks with the Bank of England, accusing journalists of overheated imaginations. But its own practitioners appeared not to be waiting for the Council to act. A palace revolution looked ripe to burst forth. Lloyd's syndicates' troubles in the US broke against a background of considerable gloom in the American insurance industry, buffeted by the same tough conditions as were the rest of the world's insurers.

The familiar ill winds of falling premium income coinciding with higher value and more numerous claims, thanks largely to the sudden upsurge in catastrophes since 1988, knocked more than Lloyd's sideways.

In the period from 1984 to 1990, 225 US property and casualty insurers went bust. In the previous fifteen years from the end of 1968, to the close of 1983, there had been just 147 US insurance company insolvencies. Of the 225 failures since 1984, some 106 US insurers had gone down since 1988; and the toll continued to rise during 1991 with worried US insurance analysts predicting that the 1990s would be a decade of massive collapses in the oversupplied, under-reserved and undercharging US market. This record threatened to make Lloyd's problems look trivial. America's problem was that, though marine and aviation insurance rates were rising quite sharply in the UK in early 1992, general insurance rates on bread-and-butter industrial liability were not. Even at Lloyd's, non-marine insurance rates were not picking up much. As a spokesman for US insurance broker Alexander & Alexander said:

There are no signs of rates hardening at all in the US and we don't expect them to in 1992. It is totally different from Lloyd's which includes marine, aviation and energy cover. Rates are not picking up on every-day, medium and smaller company business.

Despite the steady stream of insolvencies in the US insurance company sector in 1992, the US market still suffered from overcapacity. Premiums had been falling for years and the downcycle had been a long one. US insurance groups, seeking higher investment income to compensate, had moved quite heavily into the property market and junk bonds in the 1980s, with disastrous consequences when the junk-bond market collapsed and the property market went into sharp decline. Those who did not immediately get dragged under, were so desperate for market share that they dared not push up their premium rates for fear of not getting the business. Analysts watching all this feared that the insurers were camouflaging their true exposure to asbestos and pollution claims and were seriously under-reserved, while Lloyd's syndicates were taking them on the chin and admitting they were under-reserved, and trying to remedy the position with calls on Names. As one US broker forecast:

They have all the problems. Lloyd's is not the only 'person' in the world to have underwritten US general indemnity business. It is written massively by the US insurance industry and US insurance insolvencies are going to be THE issue of the decade.

Big US insurers already to have bitten the dust included the Mission insurance company, the Integrity, Transit Casualty, Ideal Mutual and the Midland insurance company, and the broker continued:

There are more to come that are quite likely to be just as serious. Everybody is bashing poor old Lloyd's but there has only been one major problem in the Lloyd's underwriting market in recent decades which is an amazing record compared with the US.

The international insurance climate began to improve in early 1992, as the industry, always cyclical, entered an upturn but little of the benefit was felt in the USA. At Lloyd's, however, premium rates began to harden quite dramatically with a 25 per cent general increase reported, with rates in its specialized fields of aviation and marine insurance rising most as the losses from previous years strengthened underwriters' arms when it came to insisting on higher rates for cover in future. Another factor pushing rates up at Lloyd's were falling interest rates in Britain. These came down steadily in 1991, from a high level, and from September 1992 the fall accelerated, after sterling left Europe's Exchange Rate Mechanism. 'As interest rates fall, syndicates need more premium to compensate for the fall in their investment income,' explained one observer. Overcapacity was blocking this remedy from US insurers. In Lloyd's, however, aviation rates soared by between 100 per cent and 400 per cent, depending on the class of business written, while marine premiums rose as much as five-fold. The world market for aviation insurance was being forecast to rise from being worth £350 million in premiums in 1990 to hit £625 million of premium income by the end of 1992, as insurers adjusted their rates to take account of the high cost of past claims.

Non-marine rates at Lloyd's were tardier, with no substantial upturn there forecast until the middle of the year, mirroring US overcapacity; but catastrophe reinsurance rates shot up, by around 120 per cent, as did private house insurance rates after the claims not only for more frequent UK storm damage but serious subsidence problems after a series of long dry summers and dry winters. Motor insurance at Lloyd's started to cost more, too, this time because of the higher incidence of car theft and a spate of joy-riding by young Britons in search of thrills in the recession-filled summer and autumn of 1991. Overall, most premiums firmed up in 1992 and 1993.

Reinsurance generally became much harder to get; while excess-of-loss cover became almost impossible to buy at once-bitten, newly twice-shy Lloyd's. Professional indemnity cover also grew dearer, for America had a new scare for Lloyd's and the insurance world. The number of companies generally going bust during the US recession had triggered aggressive action by aggrieved shareholders, who started to sue the firms and their officers.

This exposed the providers of the companies' professional indemnity and directors' and officers' cover – much of it underwritten by Lloyd's Errors and Omissions insurers – both to the legal battles and to bills for any awards against the insured. 'It is predicted as the new asbestosis of the 1990s,' said a Lloyd's insider, as syndicates whacked their annual premiums up fast to companies either seeking this cover for the first time or coming round for the annual renewal of their policies. Forewarned would, it was hoped, be forearmed this time.

12
Keep the Aspidistra Flying

Keep thy shop and thy shop will keep thee

(GEORGE CHAPMAN, *EASTWARD HOE*)

At 11 a.m. on 15 January 1992 the chairman of Lloyd's, the chief executive Alan Lord, and David Rowland, the head of the Task Force appointed a year earlier by the Council of Lloyd's, started what chairman David Coleridge called 'one of the most important press conferences ever held at Lloyd's'. It was in the Society's old home, the 1958 Lloyd's building reminiscent in design of an ocean-going liner and now a hive of administrative functions, across the road in Lime Street from its shiny new establishment. David Rowland was about to announce to the financial press the results of his Task Force's year-long deliberations into the market's long-term future.

Appointed in January 1991 by an anxious Council aware that trouble was looming for Lloyd's in the form of huge losses against a background of tough competition, the Task Force had been given a year to look under every stone and find a way forward for the insurance market. It was, in effect, briefed 'to think the unthinkable' and report back.

In the course of their researches, the fourteen-man Task Force took a long, cool, clinical look at the events behind the losses and dramas, examined the background to falling standards in the market, explored the outlook for the industry generally to see what growth prospects there might be within it for Lloyd's own unique market, and scrutinized the way Lloyd's ran itself – before finally recommending how the old insurance market could best put its house in order this time around to try and secure a sounder future. The Rowland Report sought to retain the basic shape of the market but to tone it up vigorously: starting with the most urgent exercises and then moving on to the long-term fitness programme. The surgeon's knife remained sheathed; but the regime was also designed to prepare the old patient for radical surgery if this proved unavoidable. It was not, however, presented as the most desirable outcome.

The Rowland Report was thorough, detailed, and pulled few punches. It pulled together information and figures from right across not only the Lloyd's market but also the wider London and international insurance markets, providing a unique data base. All its source material was lodged at Lloyd's with the final report. Its tone was measured but the message was clear: Lloyd's had got fat, lazy, complacent. In a world that was changing and growing rougher and tougher outside the precincts of the oracle of insurance, its own practitioners had grown overpaid, overconfident and had over-reached themselves. Often, Names had been treated with little of the respect owed to the people whose money made the market possible and without whom there could be no Lloyd's of London. All that had to change.

A drastic reassessment of practitioners' attitudes, charges, and dis-closure of information was required at once. Retrenchment into a cosy club of niche business away from the trials and tribulations of the outside world was not the right reaction, the Task Force also concluded. There were good growth prospects within this volatile industry and if Lloyd's shaped up, shed weighty costs, improved the professionalism of its practitioners and the market, raising underwriting standards, and considered new ways of attract-ing additional capital and business it had a good chance of trading its way out of trouble into a bright future.

But it had to move fast.

The Task Force had invited submissions from interested parties by the end of March 1991. Some 290 people took up this chance to register their views, suggestions, hopes and fears about Lloyd's. Market practitioners got in their points first but submissions continued to pour in from Names long after the Easter 1991 'closing' date, finally outnumbering those from people working within the market. All were studied.

The subject causing most concern and alarm, in the face of the terrifying losses reported in 1991 and even worse figures due in mid-1992, for the 1989 underwriting year, was how to find some way of limiting Names's blanket liability: either through creating a pooled fund ('mutualization' in Lloyd's jargon) to deal with high claims, or by some other means. Of the 290 submissions, 156 raised the subject of limiting liability, 76 in favour of some sort of mutualization and the rest favouring other routes. 'The strong message which came through . . . was that the current large losses were making Names question their continuing membership of Lloyd's,' the Task Force reported.

Urgent action was needed to avoid meltdown. News of the 1988 year's £509 million losses broke half-way through the Task Force's deliberations and, as talk gathered of anything from a £1.25 billion to a £1.75 billion loss for 1989 – understimates, as it turned out – and of more losses to come for 1990, Names were resigning in their thousands.

From boasting 32,433 actively underwriting Names in 1988, Lloyd's started 1992 with just 22,500. But it was worse than that. In 1990, when the number of active Names had dropped to 28,770 it actually had 35,170 members on its list. The other 6,400 were lying dormant, unable to resign because they were stuck on at least one open year, and another 10,000 or so of the active Names were also on one or more open years. In other words, the Task Force had discovered that by 1990 half the entire membership of Lloyd's had some exposure to losses that could not be quantified, might continue to roll up year after year, and from which they could not escape. No wonder unlimited liability, supposedly the feature that made Lloyd's both unique and supremely reliable for those insured there, had become the single most worrying aspect of the market for the Names who provided its capital base.

Restoring Names' confidence in the market was paramount if it was to stay in business. The Task Force quickly widened its own brief to see how this could be urgently achieved. It appointed management consultancy Kinsey to help it with the number-crunching and studied seventeen different ways of revamping the market's capital base, and a variety of solutions to all the other issues unearthed. Because speed was now vital to the market's recovery, the Task Force presented its conclusions in *Lloyd's: a route forward*, as a two-part strategy to secure Lloyd's future.

The first part concentrated on rapid remedial action – proposals that could be implemented at top speed through new Lloyd's by-laws in time for the 1993 underwriting year, and did not require lengthy new legislation. The second dealt with reforms that would need changes in legislation in the form of a new Lloyd's Act which would almost certainly take several years to progress through to the statute book.

The Task Force saw no point in doing away with the strengths that unlimited liability and the concept of a market composed of sole traders had brought to Lloyd's in the past. But it did try to limit the pain this could bring when truly exceptional losses pounded the market. The most radical proposal in the urgent, remedial, category was a plan for a compulsory high-level stop-loss scheme, to be operational from the start of 1993, that would provide a rainy-day fund to reinsure the top slice of worst-hit Names' vast losses on bad years after year four. Only losses of more than 100 per cent of the premium limit would be covered, however, to prevent abuse of the system by unscrupulous underwriters trying to use it as an easy way to get reinsurance. The scheme, to be funded by a compulsory annual levy of 0.25 per cent of each Name's premium limit, would ensure that no one could be left high and dry on an open year for more than four years – with one small proviso. If losses on claims coming in ever proved so vast that they drained the fund, liability would have to revert back to the original Names in the last resort. 'It's not perfect but it's a darn sight better than anything Lloyd's have considered hitherto,' was one Council member's private assessment of the proposal. Spurred on by the need to stem the outflow of resigning Names and try and entice some new ones into the market – only a handful had dared to sign up for 1992's underwriting year while 4,000 left, after all – the Council raced to consult Names and get the new proposal on to the rule book as a new by-law in time to cover all members underwriting business from 1993 onwards.

Another remedial move was a plan to offer smaller Names, writing under £500,000 of premium income a year, the option to pool their limits into new, unit-trust-like funds called Members' Agents Pooling Arrangements (MAPAs) that would spread the Names' resources and their risk into larger more cost-effective – and hopefully, safer – lines of underwriting than they could manage alone. Profits would be divided pro rata between them.

The second wave of longer term reforms, the ones needing a new Lloyd's Act, included a revolutionary plan to bring in a new category of Corporate Members of Lloyd's, *with* – for the first time – *limited liability* but also much higher deposit requirements to support their underwriting activity; and to make participating in a MAPA, as described above, compulsory for all Names on the first slice of their underwriting activity. Along with this would go a restructuring of members' agencies in particular, and managing agents to a degree. The Task Force report also suggested creating a way of putting a price on belonging to a Lloyd's syndicate and being able to sell your seat on it to an incoming Name. There was also a very detailed proposal on how Lloyd's governing body should be restructured. This ruffled the Council's feathers and, alone among the positive proposals, sparked quite a row over the following week.

Nearly all of the sixty-five conclusions were radical, and all but one – the 'governance' proposal – were welcomed by the Council, which promptly initiated studies on how they might be implemented. A plethora of new and existing working parties were detailed to research a proposal each and come up with a recommendation of whether, when and how to implement it. David Coleridge hoped to have plenty of news to placate worried Names at the next annual general meeting to be held that June.

There was also the question of what the Task Force did not recommend changing or doing. It wanted to keep the three-year accounting system which seemed the fairest way of being able to make an assessment of what the reinsurance to close premiums should be. Closing each syndicate year at the end of its calendar year could lead to huge claims being fed straight through via the reinsurance to close to new Names joining the following year, with no way of knowing if the reinsurance premium paid by the old year into the new one was really adequate. If it were too high, old Names who were leaving would be penalized, if too low, the incomers would suffer. A three year pause sorted out most of those issues – and was also used by the big insurance companies for assessing their own marine, aviation, transport and treaty business in their internal accounting systems.

The Task Force also came down against divorcing the ownership of members' and managing agents, provided the market had access to enough independent managing agents to keep the linked, owned or otherwise tied ones on their toes. And it said the previous switch, laid down in the 1982 Lloyd's Act, to divesting Lloyd's brokers' ownership of managing agents should be reversed. It had pushed up costs to the market and diluted expertise. Allowing them to forge links again would create greater flexibility and help syndicates to pursue new avenues of gaining business, especially in the light of changes in technology that could allow direct, on-screen under-writing of some lines of business. The ban on such link-ups was, Rowland told the press conference, 'a foolish and unnecessary restriction now, though understandable when introduced because of past misdemeanours; but we cannot base our plans for the future on an assumption that there will be misconduct as a norm.' Divestment had been forced upon the market-place in the 1982 Act in the wake of the abuse of the previous arrangement by a hard core of fraudsters.

The proposal won particularly keen support from Sir David Walker, a Council member at the time by virtue of being the head of the Securities and Investment Board (SIB) which oversees securities trading and the life insurance industry in the United Kingdom. He pointed out later that the Stock Exchange had benefited greatly by allowing investment banks and similar combines to own both stockbrokers and market-makers. As a result of the powerful new groupings they formed, London's share of the market in international securities had 'skyrocketed' (aided too by its abandonment of a trading floor for a screen-based system that allowed offices from all over the world to trade shares at a keystroke). Sir David foresaw similar opportunities for Lloyd's if divestment could ever be reversed. But this too would require legislation, and other reforms were more immediately pressing.

Most controversially of all, the Task Force found no new way to help the beleaguered Names already facing continued calls on loss-making syndicates' existing open years. These were going to have to remain open – which conclusion understandably upset many Names in financial difficulties, who felt terribly abandoned by Lloyd's. Despite recognizing the need to alleviate the impact in future of exceptional losses of the sort these Names were clearly suffering, the cost of making the 1993 stop-loss scheme retrospective to help these people was felt by the Task Force to be too hard to quantify, and therefore impossible to calculate the necessary reinsurance premiums.

That morning in the 1958 building, Chairman David Coleridge praised the report's 'evolutionary approach', calling it 'practical, pragmatic and prudent'. The sole recommendation to be rejected instantly by the Council of Lloyd's was one to change the way in which the market was governed, replacing the then Council and its host of sub-committees, policy bodies, and various Market Associations with a more elegant, two-tier structure. By turning this down without further study, the Council sailed into a very dangerous squall – this time whipped up amongst the 'insiders', the market practitioners – and one that rapidly threatened to undo the goodwill generated by the Council's warm welcome of the rest of the report.

The Task Force wanted to see a new parent body, a Lloyd's Market Board, created to attend to day-to-day business and oversee administrative matters via a smaller number of subsidiary boards or sub-committees; while a separate new Regulatory Council concentrated on the rule book and future policy. It also recommended that though the Chairman of Lloyd's should be on both bodies, he should not chair the Regulatory Council. Instead it should have its own part-time, nominated chairman and there should also be a full-time head of regulation who would sit on the Regulatory Council. The Task Force report also suggested that, though he would probably still be elected from among the senior Lloyd's practitioners, being Chairman of the Society should be a full-time, paid post with a several-year tenure instead of having an element of Buggin's turn about it.

The Council later said it had discussed the proposal at length before deciding that implementing it all would divert time and energy from organizing other, more urgent reforms, one of which – to rush out the new stop-loss scheme in time for 1993 – it particularly wanted to press ahead with rapidly. It also feared, but did not publicly say so, that legislation to implement the Rowland proposals could all too easily be hijacked by the politicians and put the regulation of Lloyd's in the hands of an outside body – the SIB, for example. Memories of the amount of work and effort that went in to the 1982 Act made Council members' blood run cold. However, by apparently rejecting the 'governance' proposals straight off, instead of putting them on the back burner by agreeing to mull them over once the more urgent work was done, the Council made a major PR miscalculation. The poorly explained move looked defensive and self-preserving and launched the Council of Lloyd's straight into a storm of protest, this time from inside its own market – and did nothing to lessen the 'risk' of outside regulation either.

Pressure, from underwriters, agencies, and Names (via the Association of Lloyd's Members), built fast on Council members to reconsider. David Coleridge, once again intemperate under fire, was coldly criticized in a leader in the *Financial Times* of 22 January for describing some of the Task Force's thinking as 'codswallop'.

'That must not be his final word,' opined the *FT*. Nor was it. The previous day had also seen chief executive Alan Lord reported as saying he would want to resign if the changes were implemented. But, within a week of its public rejection of the proposal, the Council backed down on 22 January in the face of pressure from all ends of the market, and agreed to have this plan studied along with all the others. (And Alan Lord did not immediately resign. He was due to retire as chief executive in June anyway, and in February confirmed that he would indeed do so.) A working group to study the governance question was promptly conjured up. It was to be led by the chairman of (entirely unrelated) Lloyds Bank Sir Jeremy Morse and included David Rowland himself who had picked his way carefully through the governance controversy. He was naturally strongly in favour of the Task Force's two-tier governance proposal, and while publicly merely 'disappointed' by the Council's rejection of it, he had privately felt the Council had been foolishly over hasty.

It would have made sense, for Lloyd's, for Alan Lord to do an extra six months or a year as chief executive during the hiatus while the Morse working party deliberated the governance issue. Instead, a three-man team, the heads of market services, regulation and finance, was appointed from June to look after the day-to-day running of the market in his stead. This arrangement would effectively concentrate more executive power, at least for the time being, in the Chairman of the Council – something that some other Lloyd's insiders were far from sure was a good thing.

The squall, which had threatened to obscure the Council's positive reaction to the rest of this important report, abated and – for the time being – blew over. But the headlines like the *FT* leader's 'Codswallop at Lloyd's' had not done the Council's image any good ('It's not helpful', sighed one leading Lloyd's broker that morning, more angry with the Council than the newspaper) and had only confirmed some unhappy Names' worst feelings about the way the market had been run to date. Observers from the corporate insurance world felt they recognized in the affair the natural resistance of a bureaucracy to changes that affect itself. This was how one senior corporate insurance man analysed the situation just before the Council's U-turn:

> Companies can cope with modest change but not with major changes, because of all the bureaucracy within a big company. Lloyd's is a market like a street market: if something big happens all the individual traders get together to do something and can inaugurate very rapid and decisive change, more than a bureaucracy can do, and we are now at that point with Lloyd's. The Rowland Report is a damned good report which they have accepted hook, line and not quite sinker. The refusal to deal with the restructuring is because you are back to dealing with a bureaucracy – the Council – which is resistant to changing itself. It's a pity because two-tier boards, as we've seen on the Continent, do create much clearer clarification of responsibilities than the UK single-tier board system. Once you get to a single board or council no one's clear about what they are doing.

With the governance row behind it, Lloyd's could concentrate on studying the rest of the report. The sixty-four other, more welcome, recommendations included bold new moves to ensure Lloyd's had sufficient capacity in future to remain a serious contender in the London and international insurance markets. These ranged from (a) the stop-loss scheme to protect Names from vast losses ratcheting up on open year syndicates in future, starting in 1993; (b) the scheme to put the first slice of Names' premium limits (the suggestion was up to the first £500,000 they wrote) into unit-trust style groupings or Members' Agents Pooling Arrangements (MAPAs). Ideally this should become compulsory for the first layer of all Names' underwriting but the facility should be made available on an optional basis from 1993 if possible. The pools would be run by a new breed of members' agent, split out from the existing set-up, a fund manager who would use the pooled premium limits to ensure a better spread of business for participants. Syndicates should be allowed to source 25 per cent of their total premium income limit from MAPAs. Fund managers would also be expected to raise new capital for the market by bringing in Corporate Members, once the necessary legislation was in place, as well as Names.

MAPAs should also put an end to the administratively nightmarish, costly and ridiculous practice of slicing insurance risks into smaller and smaller lines of business and scattering them like confetti round the market. Some had been cut up into so many bits, just on the primary insurance, that a broker could spend half a day trying to get someone to underwrite a £100 line of a much larger programme. Instead, the MAPAs could soak up larger lines to the collective benefit of lots of small underwriting Names and the administrative cost to broker and syndicates would be considerably less.

Other changes to ensure future survival were (c) the concept of the Super Name, writing business exceeding £500,000 a year, whose upper layer of underwriting would be carried out in the normal Lloyd's sole trader fashion, and who could consult a new breed of independent advisers, also evolved from members' agents. In addition to the advisers and the fund managers there should eventually be six to eight 'competing administrating utilities' that Names could appoint to handle all their administrative work, collect profits and losses for them and deal with their Lloyd's-related tax affairs; and (d) longer-term, the market should look into allowing insurance companies, or stockbroking firms, investment banks and fabulously wealthy individuals to become Corporate Names with limited liability, but who would have to put up much higher deposits than ordinary or Super Names to back their underwriting programmes. At the time it was thought that this would require a new Lloyd's Act, but subsequent legal advice says that it won't.

Insurance companies were lukewarm about the idea but anticipated that stockbrokers and investment groups such as unit trusts might be interested in corporate membership as one more vehicle to offer their own clients. 'I would be very surprised if it ever contributed a really significant element of capital to the market,' said one senior corporate insurer after studying the plan. Sir David Walker, familiar with the investment community, also felt Lloyd's future still lay more with the individual Names than with corporate membership.

Also needing legislation, before it could be implemented, was another radical idea: to devise a system that placed a value on belonging to a particular syndicate. Like a share, this value would rise or fall depending on the profitability, popularity, and skill of the syndicate. Thus if a Name wanted to resign from Lloyd's he could sell his seat, as it were, on a syndicate to another Name seeking to join it. This would be quite separate from his normal Lloyd's deposit, agency fees et cetera and should help to reduce (but not totally eliminate) the risk of favouritism being shown to certain Names trying to get on to popular syndicates while others find it hard to get aboard.

Transactions would be on a 'matched bargain' basis, of existing Names to the incoming individual, though in practice the highest bidder would tend to get the slot, as the retiring Name would presumably be looking to maximize the benefits of his Lloyd's membership to date. The price would reflect the degree of demand and eagerness to join that particular syndicate – or not. However, the system would be quite challenging to set up and administer and this proposal was on the list of longer-term ideas.

Other proposals involved: proper growth targets for Lloyd's capacity, which were sorely needed. To ensure enough capital flowed into the market for it to maintain, let alone grow, its market share, it needed to restore the interests of Names to the forefront of the market's consciousness and practice via a host of new rules and five new rights. The latter included the right to stay on a syndicate and not be given notice to quit by the managing agent 'except in exceptional circumstances'; the right with (say) a 75 per cent majority vote, to ask the Council to change the syndicate's managing agent if it was felt to be unsatisfactory; the right to have direct access to information about the syndicate they joined; the right to be consulted on and to approve major transactions by the syndicate; and the right to attend an annual general meeting of their syndicate(s) which it would be mandatory for the managing agent to arrange each year. Members' and managing agents would have to provide Names with much better and more frequent information about where their money went, and how syndicates were performing.

There was also a recommendation that additional reserves held by each syndicate should no longer be calculated in the light of its overall premium limit and risk exposure and averaged across all its Names, but worked out pro rata to reflect each Name's share of the underwriting so that he or she had adequate reserves for their particular exposure. These would be 'equalization reserves', held at the level of the individual Name.

Furthermore Lloyd's should change its membership rules to ensure that Names put up an extra 10 per cent 'cushion' over and above the normal 30 per cent deposit, to be in the form of liquid, easily realizable assets. This would improve the market's liquidity and reduce its heavy reliance on bank guarantees given against assets that were difficult to realize, such as a Name's farmland. This had only resulted in calls on the assets meaning the Name had to sell up to meet his obligations, which took time and could delay the settlement of claims, causing distress and resentment both to Names and to claimants.

In addition, the remuneration of agents should be thoroughly overhauled, and in particular there should be a clawback into the syndicate of profit commission paid to the agent on year X's business if huge claims subsequently struck year Y from year X's reinsured business to close. This would help to concentrate underwriter's and members' agents minds on the quality of the business being written and the adequacy of the reinsurance-to-close premium paid into the new year, too. It was not so much that agents were always overpaid, as paid in the wrong way, Rowland said later.

Equally, the report also insisted that a major cost-cutting drive was urgently needed across members' agents and managing agents and the Lloyd's establishment. All told, it was costing Lloyd's and the managing and members' agents £100 million a year to operate the market, Rowland's researchers and number-crunchers had calculated, which was on average a staggering 30 per cent too high for Lloyd's to be sufficiently competitive to achieve the growth targets the Task Force had identified as vital to Lloyd's of London's survival as a serious player in the international insurance industry.

To stay the same size in 'real' (that is, post-inflation) terms, Lloyd's capacity needed to grow from £10 billion in 1991 to £13 billion in 1997; but to keep its market share in line with the underlying, 'real' growth anticipated in the whole of the non-life insurance industry, the Task Force calculated that Lloyd's capacity to underwrite business would have to expand to £17 billion by 1997.

Given an average Name writing £500,000 of premium income a year, that meant tens of thousands of new Names would have to be attracted in over a five-year period and, from where Lloyd's was placed as 1991 ended, that did not look as if it were going to be easy – and which was why the Task Force thought Lloyd's should lay the groundwork at once for legislation to allow access to new capital from Corporate Members: a new Lloyd's Act would take five to seven years to progress through and, Rowland advised, it would be wise just to set up the mechanism in time to be able to use it later in the decade if needed.

'Changes must give confidence for the future to attract Names. The Society has a real duty to provide Names with a way to leave and new Names won't join if they can't see a means of exit as well,' Rowland told the press conference.

This was the pivotal concern that had generated one of the Task Force's key recommendations: the plan to end the trauma of open years and limit the pain of huge losses for unlucky Names in future, from 1993 onwards. First the scheme should be set up to provide 'high level' stop-loss cover for every Name who lost more than 100 per cent of his premium level on any year that still could not be closed at the end of year three, but remained open in year four.

The scheme would be funded through a compulsory annual levy of 0.25 per cent of every single Name's premium limit, and the levy should begin in 1993. By 1997, when the first if any stop-loss cover would actually be written for high loss-making syndicates – on 1993 syndicate years that had failed to close in 1995, and remained open at the end of 1996 – it should have built up nicely both via the levy and with investment gains and reinvested investment income. Once the stop-loss cover was granted, further claims against that open year's under-writing would then be met by the fund, and Names could either be free to resign, or to start afresh. But, if the claims ever got so huge that the fund was drained, then the remaining liability would revert back to the original Name just as it did when an individual's personal stop-loss policy was exercised up to its limit in the past.

The reason for this was simply that, after much study, the Task Force could not find a way round the British law of liability regarding sole traders, which is what Names are, so the liability would ultimately have to revert to them. But the scheme would at least spread the burden of 'excessive' losses across the whole market for the greater good of Lloyd's future. The suggested trigger point for the stop-loss cover was set high, to avoid the 'moral hazard' of 'unscrupulous underwriters' seeking to use the scheme as a cheap way to get reinsurance by keeping a year open for an extra year and waiting for the new fund to take up the claims burden. No underwriter worth his salt is going to want to lose his Names 100 per cent of their premium limit just to get reinsurance. 'He'd go out of business first,' said Rowland. In the end, an 80 per cent trigger was adopted. The Task Force also proposed: better help in future for Names stuck on open years or run-off years not falling into the 100 per cent loss category. Lloyd's should put less pressure on syndicates to close difficult years, but accept that sometimes it was fairer to Names coming into the new trading year that a difficult previous one should not be reinsured to close into it. Instead the CentreWrite fund, only recently established to try and reinsure syndicates with open years, should switch its emphasis from tending (so far) only to look at small syndicates with minor difficulties to offering individual Names a reinsurance policy that allowed them to settle their exposure. It should also seek 'to ensure that there is an effective and fairly priced Estate Protection Plan available to Names'. In 1993, it did so.

Other, technical proposals were designed to give Lloyd's syndicates greater access to insurance business that was not reaching the market. The Task Force concluded that only between 5 and 20 per cent of business generated by the ten main broking groups flowed into the Lloyd's market, via their Lloyd's broking subsidiaries. The remaining 80 to 95 per cent of the insurance they placed, went elsewhere: a vast pool of untapped business that Lloyd's could access in due course if it worked on ways of improving its relationship with the wider broking combines. Developing a common technology could be a way forward here, allowing brokers direct on-screen access into the Lloyd's market to place the more straightforward and smaller lines of business without insisting on individual brokers running around from box to box in a time-consuming search for takers of small or simple, fairly standard lines of business.

Many practitioners thought on-screen trading was not suitable for the insurance market since underwriting risks involved tailoring a premium to a given situation (whereas an ICI share is the same the world over whoever owns it). But there remained a good argument for devising an on-screen system that could offer, for example, standardized cover for a 747 aircraft, with pre-set exclusion clauses. If the airline wanted specialist tailored cover, it could still send its broker round the market as before – or get him to pick up the telephone.

Allowing syndicates to deal directly with non-Lloyd's accredited brokers in new overseas markets, provided they were 'major broking groups of international standing' was another suggestion. In the short term, the Task Force proposed more flexible use of Names' capacity by letting syndicates invite Names to increase their premium limit half-way through the existing year, as well as at the start of each new year. It also suggested that the syndicate's quota share reinsurance of up to 25 per cent of its premium limit, which is the slip placed outside the Lloyd's market, that is with insurance companies, should no longer be counted in the syndicate's premium limit – freeing that capacity for it to write more business provided, however, that insurance rates were seen to be hardening and not the reverse.

The 240-page report was posted to all Names and 32 meetings to discuss its contents were set up world-wide between Lloyd's officials and Names – in America, South Africa, Australia, New Zealand and Eire as well as in the United Kingdom. Lloyd's officials going on these roadshows were given intensive media-training sessions before they went, on how to cope with a roomful of several hundred hostile Names.

When the Task Force had been appointed at the start of 1991, the Council gave it a brief to 'look beyond the immediate future and identify the framework within which the Society should, ideally, be trading five to seven years' hence' and report back at the end of the year. Led by David Rowland, it was a team of fourteen, plus two secretaries, drawn from within and outwith the insurance world, and backed up by the team from McKinsey & Co.

On his Task Force were: one other Lloyd's broker, Michael Wade; four leading underwriters, Andrew Beazley, David Mann, Stephen Merrett, and Elvin Patrick; a couple of members'-cum-managing agents, John Gordon and Robert Hiscox; Council-nominated member Matthew Patient; Anthony Haynes who was the chairman of Names' ginger group the Association of Lloyd's Members (formed in 1981 by Names concerned about the quality of information available to them); Andrew Duguid the head of market services of the Corporation of Lloyd's; director of the Prudential Corporation (Britain's biggest insurance company) Ron Artus, representing the insurance world outside Lloyd's; and appearing for the rest of the world, John Kay, Professor of Economics at the London Business School – who apparently listened hard and said little but whose occasional interjections were to provide some of the report's most radical long-term suggestions, notably the idea of introducing a way of placing a monetary value on syndicate membership and making it tradeable. Their brief from the Council said:

> The group will have regard particularly for the long-term competitive position of the Society. [It] will examine and assess the advantages and disadvantages of the present basis on which capital is provided to support underwriting at Lloyd's and consider:
> (a) The tension between the one year syndicate and the need to reserve, plan and invest for the future of an ongoing business; its effect on Lloyd's competitive position.
> (b) The attractions and drawbacks of individual membership and un-limited liability to Names and policy-holders and the extent to which the Central Fund and other vehicles lead to the mutualization of liability.
> (c) The organization of the capital supporting the underwriting to facilitate an effective response to fluctuations in the insurance cycle.

The group should, taking into account the legal, accounting and taxation consequences, recommend a framework for the future and the methods by which it might be achieved.

The group will keep Lloyd's Council informed of their progress and aim to submit their report by the end of 1991. Written submissions will be welcomed from anyone interested by 31 March 1991.

Rowland was not only a Lloyd's broker but himself a Name, stuck on one of the worst-hit open years, syndicate 90's 1982 year, so he was painfully aware of the problems from both sides of the business.

There was much unhappiness amongst existing Names in difficulty about the report's view that Names who had lost money on old open years could not be assisted along similar lines to the 1993 stop-loss plan. The thorny question of the Names already on loss-making open years was a tricky catch-22 for the Task Force. Considering what to do about existing Names was not in its remit. On the other hand, the future of Lloyd's was and that hinged on potential future members' perceptions of the market and its conduct. So it examined the problem and as David Rowland said later:

We agonized over it right up to the final month to see if the 1993 idea could be made retrospective. It seems simple but the more you go through it, like peeling an onion, you see the difficulties. You cannot properly scale the old-year problems because you don't know what the liabilities on things like asbestos and pollution are. The uncertainty depends on decisions in the US courts, and they are unforecastable. There are a number of decisions which do look more rather than less favourable, but it will take five to seven years before you can be sure. The pollution liability could be zero, or massive – how do you find a reasonable point to work out what people's share should be, to help? Don't forget that reinsurance to close is just reinsurance – you are still liable. Nobody can escape from a Lloyd's policy.

The problem was that, if everyone clubbed together to create a much bigger stop-loss fund for the old years to bail out the 17,000 who had already lost in aggregate sums equivalent to 150 per cent of their premium limits, no one knew what bills this could mean in store for the 17,000 Names who (by 1990) had not so far been plunged into loss and who could be understandably reluctant to shell out large sums for others' misfortunes.

The prospect of having to dip into their pockets at once to fund other people's old losses might also scare off new Names. The Task Force studied a host of different proposals but in the end could not come up with a workable scheme to help the 17,000 people stuck on one or more open years, some of them no longer able or willing actively to underwrite new business but trapped in their Lloyd's membership until the open year(s) finally had a line drawn under them. As Rowland elaborated later:

> Morally and legally there is no way without consent that you can get those not involved to share in the ills of the other 17,000. Individuals who are not in trouble feel it was because of their skill and choice [of syndicate] and are not prepared to pay £100,000 for the future good of the whole. Uncertainty is the problem. If you could say that to deal with the old-year problems you pay £1.00, or £100,000, there might be a way – but you cannot properly scale the old-year problems. We tried very hard.

At the heart of the sixty-five proposals the Task Force did make, however, was the basic tenet that in future the Names' interests must be paramount. As David Rowland himself pointed out, the market practitioners had forgotten that without the Names' money as capital for insurance underwriting, there would be no Lloyd's. Names had been kept too much in the dark about what was being done with their money, costs had grown way out of proportion to premium income, and practitioners had spent more time thinking about how to make money for themselves than for their Names, in a climate of low premium rates and stiff competition from other insurance providers, by turning to mechanisms such as the LMX spiral.

This was damning stuff, though delivered calmly within the report. Some people felt the 1982 Act's enforced divestment of managing agents from Lloyd's brokers was partly to blame for this climate. The process of organizing management buy outs of agencies had got the participants thinking more in terms of what was good for them, and would make money for them, than of the quality of service that the Names should be able to expect from them. Weak premium rates had not helped either. As Rowland later observed:

> We are all barrow boys in pin-striped suits and like making money. Therefore when there's a market and people don't perceive profits, it's much more fun trying to make money for each other – for example by recycling business – than for the Names. A lot of practices that had grown up at that time were about that attitude.

The first step if Lloyd's were to have a future, the report said, was 'to ensure the primacy of interests of Names' so that wealthy individuals would feel more confident about becoming – or remaining – Lloyd's members. The nearly 4,000 resignations in 1991 left Lloyd's with a rapidly shrinking pool of actively underwriting Names and though a few people, anticipating better times ahead as premium rates hardened internationally and at Lloyd's, had increased their premium limits, many others were on reduced ones. The brave few did not quite plug the gap, and capacity shrank for 1992. This was not an immediate problem as there was not expected to be enough business to take up all the capacity that year anyway, but it did mean the prospect loomed of a shrinking capital base curbing Lloyd's ability to compete in future; and fewer Names to share any large losses, and finance the stop-loss fund too. It was the prospect of the exodus deteriorating into meltdown that had everyone moving so fast to try and implement the Task Force's main remedial recommendations. Ancient City institutions can be very fast on their feet to correct long-festering problems once they realize their own livelihood may be at risk. The question now was whether Lloyd's could be fleet enough, or would fail in the attempt.

By not including the current Names in the new stop-loss proposal, the Task Force was in effect isolating Lloyd's future from infection by the known problems from the past. Not everyone was convinced this would work. Critics said the failure to help old Names would put off new ones. Supporters said new ones would not come forward, and the 17,000 current ones not facing losses would leave if they did have to stump up for other people's losses.

The critics also claimed that as Names sought partial redress under stricken syndicates' Errors and Omissions (E&O) cover, massive claims would begin anyway to affect so-far profitable syndicates and spread the malaise right across the market into the 1992 and 1993 years and beyond. Syndicates' auditors were also in danger of being sued by angry Names for allegedly failing in their duty of care to the Names – who were, after all, their clients – and receiving claims on their professional indemnity (PI) cover, itself largely written within Lloyd's.

'Lloyd's will have to pick the PI cover up too – it's all in the Lloyd's markets. Lloyd's will run out of money and there will have to be a market-wide levy to meet it,' forecast Michael Freeman, the lawyer advising Names on several problem syndicates, mainly LMX casualties. In November 1991 in *Lloyd's List*, the market's daily newspaper, he forecast that Lloyd's would have to impose a £40,000 levy on all the 1992 underwriting Names to boost the Central Fund (whose existing brief was to help policyholders by assuming responsibility for the insurance underwritten by any Names who went bust and could no longer meet their liabilities). This would raise enough money to invest to meet future claims on the open years. Alternatively, he said, Lloyd's could 'mutualize' the losses just across all the 1991 Names, who would then face a cash call of £63,000 a head.

In January 1992, he repeated that:

Each Name who does not pay a levy is less money in the Central Fund which is falling by the week. Even if Lloyd's sued those who can't pay or won't pay their calls, it would take ages and they would have had to top up the Central Fund meanwhile. A levy of £63,000 per Name on average – though in practice the big ones would pay up and the little ones would get money back – would clear the slate.

Despite the Task Force's conclusions that hopes of help for the old-year Names were at an impasse with no way out that spring, Freeman still thought there might have to be a rescue plan before the summer of 1992 was out.

Observers from the City of London and on the Council felt that the Task Force was right not to shoulder the 1992 Names with the burden of sharing the old-year losses. The only hope they saw for this 300-year-old market to make it to the twenty-first century was to raise a barrier between the pre-1993 old-year losses and the future, and trade out of trouble. It would be a race against time. Task Force chairman David Rowland had grown to see overcoming the effects of the 1988 and 1989 losses as

like crossing an enormous ditch full of wild animals and snakes – and which we still might not be able to cross. Painting Utopia on the other side is not much good if you can't get over the ditch – and nothing in the report says we can.

There were no absolute guarantees that the Task Force recommendations would save Lloyd's, but at the time they were seen as its best chance, and a fighting chance too. If the old market could drag itself over that ditch, it should have a vigorous new life ahead. In January 1992 the desire to live seemed to be galvanizing the market into action. It resembled nothing so much as a corpulent old City gent suddenly learning from his doctor that he can expect a fatal seizure within a few short years, or even months, if he doesn't change his regime, lose some weight and get fit fast. You could almost hear the cry of 'Lead me to the gym!' and the thud of brandy bottles being dropped in alarm. But, implementing a new regime does not always come easy; and there were pitfalls ahead.

13
Brave New World

| *The aim of all legitimate business is
service, for profit, at a risk*

(BENJAMIN C. LEEMING, *IMAGINATION*)

Lloyd's needed a lifeline: it found a potential one in new technology, but late in the day. By early 1992 exciting new systems were being tested that, it was hoped, would give not just Lloyd's of London but the whole London insurance market the leading edge over other insurance markets and attract vital new business. Lloyd's needed it to recover its poise; the companies needed it to keep London's draw if its lodestone Lloyd's crumbled.

The idea was to bring in a computerized system and network that would allow straightforward insurance risks to be placed in the London market by brokers without the time-consuming and expensive process of trotting round the Lloyd's boxes or the insurance companies' City offices. Traditional face-to-face business could still be conducted for the larger and more complicated risks, but the new system would also speed that up by allowing broker and underwriter to call up all the details of the particular cover on the underwriter's personal computer (PC) at the box instead of poring over slips of paper. Alternatively, the two could chat by phone about any wrinkles that needed discussing, while viewing the details on their own screens. The cost-savings and speed would help to restore Lloyd's competitive edge and stop business from going elsewhere.

As one of the people involved in testing the new service said, early in 1992:

> It is a huge undertaking. Nothing like this has ever been done before. It's a vast communication network, breaking new ground after 300 years of fuddy-duddyness which is going out of the window. It will cut out a lot of the traditions, which upsets some people. But it will put London in the forefront of the insurance world.
>
> People are a bit worried about it until they see it working for them. Then they want to know (a) will it make us money? and (b) will it save us money? It should allow cost-cutting, even some reduction of staff, and pull in more business by eventually speeding up the whole process.

The plan was to move on from the piecemeal development of computerized systems that had taken root so far at Lloyd's and find a common system that would work right across the London market, unifying the existing hotchpotch. By the late 1980s there were four separate outfits logging and handling claims and information about cover written at Lloyd's alone. In addition, many Lloyd's underwriters, brokers, and the insurance and rein-surance companies clustered in the City had developed their own in-house systems or bought a wide variety of ready-packaged software. Lloyd's had become a babel of PCs that couldn't talk to each other.

Though underwriters were experimenting with computerized record-keeping and (gradually) some analysis for their syndicates, the Lloyd's Policy Signing Office (LPSO) was the central keeper of records of all slips initialled by underwriters agreeing to a line of cover. It checked, signed and sealed them on behalf of the syndicates involved. It also acted as the interface between Lloyd's brokers and underwriters each month when it came to settling up, receiving premiums and paying claims. Started with a punch-card system, Lloyd's massive centralized records were still being kept this way long after the advent of more sophisticated computer systems.

Three different claims offices handled and processed the actual claims against Lloyd's policies – each for a different sector of the market. Thus there was the Lloyd's Underwriters Non-Marine Claims Office known as LUNCO, the Lloyd's Underwriters Claims and Recoveries Office – LUCRO – which served the marine market, and the Lloyd's Aviation Claims Centre or LACC. They had grown up to centralize the laborious process of each underwriter having to issue his own policy, collect the premium and pay the claim. Each had its own computer system and its own custom and practice. As one Lloyd's man explained:

> It still works but in a world where technology is advancing so fast, and where the consumer expects prompt and efficient delivery – insurance is selling a product – and the ability to pay a claim swiftly and efficiently, plenty of customers were noticing that it takes a long time for Lloyd's to settle a claim. Really big ones, like Piper Alpha, are settled fast, but smaller ones take longer.

By the late 1980s Lloyd's underwriters were writing insurance business from around the world worth around £20 million in premiums per working day, in business brought to them by over 200 Lloyd's brokers. With each risk spread between perhaps 15 different syndicates, that meant a lot of administration, and more so if some lines of a risk which later generated a claim had been underwritten by one or two of the big insurance companies outside Lloyd's.

Not to be outdone by LUNCO, LUCRO, and LACC, the Lloyd's Insurance Brokers had also formed their own Committee: the LIBC. And, following Lloyd's example of creating claims bureaux to simplify administrative functions, the insurance companies had banded together as well to set up their own pooled service. First to do so – back in 1884 – were the companies writing a lot of marine, aviation and transport business, forming the Institute of London Underwriters (ILU). Some 100 years later, the ILU had more than 100 members including all the major UK composite insurers such as Commercial Union, General Accident and other household names, and accounted for roughly half the marine business written in London and more than two-thirds of the aviation cover. In 1987, the year of the first big UK windstorm, its members pulled in £2 billion worth of premiums net of brokers' commissions, mostly in US dollars.

Much later than the ILU – in 1977 – the insurance companies writing non-marine and reinsurance business formed a Policy Signing and Accounting Centre, now known as the London Insurance and Reinsurance Market Association or LIRMA. It is owned by its members, who in 1987 wrote premium income of $1.4 billion plus £700 million from UK and other international insurances. Lloyd's brokers – the LIBC members – not only placed insurance at Lloyd's but with ILU and LIRMA members too, and in the late 1980s were bringing in over £5 billion worth of business a year to these three organizations which together effectively compose the London insurance underwriting market.

All these bodies had been formed to cut costs and to speed efficiency. But with the passage of time they too began to look unwieldy, especially in the light of moves by American insurers to use new 'data systems' to keep their overhead costs down. By 1979 the then chairman of Lloyd's was concerned that his Society would lose its competitive edge, and began an intensive campaign to try to persuade Lloyd's underwriters and brokers of the wisdom of switching away from manual record-keeping and amassing a mountain of paper, to using electronic methods of processing business, keeping records and doing accounts.

It met with little success at first. People were, in the main, making good money at Lloyd's just then and cost-control and analysis were not great priorities during the drive to recruit more Names to provide the capacity to write all the business the market was sure was out there. It was only when insurance rates came under increasing pressure around the world as the industry went into oversupply; and as the extent of the asbestos, pollution and catastrophe losses dawned on the market that underwriters felt it was worth applying late-twentieth century technology to this seventeenth-century society; and the idea of co-operating and pooling resources to explore the application of a unified approach really took root. By this time, speed was essential – and with up to 400 syndicates, plus the 220 Lloyd's brokers who would also need to participate in any major technological development in their principal market-place, and given the complexity of assessing and underwriting many insurance risks, any form of computerizing the business of insurance was going to be a major task. Having been slow to accept the need, the market went into overdrive in the early 1990s to develop a practical system.

Many Lloyd's brokers are owned by or part of much larger insurance broking groups that place business all over the world with powerful overseas insurance companies as well as UK ones and Lloyd's of London. Many of them had already developed in-house technology of their own, and direct computer links with the insurance groups who were frequent takers of their business. The insurance groups also had their own systems. It therefore made sense for Lloyd's and its coterie of Lloyd's brokers to get together with all the companies at an early stage to collaborate on developing a system that could talk quickly and efficiently to everybody right across the London market.

So, in June 1987, Lloyd's of London, the LIBC, the ILU and the forerunner of LIRMA had all agreed to form a body that they christened the London Insurance Market Network or, sticking to the industry's fondness for initials and mnemonics, LIMNET. The idea was to establish an electronic exchange-of-information system between all four participants. US computer giant IBM was roped in to provide the basic facility that would allow their various existing computers to interconnect – PCs as well as mainframes – and into which underwriters with their own computerized in-house record-keeping systems could plug their PCs for access to the new network. Creating a network like this also made it easy to add in additional services like access to information services such as newswire Reuters, financial news gatherer Extel, and on-line newspaper and magazines article library service Texline; and of course to on-line information from the market's very own newspaper, *Lloyd's List*.

The central aim of the LIMNET project was to improve the service and efficiency of the wider London insurance market, cutting out unnecessary duplication of information, reducing the paper mountain, and widening the scope for the London market to bring in more business. To lay the groundwork for this bold project, Lloyd's decided to overhaul its own three-tier claims services to develop a single, unified claims office based in the 1958 Lloyd's building out of which the underwriting room had moved to start business, on 27 May 1986, in the high-tech new building put up on the site of the market's previous, 1928 home.

In preparation for the switchover to a unified claims office, all syndicates would first have to form up in groups as members of the existing claims office serving their principal market (aviation, marine, non-marine), the Committee of Lloyd's (which oversaw the general business of the Society) announced in September 1988 – and they would be required in the course of 1990 to join the new London Insurance Market Network.

Gradually the project gathered momentum. The four bodies behind the initiative held a workshop in March of 1990 on the electronic placing of insurance business, and concluded that a common design of system was definitely the right path. So they set up a feasibility study which in May spawned a project steering group, a broker/underwriter business panel and a system working party to start beavering away on the idea. By November 1990 the London Network Management Committee or LMNC (Lloyd's spawns almost as many bodies and initials as it has underwriting syndicates) had produced a detailed proposal for a system that would allow the electronic placing of insurance risks across the whole London market. Assessing and planning the new system was itself becoming quite an industry. In early 1991 'the Network Steering Group (NSG) established a Placing Working Group (PWG) whose initial task was to consider how Lloyd's should proceed with the implementation of the Joint Market Initiative (JMI)', a briefing document solemnly announced. The working group reported back to the steering group that April, which in turn put the proposals to the Business Issues Committee of Lloyd's and thus they percolated up to the Committee of Lloyd's for approval that May: a stately, but no longer slow, progress.

Picking one's way through all the different initials and functions was like picking a path through a tangle of computer cables. But, considering that the entire project now involved developing a system that could be accessed by and handle the needs of 350 Lloyd's syndicates, 117 insurance companies belonging to the ILU, another 134 belonging to LIRMA and 220 Lloyd's brokers (total: 821 organizations), plus the surveyors, loss adjusters, lawyers, assessors and others who were likely to want to be able to plug into LIMNET as well, things were now actually happening quite fast.

The Placing Working Group had concluded that the electronic placing system should be developed in two stages. Phase A would work out what was needed to get to a basic system of electronic placing of firm orders, telling the signing office what lines had been written by whom, updating the underwriters' record and getting information and the update back to the broker – including the legal and auditing considerations of switching to electronic information systems. Finally this phase would also involve consciousness-raising in the market so that practitioners became aware 'of the potential of networking' and traditionalists' scepticism could be overcome.

At Lloyd's, some underwriters had custom-built in-house computer systems, some used computer bureaux services' packages, with links into the LPSO for signing the 'messages' that replaced slips, while others just had simple back office links to their own boxes in the underwriting room. All these had to be able to access each other via LIMNET, as did the brokers' systems, and the network needed to be flexible enough to allow communications ranging from the Lloyd's broker's PC talking to the underwriter's PC – which would be one of a wide variety of on-screen record-keeping systems being used by many underwriters at their boxes – to being used at the box or insurance office by both broker and underwriter together.

As a market-wide switching system, LIMNET also had to be accessible to the insurance companies with whom the brokers also did business. Ultimately, all claims and premiums would be processed via the network, and this too needed to be integrated with the new electronic gadgetry of the largeinsurance companies that was going into a big new London Underwriting Centre (LUC) – created by the large insurance companies, who in 1988 had decided to club together to find and share underwriting office space efficiently in a new building close to Lloyd's.

Having established what was needed, Phase A moved to a pilot scheme for electronically placing fairly standard risks and began to operate, with the help of committed guinea pigs from Lloyd's who participated first in a series of dummy runs. This allowed brokers to put the risks on offer on screen, let underwriters access them, indicate if they were interested, ask for further information or even a visit by the broker, or set a premium and then confirm, or decline the risk. Eight Lloyd's brokers (including Sedgwick, Willis Faber – of Willis Corroon – Minet Group, and C.E. Heath) and underwriters from some fifteen managing agencies (including giants Merrett and Sturge), covering forty to fifty syndicates between them, took part. Once any gremlins had been dealt with on a series of dummy transactions, the pilot was to go 'live' in the spring of 1992 with the guinea pigs using it to place and underwrite real insurance risks in legally binding deals.

If all went well thereafter, the hope was that Phase A would go market-wide for those who wished to plug into LIMNET; and would allow underwriters to log their transactions using fewer but more expert staff, cutting administration costs while speeding up the processes and cutting out laborious paperwork, thereby freeing both underwriters and the brokers to spend more, better quality time on the difficult risks and to generate more business for the London market. No one's need was more urgent by this stage than Lloyd's own.

Meanwhile Phase B would look into an electronic system for getting a range of quotes for a line of business, settlement and claims procedures. Experimenting with this depended 'on getting Phase A bedded in' but hopes were high that the pilot for Phase B could be started by the autumn of 1992.

Lloyd's underwriters were not the only ones needing a mixture of encouragement and arm-twisting to accept that there could be benefits from using new technology. ILU members – the companies insuring or reinsuring chiefly marine and aviation risks – also found some of their older underwriters preferred to rely on the human brain. Techno-fear was rife; but their Institute set to, with training programmes for underwriters and for brokers. With a huge upsurge in losses at sea in 1991 in the wake of already loss-making 1988, 1989 and 1990 years, and with many costly claims coming in from non-marine insurance, written perhaps too willingly as part of a wider package deal for a broker's client when there was plenty of rivalry for his business, the corporate insurers and reinsurers began to find it useful to make clearer breakdowns of what they had been covering and see where the claims had notched up.

At Lloyd's, too, managing and members' agents were grudgingly beginning to recognize that greater computer-aided analysis of business written could be a very useful tool in assessing likely claims and calls and helped underwriters know just where they were at any one time. But there was no intention of doing away with the Lloyd's underwriting room nor of corporate insurers totally replacing face-to-face dealings between underwriter and broker, which would still be required by all parties for complex risks that needed a lot of discussion and assessment. Indeed it was to facilitate brokers getting around the company and the Lloyd's markets, and to pool the high costs of office space in the City of London, that insurance companies belonging to LIRMA (companies writing non-marine business) had decided in 1988 to band together to establish and fit out the new London Underwriting Centre.

They picked a modern gothic creation, all high-pitched roofs and a honeycomb of pink cladding, that was being built as an investment by the life insurance group, Prudential Corporation, just a stone's throw from the Lloyd's building and not far from the ILU home of the insurance groups writing predominantly marine and aviation risks. (The Pru had lent Lloyd's the money for its new building a decade earlier.)

Twenty-four LIRMA companies formed a property investment company, prosaically called Market Building Limited (MBL), and took a lease on the building, at 3 Minster Court. Taking it over at the shell-and-core phase, in order to kit it out to the insurance underwriting industry's special needs, MBL embarked on an ambitious £46.3 million fitting-out programme. Between 80 and 100 of LIRMA's 134 insurance and reinsurance members, including overseas groups, agreed to move their City of London underwriting operations into the new building and were allotted their floor space in a ballot run by author (and Lloyd's Name) Jeffrey Archer in May 1990. Others took office space at numbers 1 and 2 in the same development, to be close by. Number 3 was supposed to be ready for its tenants to move into in the spring of 1992, complete with high-tech touch screens in brokers' offices and sophisticated cabling systems and floor boxes for links into and out of the building with third-party services . . . and, of course, coffee shops, harking back to the insurance industry's collective origins. A commission for a sculpture of three large horses in the building's courtyard was promptly nicknamed Sterling, Dollar, and Yen. But, just as the fitting-out of the building was nearing its final phase – and after £26.3 million had been spent on the work so far – a disastrous fire broke out on 7 August 1991 on the upper ground floor of the building. Found at 7.20 a.m. by security staff the blaze rapidly turned into one of London's worst fires that year and, though firemen were there within seven minutes, took 100 firefighters with 20 fire engines until 10.45 a.m. to bring under control.

The fire burned straight up through the central atrium, wrecking upper floors, until the atrium finally blew out with the heat, and the fire was vented – leaving the building's twenty-four lead tenants, who had also insured it, and their reinsurers, with a £110 million bill for the damage and fears that it could finally be a £150 million repair job. Commercial Union's share alone of the tab after reinsurance was £11 million. Horses Sterling, Dollar and Yen were not affected by the drama. But the fire 'sets the LUC back a long way from having it up and running,' said a rueful Victor Blake of CNA Reinsurance, the chairman of the LUC and of MBL and the man whose vision the new market-place had really been. The new centre would not now be open before the autumn of 1993, he thought.

But there was one positive aspect to the delay. It opened up the possibility of bringing ILU members into the refurbished building as well as most of LIRMA's, turning the LUC into a market-place where marine and non-marine business could all be conducted under one roof, just as they were by the brotherhood of syndicates over at Lloyd's. Brokers would only have to trot between two buildings to conduct face-to-face business: one housing the corporate insurers and the other the market composed of groups of sole traders at Lloyd's. Costs and time would also be saved.

For things had changed since the LUC plan had been conceived – market forces had taken their toll of the insurance company sector. The same tough competition for underwriting business and downward pressure on insurance premiums that had weakened Lloyd's in its hour of need had had a similar (though less life-threatening) effect in the four years since 1988 on members of LIRMA and of the ILU. Losses from the catastrophes in particular had been painful for them, too, though they had the advantage over Lloyd's in a sense of being able to report those at the end of the financial year they happened in and take the losses on the chin before Lloyd's, with its minimum three-year accounting for all risks, could do so.

Marine insurance was not growing. Recession in the shipping industry had seen to that. Aviation had taken over and there was therefore a diminishing base of business for the marine underwriters belonging to the ILU. Weaker companies had ceased writing new business in London or found merger partners to create stronger new combines. Others had consolidated their own subsidiaries into larger single units. The net effect was a dip in the ILU's membership to 101 by the start of 1992, with one more member expected to leave in the course of the year. Some companies with both marine and non-marine divisions belonged to the ILU and to LIRMA anyway, and the trend in both bodies of the number of corporate insurers metamorphosing into fewer but stronger players looked set to continue in the period leading up to the LUC's new late-1993 target opening date. As a result, its champion Victor Blake reckoned that

> merging could now get two pints into a one-and-a half pint jug, with a bit of tailoring and streamlining.
>
> On the day of the fire we had 94 per cent occupancy planned and about sixty subtenants signed up [in addition to the 24 shareholders in the enterprise] but now we have some duplication of space and some tenants won't proceed because their own circumstances have changed. So occupancy is down to 75 per cent and that leaves 25 per cent available to the ILU and with amalgamations that gives a further saving so we could get the two in together okay. The ILU occupies between 60,000 and 70,000 square feet and 25 per cent of the LUC is 50,000 square feet. It's in the lap of the gods and could take a lot of persuasion and negotiation but no one is quarrelling with the logic of the idea.

ILU members, early in 1992, were less excited by the idea, but not totally dismissive.

Lloyd's, too was suffering from mergers and consolidations, closing one floor of the underwriting 'room'. Like it, ILU members had been dealt a hefty blow by the catastrophes and high accident rates of 1988, and 1989 and 1990. By the close of 1992 ILU members (of whom around 60 per cent were large foreign insurance or reinsurance groups) accounted for about 60 per cent of the marine insurance written in London: stealing quite a march on Lloyd's traditional patch. But it was not profitable business because of the increasingly high rate of casualties at sea.

Structural failure was often suspected to be the cause of this rising tide. The age of many ships, cost-cutting by shipowners in the teeth of recession resulting in poorer quality maintenance and crew training, and the new corporate breed of shipowners putting more pressure on captains to cut corners and bolster profit margins than old family shippers would have done, all played a part.

In 1991 total losses at sea were the worst since the mid-1980s in terms of the number of ships, and the worst since 1980–1 in tonnage terms. That year 182 ships were lost, up from a bad-enough 130 in 1990, a 30 per cent increase and the highest loss since the marine insurance industry's worst ever losses in

1979 and 1980. In terms of tonnage the loss was even greater, at 40 per cent and 1,708,464 tons gross. Then there had been a clear reason (tankers exploding while in ballast, 'solved by underwriters insisting on inert gas systems being installed,' the ILU recalled). Not so this time.

Claims in 1992 just against ILU members totalled £4.069 billion against premiums written of £2.21 billion. Realizing that they could not go on taking hits like this, the marine insurance industry managed to push to turn the tide of falling marine premium rates, but not yet by enough. Preventive action was also needed, and in January 1992 the ILU introduced new guidelines for underwriters on when to seek warranties on a ship's structural condition and insist on checks. Tanker and bulk carriers of 12 years old and more were prime candidates and all other vessels aged 15-plus. The insurance industry often finds itself in the role of the setter of safety standards for an industry, by refusing cover on risks that do not meet certain requirements – usually after a run of bad claims, however.

Exploring the benefits to its own business of investing in new technologies, and ending the duplication of cost and effort by concentrating on a unified, market-wide system, fitted the same pattern. When losses get too great, the insurance industry can be very agile and inventive. For the companies, the move had been left a little late, but not too late. Lloyd's was in deeper trouble than the companies, however. For one thing, they felt very little impact from the asbestos problems that had dealt Lloyd's such a blow, and only some hurt from the mounting pollution question in the USA. But they did share in the industry's other problems: the cost of the recent upsurge in catastrophes and other accidents; and how to raise insurance premium rates. They also had another problem, one related to Lloyd's but not quite the same. Lloyd's had for so long been the focal point of the London insurance market, particularly in the USA, that its troubles impacted on everyone else's image too. The fight was on to prove to US clients and brokers that the rest of the London market was still alive and well, and at the forefront of developments in the international insurance industry, whatever happened to Lloyd's of London.

14
Staying Alive

*A person seldom falls sick but the bystanders
are animated with a faint hope that he will die*

(RALPH WALDO EMERSON, *CONDUCT OF LIFE: CONSIDERATIONS
BY THE WAY*)

February 1992 was not a good month for the Council of Lloyd's. The scene was set for a rough ride ahead at the end of January, when the independent forecaster, Chatset, predicted that Lloyd's total losses on cover and reinsurance written in the four years between 1989 and 1991 inclusive could rapidly top £3 billion and continue to rise over a twenty-year period (during which Names on open years would be trapped) to as high as £6 billion. Lloyd's, it said, was effectively insolvent and could go belly-up very soon.

Then the Outhwaite settlement of 11 February, designed to resolve one problem, merely fuelled new ones. The working Names who had toed the party line and not joined in the legal action were none too pleased at being left out when the E&O insurers capitulated at the chairman of Lloyd's request and paid out those who had run the gauntlet of the Council's scorn and sued.

'The mood in the glass house is very sour,' reported a Name from the Feltrim Names Association, whose membership was growing daily as people from all walks of life joined in haste for fear of missing out on any settlements that might emerge for Feltrim litigants post the Neill loss review report now expected that spring. Rebellion was brewing in the coffee pot and the mounting pressure lifted the lid dramatically. On 12 February Labour politicians, rarely the friend of the fleeced rich, sprang into the attack on practices within Lloyd's that had contributed to the huge losses.

Tory MPs who had themselves lost money on stricken Lloyd's syndicates had, a newspaper report said, 'declared political war on its management' and handed copies to new Labour allies of a thirteen-page briefing document on the allegations of insiders creaming off the best business for favoured syndicates and dumping the dross on 'dustbin' syndicates composed largely of external Names. Labour MPs Brian Sedgemore and Dennis Skinner – habitual scourges of the financially dodgy who, now that conman Peter Clowes of Barlow Clowes who defrauded thousands of elderly savers and had just been jailed, were short of a target – promptly tabled five Commons motions on the contents. Labour's City affairs spokeswoman Marjorie Mowlam wrote to the Tory Minister for Corporate Affairs John Redwood – on the eve of a meeting he was to hold with Tory MPs and representatives of Names action groups – urging him to mount a full-scale independent investigation into the conduct of insurance underwriting at Lloyd's.

'Lloyd's should be brought under an independent financial regime equivalent to the Financial Services Act,' she told the *Independent* newspaper which on 13 February led the front page with the banner headline, 'Tories declare war on Lloyd's.'

It was the Council of Lloyd's own worst nightmare – bar the actual meltdown of the market. It had spent the whole of the 1980s trying to avoid being landed with an external regulator. Now it had enraged its natural political friends, the Conservatives. Fingers were pointed once again at Chairman David Coleridge's poor PR skills. He had been given a rough ride only a few hours after the announcement of the Outhwaite settlement, at a meeting of the Tory backbench finance committee, and had, by all accounts, not made a good impression on his audience. Once again Lloyd's had come across as being arrogant, insular, and unconcerned about putting the 'primacy of client interest' above the interests of the boys making the market. One Name said, 'They don't seem to know what a conflict of interest is.'

Meanwhile the Names following Michael Freeman's advice were refusing to pay their calls, and seeking injunctions to prevent the money being drawn-down from the funds held on their behalf at Lloyd's. Accusations were bandied about that the insider 'baby' syndicates of the best business, banned in the 1980s, had not ceased but graduated to less recherché but still pretty exclusive 'adolescent' syndicates, offered the choicest business by brokers who were also Names on them.

Lloyd's faced Valentine's Day that year in receipt only of brickbats and no bouquets. It had been a traumatic period since the 15 January unveiling of the Task Force report: the Council's enthusiastic reception of most of the recommendations had been totally overshadowed by its inept handling of its rejection of the 'governance' section and then its rapid capitulation and agreement to study it. On 29 January 1992 it sailed into a fresh storm over whether the 1991 year would show a recovery in its underwriting fortunes or fresh losses, as predicted by Chatset, the widely followed independent analyst of business at Lloyd's that had been launched in November 1981 by a breakaway group of Names who were worried then about Lloyd's lack of analysis of the business conducted in the market.

Two weeks later the Outhwaite settlement was hailed as a tacit admission that all had not been well in the way US general liability reinsurance had been placed in the past, with Names being taken for an expensive ride by a market which had thrown the concept of *uberrimae fidei* to the winds. And now the market's Tory heartland had joined forces with the rabid left and was out for its blue blood.

'David Coleridge is simply unable to deal with the situation, and I believe the government, whether Labour or Tory, will have to step in and deal with it after the election,' said Canadian Ken Lavery in February, watching the furore from his Florida holiday home.

Lloyd's had been livid when Chatset's moving forces Charles Sturge and John Rew (founder members of the original breakaway group's other creation, the Association of Lloyd's Members) had told their press conference on 29 January that they believed continuing calls and provisions at Lloyd's during calendar 1991 on business written by syndicates in 1988, 1989 and 1990 would take the market-place's combined losses on those three years' underwriting through the £3 billion barrier. It based its prediction that the tally could rise gently over the following twenty years to between £4 billion and £6 billion on a guesstimate of the sort of claims that might still trail in against the business written and reinsured during the 1980s' old and open years.

'We expect Names' deposits to be wiped out by 1994 when the 1991 account is calculated,' they announced, declaring that this meant Lloyd's was continuing to trade while insolvent.

This was dramatic and pretty sweeping stuff. Lloyd's was furious and disputed the figures hotly. It was terrified that these forecasts would wreck its rearguard action to convince present members and the potential future Names it was so anxious to tempt out into the open, that Lloyd's would once again be a safe and profitable haven for their wealth once the faster-track recommendations in the Rowland Report had been implemented.

A new, politically inspired investigation and Lloyd's Act might slow that urgent remedial action down, and without new capital flowing in with which to write new business, and earn an income for syndicates to pay claims out of, Lloyd's really could be looking at meltdown – particularly if thousands of Names rebelled that summer and refused to pay their calls. The Central Fund did not have £1 billion in it to meet all the troubled syndicates' needs, which is what it would have to do in the short-term to maintain Lloyd's tradition of having the funds ready to meet claims quickly; and it would take months if not years to try and wrest the money out of recalcitrant Names through the courts. This would also be bad publicity and offputting to potential new Names, assuming Lloyd's survived round one of this scenario.

If the whole burden of the £750 million to £1 billion shortfall between syndicates' estimated liabilities and the £350 million assets called so far fell on the Central Fund, the levy on Names that financed it would have to be increased dramatically as Michael Freeman had forewarned. But would the dissidents pay it, and would the docile ones rebel at being stuck with the bill for the others' losses? It was a very sticky question.

Far from the small return to profit tentatively being forecast by Lloyd's practitioners for the 1991 year of underwriting that had just ended, Chatset anticipated a fourth year of massive losses in the pipeline on that period's underwriting. It also reckoned 1990's losses could prove far worse than everyone else expected when its final reckoning was done in early 1993. Even its more immediate estimate for the 1989 year's global losses of Lloyd's syndicates, due to be revealed in June, exceeded Lloyd's own predictions. Chatset thought those losses would be not less than £1.35 billion. Though admitting that news of a record loss was in the offing, Lloyd's itself was talking more in terms of £1 billion – some £350 million less than Chatset's figure.

Chatset claimed that Lloyd's would not be properly back in the black ink until its 1992 year was closed. Rates were at last hardening, costs reducing, and better quality underwriting should be drawing in enough cash again to cover insurance claims and leave a profit for the Names once more; but under Lloyd's three-year accounting system, they would have to wait until 1995 before the return to profitability could be confirmed and the surplus parcelled out to Names. In the meantime, the spectre of three more years of gloomy results news stalked the gleaming escalators of the Lloyd's building.

Chatset's prognostications were bitterly contested by Lloyd's; but the fuming Society was handicapped by its own lack of in-depth analysis of what was afoot in the market, relying instead on the gut feel of its better underwriters to give the lie to Chatset's forecasts and hope to be vindicated later. 'We just don't have the figures,' one insider bemoaned to another.

Chatset's estimate of a £1.35 billion loss on 1989's underwriting included forecasts of 'pure' losses for that year of £610 million on marine underwriting, a £385 million shortfall on non-marine business but modest profits of £30 million from the motor account and of £85 million from aviation insurance, the only two areas of Lloyd's reach seemingly in reasonable shape. In the event, the figures announced on 24 June to a shocked 5,600 Names who had gathered in the underwriting Room to hear the 1989 results were of a £2.06 billion loss by the market on that year's underwriting. Just five syndicates – Rose Thomson Young's 255, Feltrim's 540 and 847, and Gooda Walker 290 and 298 contributed 34 per cent of the £2 billion loss, while between them syndicates run by just two managing agencies, Gooda Walker (at 25 per cent) and Feltrim (at 12 per cent) accounted for 37 per cent of it.

The extent of the Gooda Walker damage had only been realized in the final days before the annual meeting, as the GW Run-Off agency, created to sort out the syndicates' troubles after the collapse of their managing agency, struggled to find order among the tangled ruins of the LMX spiral.

The £2 billion loss included a 'pure' underwriting loss of £1.373 million (compared to a £431 million profit in 1988), a £398 million strengthening of reserves (£578 million in 1988) and personal expenses of £292 million. Motor and aviation business had made profits of £52 million and £16 million respectively, and 146 syndicates of Lloyd's then 487 syndicates had actually made money for their Names. The other 244 actively underwriting syndicates had not. (Another 97 were in run-off in 1989 and therefore had not been underwriting any new business.)

Two-thirds of the 1989 Names had lost less than 15 per cent of their annual premium limit – but others, especially on some LMX syndicates, were knocked sideways. There was a huge disparity in the success or failure of LMX syndicates: some had made a profit of 25 per cent of Names' premium limits; the worst had lost 368 per cent of its premium limit.

Marine underwriting had made a market-wide (or 'Lloyd's global loss') of £821 million, and non-marine syndicates had between them lost £1.149 billion. Reserves made by stop-loss underwriters against potential claims feeding on through to them also created a £125 million double-counting effect at syndicate level, which did not feed through to the global results.

Syndicates' losses in 1989 on four major catastrophes were calculated at: $1.5 billion for the Exxon Valdez oil-tanker spill, $5.8 billion for Hurricane Hugo, $1.5 billion for the San Francisco earthquake and $1.5 billion for the Phillips Pasadena oil-refinery explosion.

David Coleridge spent over six hours explaining the results and answering every question raised by Names that afternoon. His marathon performance won praise from some of his listeners. Emerging to meet the television cameras afterwards, he looked drained.

The market's extreme peril had now finally sunk in. But when an extraordinary general meeting (EGM) forced upon the Council by rebel Names was held a few weeks later, Coleridge's team won an overwhelming postal vote of confidence in the Council, which endorsed its plans to press ahead with introducing the Task Force recommendations. Initially the Council had only meant to take a show of hands at the EGM; but earlier protests from Names had persuaded it of the need to hold the postal ballot. Now Coleridge had a clear mandate for the changes he planned for the second half of his final year in office.

In its estimates for 1990's final result, due in mid-1993, Chatset had forecast 'pure' losses of £700 million. As for 1991, though it was early days yet, Chatset reckoned the year could ultimately lose another 4 per cent of Lloyd's combined premium limits (or its 'Stamp') or around £400 million. And that was before taking account of four major catastrophes that had struck in the final quarter of 1991, including Japanese typhoon Mireille which could cost the London market (companies and Lloyd's) around $450 million, though most of the bill rested with domestic insurers. There were also C$800 million of damage from a hailstorm in Calgary, Canada though again not all of that would trickle through to London; fires in Oakland, California; and the 'medium-sized' Hurricane Bob with which to conjecture. If Chatset were right, Lloyd's (if it still existed) would be dogged by cash calls and bad news of high losses on recent underwriting until nearly half-way through the decade.

Lloyd's went into attack. The 1991 forecast in particular was 'conjectural', 'reckless', 'a stab in the dark' (and, officials and practitioners clearly felt, in the back too), 'irresponsible' and 'deeply disturbing for Names'. Lloyd's officials and large underwriters were wheeled out to reiterate their conviction that the 1991 year should turn out to be profitable. But, by early 1993, it was clear that both 1990 and 1991 would indeed lose large sums.

Insurance rates had finally taken a turn for the better around the world. Underwriters were warier of the business they underwrote and the terms of policies were improving. But the flood of calls to build up reserves to fund feared future asbestos and pollution claims was still rising and infecting previously sound syndicates, which had provided the stop-loss and E&O cover for the damaged syndicates and now feared high claims.

There was an outside chance that, if important US Appeal Court cases on whether or not pre-1986 general liability policies did cover persistent pollution went the insurers' way, with such big reserves now in place, syndicates would be able to pay out a higher proportion of their underwriting income in future. The switch from wallowing in stormy seas to catching the favourable wind and sailing into profit could, when it came, be fast and extremely welcome. But how likely was a change in the insurance climate to help Lloyd's; had the old market like some of the ships it insured, patched over too many holes too haphazardly in the past to take the cannon fire coming its way now and remain seaworthy?

Others outside, but nevertheless close observers, of the Lloyd's market thought the old tub would find room for manoeuvre on that front yet.

Oliver Carruthers, a consultant to Chatset whose own private publishing venture the newsletter *Digest of Lloyd's News* was one of the few sources for Names of news about events and developments at Lloyd's, reckoned he could pinpoint 'the start of the avalanche' of cash calls to 26 April 1991 when an underwriter called Ian Agnew had announced that he planned to make huge reserves to cover any advices of claims on pollution cases outstanding to cover his syndicates' backs.

'From that point on everyone started making provisions,' Carruthers pointed out. 'It was the trigger point. It was the reserving that gave us the 1988 loss announced in 1991. We had a pure year profit until then.' If the need to make such big reserves faded away, profits could again be the order of the day. But which day?

Even in the fateful year of 1988 Lloyd's syndicates had earned £431.5 million after claims on that year's underwriting. True, this was quite a drop from the £1,305.6 million – just over £1.3 billion – earned on the insurance cover written in 1987, but then 1988 had been a year of exceptional catastrophes. Reserves had been substantially strengthened in 1987, too, by £796.4 million in fact, but that all came out of the £1.3 billion profit and still left £509.2 million over to be distributed to the Names. No problem; no panic. Even during the early months of 1991, Lloyd's had been anticipating a similar pattern and a profit of some sort on 1988's underwriting year when the sums were done at the close of 1991.

Then there was a sudden change of sentiment. A black pall of pollution worries blew into the City, settled over the market and blotted out its profits, when more managing agents decided that spring (or were advised by their auditors) to beef up their syndicates' reserves against US pollution clean-up costs that might be claimed for under old general liability policies already reinsured into the 1988 year. If decisions in the US courts went against the insurers, Lloyd's £431.5 million profit would not be enough to foot the bill. So, in 1991 Lloyd's syndicates hastily made huge additional reserves for 1988's old and open year liabilities, of £941.2 million, that is in addition to the sum set aside for 1987 – 'and only time will tell if they over-reacted,' says Carruthers. But time was running out.

Over-reaction or not, the drama caused by the high reserving, and the huge cash calls to meet it, added urgency to the Task Force report and force to its conclusions. Without these losses focusing minds at Lloyd's on the market's other problems – its excessive and uncompetitive cost base which had been rising when insurance rates were weak or falling, squeezing the potential profit out of the market like the cream out of a squashed éclair; the old guard's arrogant and out-dated attitude to Names and managing agents' secretiveness and reluctance to provide useful comparative information about syndicates' performance; their resistance to modern analytical techniques just when Lloyd's most needed the savings, efficiency and edge to be gained from embracing new technologies; an inwardness and reluctance to measure itself against competitors and the loss of business that resulted – all these might not have been examined quite so seriously, nor the need for some rapid changes been so quickly accepted when the Task Force reported. At first it looked as if the exodus of old Names caused by these losses, and the spectre of no influx of new ones to provide the market's capital base for the future, had galvanized the old guard into action to the relief of the brighter younger practitioners who were growing fearful that the older generation had squandered their inheritance and their future. But the events between 15 January and Valentine's Day 1992 threatened to turn the young guard into palace revolutionaries. Members' agents who had toed the Lloyd's line, and advised Names not to get involved in what had promised to be lengthy and costly Outhwaite litigation with (said Lloyd's) no chance of winning, were particularly angry. They now faced possible writs from their Names for negligent advice. The Council was in very bad odour with these agents now.

Some things had already self-corrected. The LMX spiral having overheated, died down to sensible rates and levels of reinsurance. After such large reserves having to be made against LMX business, reinsurance became harder to get on certain business and cost more. This priced silly business out of the market. The swing was already under way in 1988. Some underwriters had also scaled back the amount of stop-loss they would write, and raised their premium rates on it, because asbestos problems had already triggered thousands of these policies in the mid-1980s and they could see the business was no longer profitable for their own Names. Sadly for many Names who had been caught up in the upward spiral of cash calls to build up reserves, this had meant many of them were advised against taking out pricey stop-loss cover in the one year when they turned out really to have needed it. Names' purchases of stop-loss had peaked in 1987, when 16,600 of them covered their positions to a varying degree this way, and dwindled to 12,500 in 1991; while the average price per policy leapt from £1,223 in 1987 to £2,408 by 1990 and rose again to £2,841 in 1991. The trigger point for exercising the policies also rose, from losses ranging between 11.2 per cent of the Names' overall premium limit or OPL that year (on average) in 1987 and 37 per cent of their OPL (after which any further losses reverted back to the unfortunate Name), to an average trigger point of losses in excess of 18.43 per cent of OPL in 1990 and up to around 50 per cent, after which any more losses again reverted to the Name. The 'excess' point eased back to 16 per cent on average in 1991 as fewer people bought this cover.

It was the sudden difficulty in getting stop-loss cover and the higher cost of it in 1988 that fuelled the suspicions of those caught up in the pollution scramble that some underwriters knew something that others did not and that they, the Names, had been legged over as a result. In the end, market forces took over – those cold, unfeeling and often violent currents finally stirring after several years of lying dormant at Lloyd's. The Rowland Committee's proposal for a mandatory high-level stop-loss scheme to cover losses of over 100 per cent of a Name's premium limit, to be run by Lloyd's itself, was designed to bring a degree of calm to this troubled water in future. But the problems of impoverished pre-1993 Names remained.

As 1992 dawned their best option, according to the Lloyd's hierarchy, was to stick around and hope to trade out of the problem – if they could still afford to and believed in a new dawn for Lloyd's. What they really meant was, stick around so *we* can trade out of trouble. The prescription looked less convincing to the patients after the Outhwaite settlement than before it. If Lloyd's was so terrified of its obligations being set down in case law that it was going to capitulate and come up with an attractive out-of-court settlement every time its practitioners looked like losing a case, then tough, purposeful, well-researched litigation suddenly had terrific allure. Lloyd's Names, once fleeced, were suddenly twice shy of having the wool pulled over their eyes.

Though doubted by most people in the market – which if the past was any indication, probably meant it was quite likely to happen – some observers still painted an escape scenario in which the need for high US pollution reserves could evaporate (given a run of court decisions in insurers' favour over there), and the calls cease overnight. Profits on subsequent years' underwriting would then be cushioned by the high new reserves and payouts to Names could be generous. Old Names who could hang on and remain in their syndicates could eventually get their money back in the form of comfortable annual distributions. It seemed a very roundabout way of getting one's money back, however, compared to the Outhwaite route. Besides, given 53 syndicates with between them 97 open underwriting years (at the end of 1991), few underwriters in 1992 dared forecast that the billion pounds in reserves against feared claims that had been built up at such a cost to Names could ever prove to be a surfeit.

Few of the victims will forget the pain and upset of the 1988 and 1989 years, and those on open years may never forgive the market. Had Lloyd's agencies generally been in better shape, leaner, fitter, more professional, more analytical in their approach to the business they were writing, less complacent and slipshod and more informative to the Names, the dramas and the losses need not have been so severe nor so painful for so many to weather. It would not have been able to escape them entirely, however; these were world-wide ills compounded at Lloyd's by arrogance, bad habits and complacency. It was a gentleman's club without many gentlemen, and not enough conscientious batmen either. The Rowland Task Force report provided Lloyd's with one blueprint to restore Names' bruised and battered faith in this 300-year-old market; and to look for new avenues of business. First his recommendations were adopted – then the man himself. He became chairman of Lloyd's at the start of 1993.

The rising generation of underwriters and brokers, men and women in their thirties and forties, are determined that Lloyd's will adapt in time to survive. As one Lloyd's man said, in the dark days of February 1992:

I don't minimize the gravity of some of the issues that face us. Lloyd's is in danger of being lost.

But the young turks who will be the next generation of leaders are not prepared to let the grass grow under their feet and wait for Buggins's turn. They have a lot of energy and are the people who can commit themselves to the future. They are not as willing or prepared as their predecessors to be content with allowing themselves to be moved by the tide, but to act as the agents of change and promote new directions through their own activities. This is very encouraging.

If they fail, Lloyd's will founder. Though a blow to the City of London's prestige, this would not necessarily be a tragedy; nor the end of London as a major world market for insurance and reinsurance, particularly of large marine and aviation insurance and cover. All the big international reinsurers are already in the City of London. The brokers who feed them business are there. The companies already do nearly half the insurance business conducted in the London market; and stiff competition has kept rates down internationally. If one big player falls by the wayside, it means more business for everyone else and less pressure on premiums. Provided they could repair the damage done to London's image by Lloyd's troubles, they might be able to cope very well indeed without it after all. These heretical thoughts were beginning to gain currency in the London insurance market in 1992.

Though Lloyd's was still regarded by many as synonymous with the London market, as the 1990s began it only accounted for 53 per cent of the £9 billion total non-life business written annually in London, with the big corporate insurers and reinsurers encroaching further and further on to its patch. While sympathetic, up to a point, they were not amused by the damage the upheavals peculiar to Lloyd's had done to the London market's image overseas and in particular in the important US market, where to most people 'Lloyd's' still meant 'London' and all who sail in her. In early 1992 the ILU, many of whose members are the London offices of foreign insurance and reinsurance companies and whose foreign-owned capital therefore underlies much of the strength of the London market, was actively promoting the company market to US clients and regulators as a vigorous alternative to Lloyd's; and members reported that some risks were indeed being brought to them, specifically as a safer market for the brokers' clients for the time being. The company market's lower cost base also helped. Though they could not escape the cyclical ups and downs of the wider insurance market, unlike Lloyd's the companies had cut their expenses back, enabling them to be much more competitive as they followed – or pushed – rates down in the late 1980s.

Like Lloyd's they had suffered from the familiar pattern of the insurance industry then: softening insurance rates, overcapacity in the industry, the wave of costly catastrophes triggering large claims and hefty underwriting losses, and more accidents as shipowners and construction groups, struggling with recession, cut corners, took greater risks and reduced training programmes. (There is always a general rise in claims put in during recessions;

fires increase, for example, some due to greater carelessness, some for more suspect reasons.)

Unlike Lloyd's, the corporate insurance market was largely untouched by the asbestos and pollution dramas, as most of the policies concerned had been reinsured at Lloyd's. On the other hand, the big UK companies did face a very nasty bill of their own, estimated in early 1992 at anything between £2 billion and £4 billion, for claims by building societies against mortgage guarantee policies issued in the 1988 housing boom that had now fallen flat, triggering a rising tide of house repossessions running at 80,000 a year by early 1992. Very little of this was reinsured at Lloyd's and for some of the big UK composite insurers it posed grave problems and serious losses just as they were trying to recover from the cost of the UK windstorms, snow damage and repairing houses with settlement cracks caused by severe drought.

ILU members also suffered what looked like being a worse marine claims record than Lloyd's on their 1992 underwriting, partly because of an upsurge in sinkings and other less grave incidents, partly because they now had more of this declining business than did Lloyd's, and partly because they (like some Lloyd's marine syndicates) had taken on some non-marine business packaged in with shipping cover and caught a cold on that. Brokers had persuaded them to do so to suit big clients wanting all-in-one cover at a time when marine rates were low and the more appropriate specialist underwriters even at Lloyd's would not take on some of the business – or not cheaply – which was thus palmed off on the ILU marine underwriters.

Lloyd's and the Lloyd's brokers had attracted nearly £1.68 billion to the United Kingdom in invisible export earnings in 1988; and the corporate insurers and reinsurers operating in London pulled in just over £2 billion, of which a fair proportion would have been attracted in originally by the lodestone of Lloyd's presence, often in lines of insurance spread between the two markets. They managed this despite being further handicapped on the world scene by a tough UK tax regime that refused allowances for the building up of strong reserves to meet anticipated calls, whereas huge European competitors such as the Munich Re enjoyed a much more sympathetic tax structure at home. This in part was blamed for some of the under-reserving that had gone on in the past at Lloyd's. Not being seen as tax-efficient for Names, the extra reserves had not been built. Managing agents taking these decisions protest too much now that it was all the taxman's fault, but there is no doubt that a more supportive attitude at the Inland Revenue now will help Names in future. In spring 1993, the Revenue transferred accounting for Names' tax from managing to members' agents – which speeds up tax relief against Names' losses. Despite its size and influence, London had accounted for just 5 per cent of the world non-life direct insurance premiums of $576 billion in 1989. America, being the biggest market for most things, took 46 per cent (Japan 11, West Germany 8 and France another 5 per cent). But of a marine insurance market worth $13.5 billion in premiums world-wide, Lloyd's of London alone took 18 per cent, and 20 per cent of the $2.4 billion premiums generated by the world aviation market.

While the corporate half of the London market shifted in its City seat at the start of 1992, lobbied the Inland Revenue, and began to position itself to cope with the side-effects of Lloyd's mounting peril, a handful of brave souls chose this moment to board Lloyd's wallowing ship. As 3,687 Names left, 118 walked up the gangplank. Why?

'Becoming a Lloyd's Name is a lonely pursuit at the moment,' agreed one of them, a youthful new working Name. 'But in 1991 underwriters have been improving their rates of premium and the terms and conditions, and likewise in reinsurance, and there is a real air of optimism for the 1992 year.' Marine rates had ceased to decline, aviation and motor were rising, and the quality of business written was improving. The intrepid newcomer spread his first year's underwriting between eleven syndicates, across all the four main arenas of business (marine, non-marine, aviation, motor) writing lines of £15,000 on ten of them and of £10,000 on the eleventh, and settling down to wait until his syndicates' 1992 year closes (he hopes) at the end of 1994 before he sees his first cheque, all being well, in 1995. But will his courage and optimism be rewarded or has he just made a ghastly mistake?

Can the changes now in progress turn Lloyd's of London round in time to survive the storms and make calm water? Opinion is deeply divided on whether it will survive much longer into its fourth centenary, or prove the biggest casualty of all of the boom and bust cycle generated in the mid-to-late 1980s. 'Lloyd's is finished,' say the siren voices of despair. 'There just isn't the money. Even if everyone wanted to pay, they can't.'

Practitioners tied to the mast at Lloyd's admit to severe difficulties ahead but argue that the market will come through the storm though in very different shape. This is their reply:

Over the centuries Lloyd's has shown tremendous resilience. With the exception of the Neill committee report into the protection of Names as sole traders versus other types of investor, all the other reforms have been self-generated. Certainly the next few years will not be easy for Lloyd's nor for the insurance industry world-wide. Lloyd's cannot escape the calamity that has befallen the world industry and which has its manifestations in the rest of our corporate competitors across the world.

Lloyd's exposes a lot at the surface because it is made up of 300 or so separate business units, the syndicates, all required to publish a report and account, while company subsidiaries can use all kinds of accounting.

But this is a market-place, and its essence and success rests on entrepreneurial spirit and ability to move at great speed. The problems are not insupportable. Ways will be found. They always are and they always will be. While history is not necessarily a precedent, three hundred years of it is a pretty good precedent and the market will change dramatically.

As Lloyd's struggled to find a way ahead in 1992, Sir David Walker of the Securities and Investment Board mulled over the final closure of the London Stock Exchange's trading floor that February, fully superseded now by screen- and telephone-based national and international securities dealings from stockbrokers' own offices. This, too, could lie in store for Lloyd's one day, as its practitioners grow accustomed to the wonders of new technology. It has brought far more international reach to the stockbroking industry than before.

The Lloyd's name may last, and perhaps the concept of sole traders grouped in syndicates; but the medium could be very different. While it might be sad for some to lose face-to-face trading one day, an end to the hothouse, clubby atmosphere might also mean a reduced risk of people quietly conspiring to look after each other before the Names.

Not long after seeing the old share-trading floor close, Sir David was asked by Lloyd's to oversee an independent working party to look into the twin allegations of 'insiders' in the insurance market protecting their own patch at others' expense by granting preferential access to some syndicates, and of boosting their income by recycling their worst risks through less-experienced players in the LMX spiral.

Lloyd's may have seen this as a necessary PR move to stave off mounting accusations from all sides, and the parliamentary fracas that had broken out; chairman David Coleridge had received a particularly rough ride from MPs and Names at a further meeting earlier in the same week as Sir David was suddenly appointed to lead the new working party. Lloyd's pointed out that a study by McKinsey, the management consultancy crunching numbers for the Rowland Report had found that insiders earned a 2.5 per cent return in

1985–8 to outsiders' 2.3 per cent. Names were not entirely convinced that these figures were correct, however, and on 4 March 1992 Lloyd's itself released data apparently showing a heavier proportion of working Names on the most profitable syndicates than on the biggest loss makers. Sir David, the man who had been very firm with the rest of the investment community on behalf of its customers, held his inaugural meeting the following day. Within less than a week of his appointment, he had told Tory MPs that he would call in a firm of outside auditors to help him check through computer records of LMX transactions; and said he would also be checking the syndicate membership of working Names' families. His conclusions are summarized in the next chapter.

It was becoming clear that Lloyd's survival would be a close-run thing. If she sank and went down fast, the down-draft and the waves would rock other insurers, reinsurers, brokers and the holders of Lloyd's policies – from British car drivers to vast companies – all around the world; to say nothing of the disastrous impact it would also have on Britain's balance of payments, in the short-term at least. If she were to sink slowly, for lack of new Names and new capital to underwrite new business, and a lack of good business on offer as brokers looked to safer carriers for their clients' insurance, the companies already clustered close to the large insurance brokers in the City of London would just move steadily into the vacuum, glad of the extra business available in a hitherto over-supplied insurance market.

As the remedial action began, there was talk that Lloyd's syndicates might seek the protection of some sort of incorporation under the Rowland corporate membership flag, with Names becoming their private shareholders and the new outfit operating as a specialist insurance company within a club of such specialist private underwriting firms. Might some wealthy Names take up the Rowland suggestion of individuals each forming a company in their own name to continue underwriting with the protection of limited liability? Would they put up far higher resources to capitalize their 'business' than the 1992 minimum requirement for 30 per cent of their premium limit to be deposited at Lloyd's? Other visions of the future included managing agencies owning specialist insurance brokers – rather than the other way round – if the 1982 Act's divestment clause were reversed.

Lloyd's Names will be more carefully picked in future; required to be richer, more able to meet cash calls easily from more liquid assets than hitherto insisted upon, and to deposit rather more of their funds at Lloyd's. But do the really rich need to take this risk with their money? And will they? The wealthier you are, the more you have to lose from unlimited liability if things go wrong, after all – and if you are filthy rich you don't need the cachet of being a Name, while the financially astute may prefer a higher return on their assets. Did Lloyd's appeal always really lie with the well-to-do rather than the rich, with people who hoped to become wealthier through their Lloyd's membership rather than those who had already hit the big time? If so Lloyd's could find a dearth of the rich new players that it has targeted as playing a vital role in its future.

Rewards on offer are usually a direct measure of the risk you are taking with your money; at Lloyd's the good returns of the 1970s and most of the 1980s were for many totally outstripped by the risks Names found they – or someone – had in fact been taking with their assets. Something very odd had skewed the risk:reward ratio way out of line. And, unlike banks or companies, Lloyd's in its 1992 manifestation could not just write off its troublesome liabilities, declare a loss, seal off the past from the future, and chalk it all up to experience. Legitimate claims against its old policies still have to be met in full. But if Lloyd's went under suddenly because Names' assets (or willingness to pay) and the Central Fund were exhausted, who would pay policy-holders' claims then?

Finally the Lloyd's hierarchy accepted that the losses of 1989, Names' solvency problems and the mounting cash calls, which many Names could not or would not meet, were indeed – as Michael Freeman and Chatset had warned – in danger of putting too much strain on the Central Fund. The fund, used to meet promptly (for the sake of policy holders) the obligations of Names who cannot pay their Lloyd's bills but who are subsequently pursued for the money, stood at around £500 million when, in the summer of 1992, a levy was announced. At 1.66 per cent on the 'stamp' of each syndicate's 1990, 1991 and 1992 years, it raised around £500 million and brought the fund up to £1 billion. The levy was met largely out of Names' funds held in trust at Lloyd's.

Liability for its old policies stays with its sole trader members, the Names. If they can't pay, and if there were nothing left in the Central Fund, then the policies would be worthless, leaving companies and their workforces, and customers, exposed. Big reinsurance groups might take on the better quality business in deals with shrinking syndicates while they still had cash to pay a reinsurance premium; but the salvage operation that would have to be mounted to pick up the pieces if Lloyd's foundered suddenly would dwarf all the dramas described in this book. To avoid that nightmare Lloyd's had to contemplate a more radical change than in any of its own previous three hundred years of life. After the shocks of June 1992, it went into overdrive to try to ensure that it would have a future as well as a considerable past.

15
Another day; Another Dollar?

| *The biggest corporation, like the humblest private citizen, must be held to strict compliance with the will of the people.*

(THEODORE ROOSEVELT, SPEECH, CINCINNATI, OHIO, 1902)

On Thursday, 9 April 1992, Britain went to the polls. In a close-fought general election, the Conservative party narrowly hung on to power for a fourth term in government. For Lloyd's, it was an even narrower squeak. Had the Labour party won, the insurance club would instantly have found itself facing the prospect of an independent regulator from outside its corner of the City of London, with *carte blanche* to shake up the place and sort out what one prominent Labour MP called its 'attitude problem' towards Names and commercial realities.

The stock market was relieved too, and shares soared the next day, putting some £26 billion on the value of the leading one hundred companies, in hectic trading. That Friday night, a week before Easter, as City workers and Lloyd's underwriters celebrated the election victory in the pubs and bars of the City of London or put the finishing touches to the week's work, a huge 100-lb terrorist bomb rocked the Square Mile. It was the Irish Republican Army showing Britain what it could do with five more years of Tory rule. The biggest terrorist explosion on the British mainland, the semtex bomb went off at 9.20 p.m. outside the Baltic Exchange in St Mary Axe, wrecking insurance group Commercial Union's 25-storey London headquarters, and blasting windows out of several floors of the Lloyd's building opposite the Commercial Union piazza. Floors inside the CU building collapsed, and glass and computer terminals rained down on to the streets. The front of the Baltic Exchange was wrecked, and offices all round the area were badly damaged. Two died instantly; ninety-one were hurt, mainly by the flying shards of glass. A third victim was found in the rubble the following day. The damage to buildings was estimated at £1 billion. Insurance claims finally totalled £300 million, of which £6 million fed through to Lloyd's.

Witness Darren Brown of Fulham was passing Lloyd's as the van containing the bomb blew up. 'I saw the building bulge,' he told *The Times* (whose staff at its own Wapping headquarters had heard and felt the bang). And Nick Phillips, general manager of the Lloyd's buildings, had this to say the morning after the blast: 'The building stood up extremely well. It obviously flexed but seems to have gone back again.'

North of the City, in the heart of the London Borough of Islington, the explosion was a dull roar like approaching thunder. A pall of smoke and debris could be seen hanging over the forty-plus-storey NatWest Tower, some of whose windows had also been shattered. The lights normally playing on the 1986 Lloyd's building had – temporarily – gone out.

The day before, when Britain's voters had taken advantage of the fine spring sunshine across most of the country to stroll out to their polling stations, Lloyd's had been privately squaring up to an increasingly explosive situation of its own and realizing that a major shake-up of its operations was now inevitable. In the previous few weeks of early 1992 there had been an upsurge of concern about new claims coming in from the USA as a result of various court hearings. This fuelled new worries that the club's aggregate losses for its 1989 year might exceed £2 billion – as indeed they did.

The culprits came from two main sources: savings and loans banks and property-damage claims for stripping out asbestos. Claims were now feeding through to Lloyd's against the professional indemnity written to cover the actions of directors and officers of American savings and loans (S&L) banks. These had run into trouble in their hundreds as boom turned to bust in the USA. The property market there had gone belly-up, taking with it many

S&Ls which in the 1980s had lent fortunes enthusiastically, but not always judiciously, to real-estate developers. The resultant collapses left stricken S&L depositors out of pocket, and the US authorities with a major save-and-rescue programme. Claims for recompense came through not only against the S&Ls' professional indemnity policies, but also against similar cover written for their advisers – their lawyers and accountants. Some claims also related to bankers' blanket bonds.

Nor was this all. Asbestosis again reared its ugly head, this time in the property damage suits now coming to a head. Bodily injury claims were still arising, but Lloyd's syndicates had hoped that US courts would not hold insurers responsible to the same degree for the full cost of stripping out the asbestos and rebuilding, for example, American schools built in the 1950s and 1960s. But by spring 1992 fears returned that US insurers and their reinsurers, including Lloyd's syndicates, were again going to be hit with hefty bills. Some estimates of the additional claims feeding through to Lloyd's syndicates' 1989 results were as much as £500 million, said market sources – which is why the new stabs at gauging 1989's global loss soared above £2 billion. Faced with potential problems of this magnitude, the Lloyd's hierarchy decided the time had come for rapid remedial action – and took the initiative in election week.

In early April 1992, faced with the new asbestosis and the savings and loans claims, Lloyd's quietly opened its inner sanctum to conversations with a 'supergroup' of the heads of the various Names' action committees about what solutions they would be prepared to support to save the insurance market for posterity (and protect its contribution to Britain's balance of payments).

Names were due to stump up to meet their solvency tests on 10 April. Early that week fears returned that the Central Fund was in sore need of beefing up to meet policy-holders' claims against syndicates with cash-flow crises. This time the talk was behind closed doors and explored whether a 'superlevy', not only on all Names but also on Lloyd's underwriters and Lloyd's brokers could be organized to keep the old tub from beaching high and dry that summer.

Desire to keep Lloyd's going in a form that would continue to attract valuable business to London, and to pull in the Names to provide the capital to keep it trading was paramount. For leading rebel Names this meant ensuring a younger, more dynamic leadership, and more Council members drawn from outside Lloyd's with wider experience of the business world – tempered by the presence of a minority of experts who understood the complexities of the Lloyd's insurance and reinsurance market. Some even favoured introducing stringent professional qualifications and standards for underwriters.

For the young turks of the market, the under-45s, the idea of a shake-up of the old guard and the arrival of their own generation at the forefront of market governance, planning its future, was equally attractive. They all got their wish. A week after 24 June's marathon, six-and-a-half-hour annual general meeting, at which Names had heard Coleridge explain the shocking plunge into a new record loss of £2.06 billion on the 1989 underwriting year, Sir Jeremy Morse's report into the question of the governance of Lloyd's was published. On the same day, 2 July, so was Sir David Walker's report on the LMX spiral.

The Morse Report endorsed the Rowland Task Force's January recommendations that the Council's functions be devolved to two new boards: a Market Board, headed by whoever was Lloyd's chairman and concerning itself with matters of policy and future direction; and a Regulatory Board to deal with the day-to-day conduct of the market. Some three weeks later David Coleridge announced that the Council's preferred choice for chairman in 1993 (subject to being elected to the Council in November) was none other than David Rowland – the man who had masterminded the January 1992 blueprint for the society's future.

In August 1992, the Council approved the implementation of the Morse Report – and in September came news of the appointment of Peter Middleton as the society's new chief executive. Most recently the group chief executive of travel business Thomas Cook, which he first ran and then sold for the Midland Bank, he had previously been (in descending order) a diplomat, a student of social studies and philosophy – and a monk. He also rode a large motor bicycle to work: not at all Lloyd's old style. His appointment, said one insider later, 'was part of a sea change of attitude' at Lloyd's, which was now rapidly gathering pace – and which culminated in April 1993 in a business plan designed to give Lloyd's a solid base from which to move forward with confidence, attract new capital and live to tell the tale of the nightmare that had so nearly destroyed it.

Middleton's appointment in the autumn of 1992 was followed by the news that the head of the new Regulatory Board and a deputy chairman of Lloyd's itself would be Brian Garraway, one of the two driving forces of the tobacco giant BAT Industries, from which he was now retiring as deputy chairman.

The new Council – including Rowland – was elected in November 1992. Its members lost no time in duly voting in David Rowland as the new Lloyd's chairman from January 1993. So this was the new triumvirate: Rowland (an insurance broker who had already made an exhaustive study of Lloyd's prospects), Middleton (bringing a mix of commercial nous and diplomatic skills) and Garraway (a seasoned industrial boss). Together they faced the daunting task of finding a rapid answer to the market's deepening problems. If they could not come up with some practical answers in time for the 1994 year of account, Lloyd's was likely to be dead in the water.

The new team set the example that it expected all Lloyd's agents to follow – by immediately slashing its own costs. Middleton cut its budget, from £144.5 million in 1992 to £117.9 million for 1993 (and later shaved it again to £115 million). The new Council had just 24 members instead of 28, in line with the first stage of the new slimmed-down governance structure – eight working members (down from twelve), five external members (previously eight) and eight nominated members (as before). Administrative staff were cut, from 2,200 as 1992 closed to 1,900 by the spring of 1993 and heading for a target staffing level of 1,600 by the end of the year.

In tandem with these cuts, in February 1993 the new Council unveiled a steep reduction in the number of market committees reporting to it, from 48 to just 17 – largely because many of their functions were now being absorbed by the new Market Board and Regulatory Board. The leaders of the society were making their operations leaner and fitter, and agents were expected to do likewise. Agents' costs – which had made up 33 per cent of the 1989 pure underwriting loss and some 28 per cent of the total £2 billion loss – had to be cut, and the competence of their remaining staff increased. The troubles of the previous two years had also seen a dramatic fall in the number of syndicates, as agencies merged, and as some syndicates went into run-off: down from 400 in 1990 to 230 by early 1993.

In March 1993, Lloyd's drove these messages home again when it appointed its own, first ever, director of finance (and of administration) – David Bruce, formerly group finance director of merchant bank Guinness Mahon and before that the man in charge of finance and administration at the London Stock Exchange. Even the Adam Room would have to earn its keep, by being let for functions. Rowland refused to hog its splendour while Lloyd's and so many of its Names were on their uppers.

As the new team worked feverishly to complete the new business plan by mid-April, insurance rates were still hardening – but mounting reserves for asbestosis claims and pollution reserves were also still causing massive cash calls and making 1990 losses look nastier and nastier. After Lloyd's disastrous attempt a year before to produce an estimate of 1989's likely out-turn, Rowland initially ruled out any official forecast of 1990's result because the market simply did not have accurate enough statistics from the syndicates to do it. He was determined this would no longer be the case in 1994.

What Rowland dubbed the 1993 'spring offensive' by Lloyd's critics produced unofficial estimates of the 1990 result ranging from a £1.4 billion loss to £2.4 billion, an even worse loss than for 1989. Insiders said that was unlikely – but, then, they had pooh-poohed forecasts of a £2 billion loss for 1989. Rowland decided to give no hostages to fortune. Market men also accepted that 1991's underwriting would now almost certainly show a loss, of perhaps between £500 million and £750 million by the time its figures were reported in 1995, while 1992's business, with luck, would at least break even. The bright spot shining like a distant pole-star through all the gloom was a confident expectation of a return to healthy profits on insurance business underwritten in 1993 – but its results would not be known until 1996. *Fidentia* was back on the horizon – just.

Meanwhile, bogged down in early 1993, not only were asbestosis and pollution claims from previous years' underwriting still looming large, but the once abnormal spate of natural catastrophes had also settled into something alarmingly like a trend. Manmade accidents were also increasing – notably, fire damage. A year earlier, giant insurer Swiss Re's *Sigma* publication's study of 1991's pattern of claims had warned: 'The last five years have shown a loss burden above the long-term trend, both in the natural catastrophe and also the major loss sectors. If this development continues, the world insurance system will face a huge challenge.'

In 1992 the USA had experienced its worst-ever year of insurance catastrophes. Hurricane Andrew had smashed through Florida and Louisiana, followed by heavy rains, which further damaged buildings whose roofs had gone in the windstorm, and which boosted the initial cost estimates of between $6 billion and $7 billion to $15.5 billion of insured damage. (Hurricane Hugo had cost $6 billion.) By the spring of 1993, market estimates were that around $900 million of the Hurricane Andrew claims would finally wash up at Lloyd's. The year 1992 had also seen Hurricane Iniki devastate an Hawaiian island, costing an estimated $1.6 billion; the Los Angeles riots, whose gross insurance cost was put at $775 million; and the 'Great Nor'Easter' winds in December, estimated to have done $650 million damage.

These natural disasters of 1992 and other, less individually large, wind-damage and related claims took the bills facing American insurers to an estimated $18 billion for that year alone – whereas in 1991, the world's insurance losses through natural catastrophes had been a (then) record of $14 billion from storms, earthquakes and epidemics. Catastrophe cover rates had risen substantially in the London market during 1992, but even a relatively small proportion of the new claims were less than welcome at a time when so many Lloyd's syndicates were still battling to improve their fortunes. Experts warned the insurance industry that what had in 1989 seemed an abnormal number of catastrophes could now be here to stay, as the world's weather patterns settled into what could be a long-term change.

Human malice also continued to destroy life, limb and property. Counting the cost of 1993's massive bomb blast under the World Trade Centre in New York, Lloyd's said in March that $300 million of claims could feed through to three policies, which were led at Lloyd's, but were spread among its syndicates and other London market insurers. And on Saturday, 24 April, the IRA struck at London again – with another bomb that killed a newspaper photographer and wreaked up to £1 billion of damage in the City of London for the second time in twelve months.

To meet all the challenges facing it, Lloyd's needed to find a way to repair at high speed the damage done to its own fractured frame by the LMX spiral, mounting claims and poor underwriting policies, before knock-on effects caused its severely damaged fabric to deteriorate further. Said new chairman David Rowland in March 1993:

> We have an enormous amount to do in a very short space of time. We have to be able to operate with a sensible capital base for 1994 and 1995. We need therefore to present the existing membership with plans that give it confidence and create a framework from which to attract new capital. We must address how to make profits for the future; create a framework for the capital base of the future in a way that is fair to the past; and make it clear how we intend to manage the old problems.

Working parties were formed during 1992 to address these issues – Lloyd's had one, under Dick Hazell, and a 'supergroup' of the chairmen of Names action groups had also teamed up to consider the problems facing their 6,000 members.

Could a way be found to offset the over-reserving per claim across the market place, resulting largely from the collapse of the LMX spiral? If so, it was just possible that not only could the spate of cash calls cease but also money might yet find its way back to Names trapped on open-year syndicates or still desperately clinging on anyway. The problem was this: though the LMX spiral was dead in the water, its legacy was still growing. Not only did each syndicate continue to make reserves to meet its own potential liabilities per risk, incurred at different and multiple levels of the spiral, but so did their E&O insurers, in case the various disputes and legal actions led to claims on them. Said Rowland:

> Intra-market disputes about E&O and stop-loss claims are the major problems. It balances itself out in Lloyd's global results – because the true loss is known – but at individual levels it becomes well nigh impossible. Until the E&O argument is settled, a liability in one underwriter's book does not become an asset in another's.

This meant that for every claim there could be several syndicates making cash calls on Names to set aside enough reserves to meet the syndicate's own 'worst case' exposure: a massive double-counting effect, which was building up while everyone argued over which bits of what claims ended where. As a result, while individual syndicates might not be safely able to claim that they were over-reserved, the market as a whole was.

A major challenge for the new guard at Lloyd's – but one that might also provide a possible route out of the impasse – was to find a way of ending the market's over-reserving of these types of claim. The best way to do that seemed to be to devise a formula for pooling syndicates' reserves for major problems affecting a large part of the market, principally asbestosis and pollution, into one, single and market-wide fund. Rowland again:

> People trapped can't be offered a route out until you have a common starting-point – and by putting old year, latent disease and pollution claims all in one place you have one single centre instead of several. The object must be to enable members that are trapped to be freed.

While E&O disputes might continue, pooling reserves in this way would at least end the syndicate-by-syndicate, double-counting effect and put a halt to the cumulative, year-by-year increase in calls on Names. It could even lead – after discounted cash-flow calculations as to what the total fund needed to be to meet the anticipated liabilities as they came through at a future date – to part of the multiple reserves money being released back to syndicates.

There were already glimmers of hope on some of the 'old year' problems on the pollution front. The first piece of good news had come in the United States a year earlier, when, in April 1992, the New Jersey state superior court (its court of appeals) had come down firmly on the side of the insurers against chemicals and herbicides company Diamond Shamrock. The company was told by Judge Reginald Stanton that, because it had 'intentionally and knowingly discharged hazardous pollutants', it could not claim against its insurers for the cost of cleaning up the long-term contamination by dioxins, used in herbicide manufacturing, on its site in the Jersey meadows. These 'meadows', running between Newark Airport and New York, had become a stinking industrial wasteland of oil refineries and chemical plants including the Diamond Shamrock site. The chemical company was also told that it could not turn to its insurers for the cost of payments to Vietnam war veterans, who were claiming for disabilities linked to exposure, while on combat duty, to the agent orange defoliant spray, used by US forces to destroy the jungle cover of the Viet Cong.

While Diamond Shamrock prepared to appeal – a lengthy process – the New Jersey ruling cheered the spirits of insurers battling on the other side of the USA, in California, against liability for any claims from Shell Oil for the estimated £1 billion clean-up costs of its Rocky Mountain arsenal site there. And, in January 1993, the California court of appeal confirmed the lower state court decision (of 1988) on this case that liability for pollution claims is indeed excluded from post-1969 policies.

It was only a partial victory for the insurers, because the court also referred pre-1969 policies back to the lower court for further consideration of matters related to sources of contamination, which might be covered by their wording. But, it was an important ruling – and a statement made on behalf of the 200 Lloyd's underwriters whose syndicates were involved in the action said they felt confident (that word again!) of victory in any retrial of the issues surrounding the interpretation of pre-1969 policies. Their legal costs thus far in the Rocky Mountain battle were $10 million; but cheap in comparison with the many hundreds of millions of dollars at stake if the syndicates had to pay for a share of the $1 billion clean-up.

Both these decisions raised hopes in early 1993 that syndicates might be able to cease beefing up their reserves against pollution risks, even without some sort of pooling deal, though it was still too early to talk of syndicates on their own being able to redistribute some of the reserves built up so far.

There was another reason for urgency in preparing the new Lloyd's business plan. Rowland hoped to provide enough comfort for Names in difficulties with old and open years to head off fresh litigation – already in the pipeline – as well as to give the market a firm base from which to move forward. Most North American litigants, including the New York campaigners, found time and again that local courts ruled that they must after all seek redress through the English courts against their agents or Lloyd's. In New York the judge also ruled that syndicates were not entities that could themselves be sued. But, in Britain, new litigants were queuing up in the wake of autumn 1992's batch of loss review reports into LMX syndicates.

These had revealed a sorry series of tales of incompetence and poor record keeping on the part of underwriters. The knock-on effects through the spiral of the Piper Alpha oil-rig explosion loomed large in several. At Rose Thomson Young's syndicate 255, for example, £55 million of a £63 million loss in 1988 was due to its exposure to Piper Alpha.

The weightiest report was the massive, three volume Feltrim Review – as a result of reading which some 700 Feltrim Names were keen to press ahead with writs against their underwriters and agents – and the most damning was the Gooda Walker one, with its succinct summary of the spiral and the Gooda syndicates' heavy concentration on XOL business. 'Certain members' agents concentrated Names' participation almost exclusively on the Gooda syndicates,' whose risk 'was further concentrated by some of the syndicates reinsuring each other,' it said. Families' risk was compounded by husbands and wives (and sometimes other family members) being put on the same syndicates. Some Gooda Names had also been put on other, high risk, spiral syndicates by their members' agents.

The Gooda loss review committee concluded that the 'planning and control of underwriting . . . was inadequate;' that 'the managing agents failed to give members' agents and Names all the relevant information on the developing losses in their possession' – particularly in November 1988 when, if the information had been passed on, some Names might not have participated in the syndicates' 1989 year of account. Neither Names nor their members' agents had appreciated the high-risk nature of the Gooda syndicates. Underwriters thought that the higher up the LMX spiral a layer of exposure to a risk was, the less hard the syndicate could be hit by any single claim. In fact, as the Walker Report had found, the reverse was true.

But there was no deliberate impropriety, and Lloyd's had also administered its regulatory requirements 'properly'. But the committee also served up several areas of food for thought for market-wide improvements in the future. These were: the lack of syndicate prospectuses, syndicates' lack of records of aggregate exposures ('an essential underwriting tool'), solvency rules that favoured reinsuring within Lloyd's instead of outside it, the lack of a risk-weighted system for controlling risk exposure and liquidity problems caused by Time and Distance policies.

By early 1993 cumulative losses to 3,500 Names on Gooda syndicates with open years was 'in the region of £925 million', reported GW Run-Off Limited, the agency created to try and sort out the mess after the Gooda Walker agency folded. There were dark puzzles over the 'purchase, use and early commutation' of some of the Time and Distance policies taken out by Gooda Walker, and the GW Run-Off board was encountering 'unwillingness of certain parties to co-operate' in its investigations.

It was also examining bonuses and salaries paid to former Gooda staff 'and in particular salary increases paid to Mr Derek Walker during 1991' (its main underwriter), said the 1 February report. The board was also trying to get back, from the liquidators of the Gooda agency, a fleet of expensive cars, which 'appears to have been charged to syndicate funds', but which had subsequently been sold under a sale-and-leaseback deal, apparently without the proceeds being returned to the syndicates' funds.

The Gooda, Feltrim, Devonshire and other loss review reports came out in rapid succession during the autumn of 1992. They followed (and echoed) Sir David Walker's July deliberations on the LMX spiral across the whole Lloyd's market. Split into two parts – one on the spiral itself and the other an analysis of syndicates' participation and exposure – the Walker Report confirmed that as each slice of reinsurance had been parcelled up and passed on, an underwriter's ability to measure his syndicate's total exposure had been eroded – not least because underwriters had not bothered to calculate their aggregate exposure to each risk, as they took additional slices and slivers of it as it passed round the market and in and out of their own syndicates.

Far from spreading a syndicate's risk and bringing it extra profits in the form of additional premiums, the spiral had the reverse of the intended effect and ratcheted up each participant's exposure to a larger and larger proportion of any single claim. Walker made a series of recommendations designed to prevent a repeat of this unpleasant, inverse effect by improving underwriters' competence and control of syndicates' exposure. These included the use of risk weightings for different classes of business, to be devised by Lloyd's, which syndicates could use for risk-weighted analysis of the amounts and types of business they were writing. This would also provide Names with a clearer picture of their own exposure. He also said Lloyd's should monitor the more risk-prone syndicates. The report recommended that Lloyd's set a limit, in Names' annual solvency tests, on what proportion of their exposure could be in reinsurance placed within the Lloyd's market. This should cap any future, nascent spiral.

In part two of his report, Walker found statistical evidence that working Names sometimes did have a slight advantage over external Names and made better returns – but not a sufficient one to suggest a pattern of fraud. The report suggested that a modest bias in favour of working Names was probably unavoidable given their 'inevitably superior market knowledge' – but Lloyd's task was to make sure this bias did not reach proportions consistent with abuse of such superior knowledge. He also accepted that if the members' agency's directors were on a syndicate their Names might benefit from their superior knowledge by asking to be put on to the same syndicate – (remember Georgie Girl in chapter three?) – but commented, too, that past results were not always a good guide to what the future might bring. Georgie Girl, meanwhile, was beginning to get cash calls from a syndicate that had written E&O and stop-loss cover for its now stricken peers.

Members' agents were castigated for cavalier conduct on the part of 'a small number' of their ilk; and should in future provide more information about their policies on allocating new capacity, for example. Regular reviews of underwriters' competence by a peer group was also suggested.

To ensure that its practitioners were capable of doing all these new things, Lloyd's was already placing greater emphasis on training and formal measures of professional competence than in the past. Since the start of 1992, new underwriters had to pass the Lloyd's Market Certificate in three subjects, drawn from the qualification of Associate of the Chartered Insurance Institute (ACII). By early 1993, with Rowland and Middleton in charge of the society, the intention was to extend this requirement to all agency directors and to bring in a Lloyd's Market Certificate Stage II, covering eight of the ACII topics. 'Continuing Professional Education' was also on the agenda to keep practitioners up to the mark in future, both in business practices and information technology.

LIMNET, the market's new computerized trading system, had been introduced on schedule, and on budget, on 30 March 1992 and was working well, though take-up was slow. Moves were afoot in 1993 to look at developing a common, market-wide software and in the meantime to reduce, from twenty-six to perhaps three, the number of software packages currently being used on in-house computers by syndicates, brokers and members' agents.

Other legal battles continued. Fights broke out between the Oakeley Vaughan Names' E&O cover providers and their reinsurers, and Oakeley Vaughan litigants waited to hear whether the Court of Appeal would back the earlier, lower court ruling that Lloyd's had not owed Names a duty of care before the 1982 Lloyd's Act (which gave the Corporation immunity from prosecution thereafter). The Outhwaite settlement ran into rough seas. There was a battle royal first over a (defeated) attempt by Lloyd's old guard to seize the settlement cash (via members' agents) to meet the Names' calls; and then over whether stop-loss providers, who had already paid Names, could claim repayment from the settlement money before, or after, the first layer of a Name's exposure was met. One court said 'after'; but the final opinion of the House of Lords was 'before'.

The net effect of this 'top down' ruling was less of the cash for the Name. First, he got whatever calls exceeded his stop-loss ceiling; then the stop-loss provider had to be reimbursed. If any more were left, it met the Name's pre-stop-loss losses. As this chunk was usually bigger than any losses above the stop-loss ceiling, a ruling the other way round ('bottom up') would have channelled more of the cash up-front to the Name. Meanwhile, the E&O providers of the settlement money were told by their own reinsurers that the latter would not pay up on out-of-court settlements.

While efforts continued to sort out this impasse, waves of Task Force recommendations were being brought in during the second half of 1992, tightening market practices and bringing in a new two-tier arbitration scheme to adjudicate in disputes between Names and managing agents (one for disagreements concerning under £100,000 and the other over £100,000). Also introduced was a market-wide Estates Protection Plan administered by broker Holman Wade but insured by CentreWrite and reinsured through top-performing syndicate, Bankside 45. It was available to Names under 45 at £360, at £650 to Names of 46–60 years and at £950 a year thereafter. The premiums are tax-deductible; and the policy provides unlimited cover after a Name's demise for the remaining open years of his syndicates (for example, to end–1995 for a 1993 syndicate) and for years in run-off.

Other initiatives included a considerable softening of the attitude of the Hardship Fund, following a review announced by Coleridge in June 1992. Though, for 1993, Dr Mary Archer retired by rotation as a Lloyd's Council member, she continued to chair the Hardship Committee. The revised guidelines for helping Names meet underwriting losses, announced in October 1992, were intended to offer Names more attractive terms than the UK rules covering bankruptcy or the tough Individual Voluntary Arrangements (IVAs) of the sort some people were striking with their banks. Schemes agreed with the Hardship Fund in future would set a limit, normally of three years, on any payments by Names to Lloyd's out of their income or from windfalls such as inheritance. Spouses of deceased Names would also be able to apply to the Hardship Committee for help.

Charges could still be taken on a Name's property, to cover larger exposures, for longer than three years – for life if necessary. But only money arising from Lloyd's-related tax recoveries, stop-loss policies or any Lloyd's-related litigation should be assigned to Lloyd's during or beyond the fixed-term agreement.

Backing these moves would be a new support fund of £50 million supplied by 'contributions' from Lloyd's brokers and underwriting agents. The fund could be used to supplement an impoverished Name's or widowed spouse's income, buy vital domestic commodities, pay nursing home fees and school fees, during a critical phase of a child's education (rather than force a change of school midway through an O-level syllabus, for example), buy annuities, pay for the basic upkeep of a house – and so on. Discussions with the Charities Commissioners about how this fund should be constituted and payments from it be allocated continued into the spring of 1993. A simplified and more readable version of the form that applicants to the Hardship Fund have to complete was also ready for publication.

'To supplement what the Hardship Committee does, yet operate as a charitable trust, the fund has to be independent and not at the behest of the society as a whole,' explained David Rowland in March 1993. At that stage, with the new fund not yet operating, the Hardship Committee's record stood at 1,977 inquiries since its inception, of which 658 applicants had withdrawn their request, 453 had been asked for more documentation, 866 were discussing terms, and just 130 had actually signed schemes of arrangement.

Lloyd's was also taking a less hard line with Names whose Lloyd's debts had been met out of the Central Fund and whom the fund had been pursuing for the money. Following the 1.66 per cent levy imposed on syndicates' 'stamps' for the 1990, 1991 and 1992 years (as Michael Freeman had forecast would be necessary and largely met from their premium trust funds), the Central Fund stood at £1 billion, of which £360 million was earmarked to cover Names' solvency shortfalls for their 1991 and prior years.

Letters went out on 7 October 1992 to 3,500 people who between them owed the fund sums totalling 'less than £10 million'. They were given just 28 days to pay. But on the 28th day – 5 November – Lloyd's relented. It was just one week after the tragic suicide of a Welsh woman worried about her Lloyd's losses. (Two Canadian Names have also taken their lives, as has a former Lloyd's underwriter.) On Guy Fawkes Day, Peter Middleton suspended for six months the issuing of writs for the recovery of money owed by Names facing cash calls. As some Names paid up anyway, the fund crept up, to £1.125 billion by March 1993, when £330 million remained earmarked to meet shortfalls on Names' 1991 and prior year solvency tests.

More new rules, which came in during November 1992, included measures to separate but not divorce the functions of managing (underwriting) agents and members' agents. An underwriter with fewer than 100 Names could be a combined agency, but larger syndicates would have to be run by a managing agency that was quite separate from the Names' members' agents. Guidelines to both types of agencies on how to set up the business plans, annual budgets, which in future – from January 1994 – would be required of them and how to monitor their own progress during the business year were also introduced.

Plans were being laid, too, for the creation of a panel of up to three members' agents to review Lloyd's syndicates' expenses and managing agents' fees from 1994 onwards. Syndicate reports were already being required to carry far more information than previously, and managing agents were instructed to make their financial accounts available to any members' agent or Name who wished to inspect them. To help practitioners cope with this sharp introduction to the real business world, training courses were being laid on by Lloyd's.

So, as 1993 dawned, a considerable amount of remedial work was under way – but Lloyd's membership numbers were still falling. Despite confident predictions that the steady rise in insurance rates, and far more cautious underwriting, would make 1993 a profitable year in due course for Lloyd's Names, just 75 people had been brave enough to join up. Some 1,600–1,700 had resigned by late 1992, and, with the normal 31 December deadline extended to 31 January, the final tally of leavers totted up to nearer 2,000 – leaving Lloyd's with just 19,603 members in 1993 on 230 syndicates. Market capacity for 1993 was around £8.75 billion, with the average capacity per Name having risen to nearly £450,000 – so some of those staying in did expect to do better out of 1993.

As they waited to see if they had made the right move, the new Lloyd's team was preparing the business plan that it hoped would steer Lloyd's safely into calmer waters from 1994. The pooling of pollution and asbestosis reserves was high on the agenda. So was bringing in MAPAs – the unit-trust-like funds recommended in the Task Force Report, through which Names' initial underwriting could be done. Creating the Super Name able to underwrite up to £3 million was another aim; and so was introducing corporate capital.

'From 1 January 1994 we must have a good capital base for the society. Ideally I see the new capital base between 10 per cent and 20 per cent of the total,' said Rowland. His own firm, Sedgwick, had set the tone for MAPAs in autumn 1992, when it announced the 'Sedgwick Standard Programme' for 1993. This allowed Names to participate in an underwriting fund with a premium limit of up to £100 million, in £50,000 units per person. These units were divided into chunks of £1,000 apiece on up to thirty handpicked syndicates and £2,000 on another ten. The forty syndicates would be chosen for their defensive, low-risk profile and with a capacity of up to £2 million.

The big question of 1993 was what the role of new, corporate capital would be. A few weeks before the team's proposals for saving Lloyd's of London were rolled out to an expectant market-place, Rowland said:

I'd like to create a scheme whereby new capital lies easily alongside the old capital, with the latter seeing an advantage in having the new capital – so the new capital must contribute in some way to the old; by strengthening the cash flow, for example, which is different from just solving the old-year problem. The providers of the new capital will calculate whether it is worth it or not. Rising premiums help.

After the horrors of 1992's revelations, 1993 is make or break year for Lloyd's of London. If the business plan works, the 300-year-old market will be able to patch up the holes below its water-line, finish restructuring the engine room and, under the guidance of her new captain and first officer, steam gently into a more profitable future. If not, she will become one more – and by far the largest – casualty on the long list of disasters to beset the insurance world so far this decade.

On 29 April – with the moratorium on suing Names who refused to meet cash calls about to expire, and just after 300 Lime Street agency Names had complained to the European Commission that Lloyd's practices breached the competition rules of the Treaty of Rome – the new offices at the helm of Lloyd's rolled out their radical, urgent proposals for its salvation.

Planning for Profit: A Business Plan for Lloyd's of London, published at 8 a.m. that morning by the new guard of Lloyd's, was tough and uncompromising; but it was accepted without dissent by the men and women working in the market. For Lloyd's was in even greater danger than earlier suspected. Losses for the 1990 year of account now threatened to be dramatically worse even than 1989's terrible reckoning. The plan was an emergency survival kit, as well as a blueprint for the future, and there was no time to waste in deploying it.

The picture was 'not good'. David Rowland announced that morning that he now expected the 1990 losses, to be finalized in June, to turn out anywhere between £2.5 billion and £2.8 billion – with a 1991 loss of up to some £1 billion yet to come. He did not mince his words.

This staggering news meant Lloyd's syndicates had collectively 'made losses of £6 billion over four years – and you have to think very hard indeed about organizations who have lost that kind of money and how they conduct themselves,' Rowland told a packed press conference that noon.

It was still not clear how much double-counting – in the sense that syndicates and their providers of E&O, stop loss and estate protection were all reserving against elements of the same potential claims – was included in this new estimate of the likely 1990 loss. But Rowland said his personal 'guess-timate' was that around £800 million fell into this category, reducing the real, market-wide loss to somewhere between £1.7 billion and £2 billion – still pretty appalling. But it was the £2.8 billion figure that hit the headlines.

Rowland and chief executive Peter Middleton made it plain that, while higher premiums meant the 1992 underwriting year could manage a modest return to profit – and that 1993 ought to be very profitable – reliance on better rates and leaving change to market forces alone were neither sufficient nor appropriate for a market that wished to attract enough capital and enough underwriting to remain at the forefront of a modern insurance industry.

While the new leaders of the market were prepared to take account of professionals' and members' views of their proposals, they were adamant that this was no discussion document but a plan for action. The market was now to do as it was told and, anxious to preserve their livelihoods – and to restore the society to its former standing in the world – its diverse practitioners were largely relieved that someone had finally taken firm charge of the situation.

The market needed new capital, and the plan proposed ways of getting it – including the introduction for the first time of limited liability, corporate members. But they would only join a market that was efficient and well run, one that could be analysed and evaluated, whose cost base was low, whose standards of professionalism were high – and from whose dismal recent losses and old-year problems they could be protected. So these issues had to be addressed urgently first.

Lloyd's practitioners were still cutting their own costs too slowly to turn the situation round in time for Lloyd's to win the new members it needed to remain a serious player. So while syndicates would continue to exist, as would unlimited liability for individual Names and – for the time being – the three-year accounting system, syndicates were no longer going to be left to act entirely as they pleased. Individual underwriters who protected their own interests regardless of the effect on the market's reputation, or at the expense of the rest of the membership, were not going to be allowed to muddy Lloyd's reputation again. Cost-cutting, better standards, regular monitoring, proper risk analysis and electronic trading were all going to be imposed upon the market, like it or not. Rowland said:

> Our over-riding virtue should be the good name of Lloyd's. It is the best brand name in insurance, perhaps in anything. Compared to our competitors, our fixed costs are low, and our variable costs to intermediaries should make us very flexible. We must seize what we have and use it for the future. But first we must face up to where we have got to and make some very difficult decisions.

Middleton elaborated:

> We are asking the market to change. We no longer think it appropriate for the businesses at Lloyd's only to look at their own interests – they are deploying our brand name, and it's a collective brand name.

Costs were to be cut across the market by £200 million by the end of 1995. The administrative functions of the members' agents would be streamlined into one central support unit, cutting out massive duplication of effort – and reducing the number of people employed in the market from 12,000 to 9,500. Most radically of all, the old-year problems would be 'ring-fenced' both to end the spectre of years of calls on the dwindling assets of trapped Names and to protect the future. This would allow the new capital to come in without being dragged down by the old problems.

The drive to attract new members would include, as expected, the introduction of both the unit-trust-style MAPAs for smaller Names and corporate capital – thereby bringing to Lloyd's, for the first time in its history, members with limited liability. Other elements of the business plan reflected a report received from a committee studying the E&O position, and one from the group of external Names led by Neil Shaw who had been looking for a solution to the open years' problem.

The quality and conduct of Lloyd's business would henceforward be subject to the same kind of scrutiny, analysis and commercial standards as that under which any other large institution would expect to operate. Said Peter Middleton:

We are bringing to Lloyd's simple practices of good management, which have been absent from it for too long, practices which most well-run companies do. The top quartile of Lloyd's is very good: we need to ratchet up everyone to that level.

What we are trying to do is not inherently difficult, though we do have the old-year problem to tackle. Facing the market is the harsh reality that the past way of doing things does not work, and that Lloyd's has a brave future if we go about it in a different way.

Asked at the press conference if angry Names who felt that the market had been managed in the past in a 'wasteful, bureaucratic and opaque way' were right, he answered simply: 'Yes.'

Lloyd's had finally been shaken from its old torpor and come to its senses. The new leadership's sixteen-point business plan concentrated on two main areas: a scheme to ring-fence the worst of the past, old-year problems in a way that was fair both to old and new capital; and a proposal to open the door to a brighter future with new capital attracted to the market by the current prospects of good insurance underwriting profits from 1993 onwards – as the insurance cycle improved, and as the market became more efficiently run. If remedial action were applied fast enough, Lloyd's turn-about could be seen as one of classic recovery. This regeneration could be swift enough to make a £900 million profit on its 1995 year, the plan said.

To achieve that, stringent professional qualifications and performance monitoring were to be the new order of the day. Shoddy underwriting that relied on 'cheaply priced reinsurance to achieve a net profit' was out. It had undermined standards and led syndicates to ignore the need for adequate risk analysis of the business they were writing. Instead, underwriters would be 'encouraged to achieve a gross underwriting profit' in future.

This 'encouragement' took a mandatory and unarguable form, which came in two parts. From 1994 onwards, underwriting agencies would only be allowed to take their profit commissions after the deduction of Lloyd's subscriptions, Central Fund levies and high level stop loss scheme premiums – not before. And the percentage level of these commissions was to be severely cut and capped, at no more than 0.5 per cent of a syndicate's capacity for 1994 and only 0.4 per cent in 1995. This, said Peter Middleton, would 'allow them to break even and, if they are running their business well, any profit is because they have made a profit for their Names and becomes performance-related pay. Other industries do this – and why shouldn't Lloyd's?'

Use of a common, computer architecture and software, screen-to-screen trading would become compulsory from the end of 1993. This was dragging the market into the late twentieth century, like it or not, though face-to-face trading would also continue for more complex insurances. Claims handling and members' agents' administrative functions would both be centralized in order to speed up business and enable the collection, to a common standard, of analysable statistics on syndicates' performance, thereby ending the duplication and variability of information-gathering by each agency.

These improvements would contribute to the £200 million cost-saving target as well as ensuring that all Names gained access to the accurate, useful and usable information about each syndicate. Proper risk analysis of each syndicate would also become both possible and obligatory – at last. Performance tables would be published so that people could see what was going on. Better market-wide information of this sort would also make it possible to spot dangerous new trends and prevent the emergence of another LMX spiral, for example – while the new obligation upon underwriters not to act in ways that would swell their own syndicates' coffers at the expense of Lloyd's good 'brand name' would see the market's regulators nip any dubious practices in the bud.

New capital could then be brought in: through unit-trust style MAPAs, as forecast; through a new class of traditional but 'high liquidity' Names; and through corporate membership. To assist the incorporated Names in their deliberations, a new breed of creatures – licensed Lloyd's advisers – would be created to give impartial advice on syndicate selection and quality.

To preserve that impartiality, although 'all members' agents will have the status of Lloyd's advisers,' no agency relationship between an incorporated Name and his own Lloyd's adviser would be permitted. Nor would all Lloyd's advisers necessarily be members' agents anyway. 'Our intention is to encourage professional advisers and banks to become licensed Lloyd's advisers,' the plan said.

Ring-fencing the old-year problems, notably asbestosis, health hazard and pollution claims, would be done by reinsuring all Lloyd's years of account up to and including 1985 into a new, separately capitalized reinsurance company – by the end of 1995. The new company would have limited liability and could, eventually, even be Stock Exchange listed in its own right.

Syndicates will first calculate their 1985 and prior years' reserves and prepare an outline of their anticipated liabilities for those years. They will then be allowed to discount the sums needed to meet the liabilities, by a formula that takes into account the length of time it could be before these potential claims turn into actual ones, the idea being that in the meantime the money will be invested and generate enough income (to be reinvested in turn) to increase the fund in line with its likely responsibilities. These discounted reserves will be passed to the reinsurance company – effectively reinsuring the syndicates' old liabilities incurred on insurance written up to and including 1985, thereby allowing open years to be closed at last. This will also allow many currently trapped Names to leave Lloyd's if they choose.

But it does not let them totally off the hook. Rowland warned that if a syndicate's reserves still look inadequate, against the guidelines to be set for this process, its Names could face additional calls to beef up their reserves to the required, discounted level. But these calls would be handled sympathetically, again with the amounts sought per individual being discounted forward to take into account the length of time that could pass before the money was likely to be paid out as claims. Names could also be allowed to pay this cash over a number of years rather than all in one go as before.

If, as a result of the discounting process, a syndicate's pre-1986 reserves exceed the estimated liabilities, the syndicate will be able to distribute the excess back to its Names pro rata to their participation in those syndicates. The earliest this can happen is after the end of 1995 when the discounted sum, needed to secure the reinsurance to close the old years, will be passed into the new reinsurance company. In this way a fund of some £4 billion or £5 billion will be created, solely to handle claims against old-year underwriting up to and including 1985. This takes in most asbestosis, pollution and impaired health claims but not LMX losses, which will be separately handled.

The fund will be managed and invested to generate an annual yield that should be enough to top it up at the same pace as likely claims rise in cost. Should this not be the case, the Central Fund would make up any shortfall. Using the PCW Lioncover fund as a yardstick, Lloyd's practitioners reckoned in 1993 that the new company could have a 26-year task ahead of it.

A full-time 'managing director, old years' would be appointed to cope with 'the complex transitional phase' in the build-up to the creation of the new reinsurance company by the end of 1995. New data bases would have to be built during this period, and a new specialist claims unit to handle asbestos, pollution and health hazard claims was to be running by the end of 1993.

The carrot was extended to Names of the possibility of shares in the new reinsurance company being allocated pro rata to those reinsured with it at the start of its life. If the fund eventually proved to be larger than needed – if, for example, more US pollution battles went the insurers' way, and these huge reserves were no longer required – its shareholders could one day receive a special dividend redistributing the excess pro rata to their holding. If floated on the Stock Exchange, the shares would acquire an easily tradable market value of their own, and they would present another way for Names to get some capital back at a future date – by selling them to other investors willing to take a view, and put a price, on the likelihood of one day receiving just such a distribution of excess funds.

As the new company takes on its liabilities, the 1993 year of account will be closing and should be able, freed from the pre-1986 liabilities, to be reinsured into 1996. For the handful of syndicates crippled by the LMX spiral and already in run-off, CentreWrite would provide reinsurance cover 'as soon as the main bulk of the exposure has been settled'. To help with those calculations, a new central run-off management company would take on the management of 'an increasing number of run-off syndicates with long-tail liabilities, and of long-tail liabilities of ongoing syndicates'. It would be built on to Lloyd's existing vehicle, Syndicate Underwriting Management (SUM), and plans were laid to license a small number of specialist run-off management companies as well during 1994 and 1995. Names who had resigned from Lloyd's, but had 'reason to be seriously dissatisfied' with the agent still looking after their final year of account, could turn to the Additional Underwriting Agencies already looking after Names of insolvent agencies.

In spring 1993, some 29,000 people were still trapped on at least one run-off year 'in respect of 1989 and earlier years of account'. That included about 11,000 who had actually resigned from underwriting before 1992 but had become trapped all the same because their final year had not closed and was now in run-off. Between the new reinsurance company, SUM and other licensed run-off specialists, and Centrewrite, the vast majority of trapped Names would be freed from the spectre of years and years of mounting calls on their money or against their estates in future.

But Rowland and Middleton could find no such innovative ways of offering a blanket solution to the litigating Names seeking compensation for their losses from their former agents. Ideas of raising a bond to lend them cash to bail them out temporarily proved a non-starter, because Lloyd's has no unencumbered capital of its own to secure a large enough bond. All its capital in fact belongs to its Names.

Names who had paid up also resented the thought that non-payers might be in some way let off their responsibilities. So the moratorium on writs against non-payers was not extended; though blanket writs would not be issued, Rowland said. Instead, he and Middleton would seek to broke a series of negotiated settlements and remove the unsettling prospect of lengthy and costly (for all) legal battles between the membership, their agents and E&O,

stop loss and estate protection providers. To that end, Middleton planned to continue talks with some action groups and to draw in all thirty action groups to similar negotiations to try and agree mutually satisfactory terms.

The business plan reminded its recipients:

> Lloyd's role here has to be one of facilitating and encouraging realistic discussion and negotiations – acknowledging the constraints on both parties to carry with them those who they represent – and this is a process in which haste can be counter-productive. A negotiated settlement of these disputes will be possible only if the parties genuinely seek to achieve one and genuinely believe that the result is demonstrably a fair one.

In summary, the sixteen-point plan:

■ Set a challenging financial target for the market to make a higher return on capital for Names, of 10 per cent on the market's annual capacity. This, it said, worked out as a 33 per cent return on Names' funds actually held on deposit at Lloyd's – and a 20 per cent return for the new class of incorporated members, which would be expected to deposit a higher proportion of their overall premium limits with the market in order to make up for having the benefits of limited liability.

■ Moved away from the traditional consensus-based decision making that had so conspicuously failed to cope with the events of the 1980s. Instead the central management team would take and impose decisions, albeit after consulting the market-place on the topics in hand.

■ Established a two-phase plan to ring-fence the old-year problems up to and including 1985; first, by setting up market-wide data bases and a body capable of managing these liabilities, and then by reinsuring the old years into the new, limited liability reinsurance company.

■ Promised to find ways of minimizing cash calls upon Names for the 1990 losses, chiefly by allowing delayed or partial payments both for topping up 'double-counted' reserves and for reserves that might not be called upon to meet disputed claims for many years; and by allowing Names to use part of their premium trust funds as a credit towards meeting their solvency tests. Names who dipped from a £250,000 premium limit to a £100,000 one would also be allowed to raise their deposit, from 30 per cent to the 40 per cent required at this lower level, in stages over two years instead of all at once.

■ Undertook to try and broke negotiated settlements between litigating Names and their adversaries, as a matter of high priority.

■ Planned a more independent regulatory regime by splitting it out from the commercial operation of the market, into a structure, devised by head of the Regulatory Board Brian Garraway, that 'replicates the operation of external regulation'. (Here was an experiment with self-regulation at arm's length, internal self-regulation having failed to avert disaster.)

■ Set new and far higher standards of professionalism and training for the market 'and new controls to prevent undue and uncontrolled aggregations of risk'. Syndicates would be expected to learn how to assess and weight their exposure to risk in future, as recommended by the Walker Report and to understand what their worst-case position could be.

■ Speeded up and made compulsory, in stages, moves to electronic processing of policies, cutting administration costs, streamlining claims handling across the market and improving the quality of management information as a result. All syndicates had to be connected to the Room's electronic support system by 1 December 1993. By the start of 1996, they must all keep a full, electronic version of insurance contracts written at Lloyd's and have moved to electronic closing.

A specialist unit would handle asbestos, pollution and health hazard claims from autumn 1993, and Lloyd's existing four claims handling operations were to be streamlined into one claims office by the start of 1994. Later, the specialist unit and the new claims office would be merged into a single, Lloyd's Claims Centre. A three-year target was set for this. Ultimately, the goal was to create 'a single London market bureau serving both Lloyd's and London market insurance companies' and the Market Board had already, by the spring of 1993, 'reached agreement with other market bureaux to work together towards compatible processing infrastructures in the longer term'.

■ Sought dramatically to cut syndicate expenses and agents' fees, which were 'still too high and not falling fast enough'. New measures would force expenses down with 'a mandatory cut in managing agent fees and detailed disclosure of total agent and underwriter remuneration', as so many Names had been requesting. There would be new controls to ensure run-offs were cost-efficient too.

■ Planned for a new central services unit 'to provide shared administrative functions for all members' agents . . . reduce duplication of effort, improve information dissemination and streamline work flows'. Creating 'the new role of licensed Lloyd's advisers [will] enhance the availability of independent analysis and professional advice primarily for incorporated Names.'

■ Confirmed the Corporation of Lloyd's programme to cut central costs.

■ Introduced moves to control the aggregate level of capacity in the market, to avoid the 70 per cent growth in capital in the 1980s that had led to too much wealth chasing too little underwriting business and had fuelled the disastrous development of the LMX spiral. Around June every year, traditional Names would have first crack at supplying any extra capital for which there was room, and then the new, incorporated Names would be invited to tender for the rest. The 'price' of being allowed to take up this additional underwriting capacity would be an 'entrance fee' set, say, somewhere between 0.25 per cent and 0.5 per cent of the additional premiums it would generate, and which would be paid into the Central Fund.

■ Created two new classes of individual Names from the start of 1994, to attract more capital from personal backers of the market. These are the MAPA-only Names; and high-liquidity Names with at least £500,000 each in liquid assets. This takes the classes of private individual Names underwriting at Lloyd's from four (as before) to six. The £3 million cap on individual Names' premium limits would also be removed. But high-liquidity Names would have to show wealth of at least 50 per cent of their premium limit and deposit 20 per cent of it (subject to a minimum deposit of £200,000) at Lloyd's. Names underwriting solely through membership of a pooled, unit trust-like MAPA fund will be allowed to reduce their funds deposited with Lloyd's to 25 per cent of their premium limits, to reflect the lesser volatility and risk of this sort of pooled underwriting.

■ Announced the introduction of corporate capital, or 'incorporated Names', also from the start of 1994. They must be structured as limited liability companies existing solely to underwrite at Lloyd's (and to manage their Lloyd's-related money and income). Because their own liability is limited, they will have to hold capital, equal to 50 per cent of their underwriting limit, as a cushion to protect holders of the policies they write. For the same reason they will be required to pay a higher levy to the Central Fund at 1.5 per cent of their premium limit than individual Names with unlimited liability, who will pay 0.6 per cent for 1994.

This very neatly ensures that, via the Central Fund, these limited liability newcomers are paying some dues to the past as well as benefiting – they hope – from the future. If the Central Fund ever had to introduce another special levy to top itself up, they would also have to pay their share of that. Having limited liability means these incorporated members will not have to contribute to the Names' high-level stop loss scheme, however. They may be Stock Exchange listed in their own right, allowing their shareholders to trade in and out of the shares at a profit (or loss!) as well as enjoying dividends paid out of the incorporated Name's underwriting earnings. Rowland said that the market had received many approaches from interested parties.

■ Brought in new, business development initiatives. Lloyd's needs to find new sources of insurance business in a world now recovering from a bad turn of the insurance and reinsurance cycle generally. It sees bright prospects in continental Europe, thanks to the European Community's single market policies, and in the burgeoning Asia/Pacific region, where insurance markets are opening up more to outside players.

■ Devised six programmes of work to implement the business plan, each 'led by a single executive answerable to the Market Board with an advisory panel drawn from the market. Progress will be reviewed monthly at the regular Market Board meetings and reported to Names every six months.'

Lloyd's set itself several other important targets. One was to make a £900 million profit on the 1995 year of underwriting. Another was to grow its capital base from around £8 billion in 1993 to between £10 billion and £12 billion by 1997, fuelled by an influx of incorporated Names, high-liquidity Names and MAPA participants as well as the traditional classes of Name. It determined to court new members in the English-speaking world and further afield. It wanted Lloyd's syndicates to be capable of agreeing insurance contracts eletronically with brokers at the far corners of the world as well as round the corner in the City of London. It wanted to restore the name of Lloyd's as the world's top brand name – to become a byword for good business, quality and profitability. Lloyd's had a major task ahead and a tight timetable. 'But we are absolutely determined that we are going to succeed,' said Peter Middleton.

This plan was indeed as bold and radical as David Rowland had initimated it would be. It represented a complete change of air at the society. For the first time during the crisis that had so nearly ended its 300-year career, Lloyd's had a strategy and a leadership in keeping with the high-tech twentieth-century exterior of the building that housed it. It could no longer be accused of being a riddle inside an enigma. But has the solution been arrived at in time? The next two years will bring the answer.

Index

229